Land and Work in

Selected Papers

Land and Work in Mediaeval Europe

Selected Papers

Marc Bloch

AAKAR

LAND AND WORK IN MEDIAEVAL EUROPE
Marc Bloch

© Aakar Books

First Indian Edition 2017

ISBN 978-93-5002-467-6

All rights reserved. No part of this book may be reproduced or transmitted, in any form or by any means, without prior permission of the publisher.

Published by
AAKAR BOOKS
28 E Pocket IV, Mayur Vihar Phase I, Delhi 110 091
Phones : 011 2279 5505, 2279 5641
aakarbooks@gmail.com; www.aakarbooks.com

Printed at
Sapra Brothers, Delhi 110 092

CONTENTS

FOREWORD by F. R. H. Du Boulay *page* vii

1. The Empire and the idea of Empire under the Hohenstaufen — 1
2. A contribution towards a comparative history of European Societies — 44
3. A problem in comparative history; the administrative classes in France and in Germany — 82
4. Technical change as a problem of collective psychology — 124
5. The advent and triumph of the watermill — 136
6. Mediaeval 'Inventions' — 169
7. The problem of gold in the middle ages — 186
8. Natural economy or money economy: a pseudo-dilemma — 230

INDEX — 245

FOREWORD

F. R. H. Du Boulay

Although twenty years have passed since the tragic death of Marc Bloch, only a few of his works have yet been made available in English, and even the collection of his writings in French, dispersed and varied as they are, has gone forward slowly. For the English-reading public *The Historian's Craft* appeared in 1954, and his biggest book, *Feudal Society*, in 1961. Soon the brilliant essay on French agrarian society from its mediaeval origins to the eighteenth century, which he called *Les Caractères originaux de l'histoire rurale française*, will appear in an English translation by Mrs. Janet Sondheimer under the title *French Rural History*.

This is not enough. Marc Bloch's claim to remembrance is not simply as the author of monographs but as a great teacher for whom history was as much a mode of enquiry as a publication of new information. Even the reports on his research were discourses upon method, written in his unmistakable rhythms of speech, confidential, poetic, and a trifle astonished at what he had to say. In articles, conferences and reviews he displayed gifts of luminous explanation and the power to ask from his subject-matter fresh and original questions. All these may still stir and instruct the reader.

The task of drawing up Bloch's bibliography was formidable, partly because it was large and scattered, and partly because his pieces were sometimes unsigned or appeared over a pseudonym. The work was put in hand by his friend and colleague, Professor Lucien Febvre, who was responsible for a preliminary bibliography in *Marc Bloch at Strasbourg*.[1] After Febvre's death there were more difficulties and delays, but the *Association Marc Bloch* continued the work, and in 1963 two handsome volumes of Bloch's *Mélanges Historiques* appeared and included a more perfect bibliography.[2] In deciding what to reprint the editors had to consider three main types of Bloch's contributions: original articles, extended reviews of a single work or of historical writings about a single country, and short book-notices and obituaries which nonetheless were of an interesting and original nature. For the *Mélanges Historiques* they thought it best to make use of the first category only, and it is upon this selection that the present volume is based.

Of the eight papers which are presented here in English dress, all but one date from Bloch's time at Strasbourg, where he was professor from 1919 to 1936. Only the short address on 'Technical change as a problem of collective psychology', given at a conference of psychologists, derives from his later period at the Sorbonne.

Two of the essays touch upon mediaeval Germany, and these merit inclusion because of the small amount of literature available to students of this subject who cannot read German. They have another kind of rarity value. Bloch himself wrote surprisingly little of his own on Germany. Although he spent the years 1908–9 in Leipzig and Berlin, and never ceased to concern himself with German history, he confined his publications either to studies where Germany was treated comparatively with other west European countries or to long collective reviews of German historical publications in the *Revue Historique*. Though the abiding interest was there, it was not directed single-mindedly upon German territories in isolation, but was forever flickering over the frontiers of country and discipline. In one way he admired the solid efforts of German historical scholarship during the years that succeeded Germany's defeat in 1918, especially the research into Hanseatic history and on the diversity of agrarian forms, but he was, on the other hand, quick to denounce the historical nationalism, the neglect of historical work done abroad, and the disdain for comparative methods which he detected among German scholars. Of course Bloch was hard to satisfy. When he read Willy Andreas's *Deutschland vor der Reformation*, a book that reacted against the old tradition of monumental erudition, he found it too *geistreich* and prodigiously irritating in its neglect of verification, though intelligent and full of ideas. But his comparative discussion of the administrative class in France and Germany is a fine demonstration of his own methods, which were to illumine the society of one country by pointing the differences with those of another. The lecture on the Empire under the Hohenstaufen is remarkable in another way, for it is the only course delivered to students who were going to be examined that he ever consented to print.[3] Bloch felt a deep distaste for the recurrent, traditional syllabuses required of candidates for *licence* and *agrégation*. He disliked limiting historical problems to political frontiers, and shrank from what he sardonically called 'teaching the breviary'.

The last four essays in this volume are concerned with more technical problems of the mediaeval economy, but they too reflect the author's passion for the comparative method and for visualising the physical realities behind the abstract concepts of which he was writing. In 'Mediaeval Inventions' he reserves a kick for rural histories whose heroes appear to do their ploughing with charters, and for administrative histories full of the great doings of a central power that rules its provinces, seemingly regardless of such mundane realities as the condition of the roads, the availability of animals for transport, the supply of fodder for horses, and the time taken to travel. For students who feel they would like to know something about money if only they could survive the buffeting from technical jargon sustained during ordinary attacks on the subject, Bloch supplies in 'Natural Economy or Money Economy: a pseudodilemma' a precise and lucid sketch of money's nature.

If Bloch's answers to the problems he raised have sometimes been superseded by more recent research, he would have been the first to rejoice. Yet what he wrote has a continuing value. The questioning tone of voice endures, appealing both to intellect and to the poetic imagination. Indeed the questions may be more durable than the answers, which is more than can be said of a good deal of historical writing.

Bloch's mind refused to be delimited within the frontiers of geography, period or doctrine. His problems could not be even posed, let alone solved, without searching far afield for similarities and differences in social structures and communal mentalities. True, he began his life-work, as any historian must, with a limited subject. But the work of early years among the archives of the Île-de-France amassed an immense collection of material to be turned to new uses in the heyday of his maturity and experience. A growing interest in linguistics suggested an analogous method for history. If widespread similarities in language-structure might help to explain common circumstances, so too might likenesses in fields and farming methods. If the linguists could speak of *iso-glosses*, he reflected with teasing pertinacity, why should not agrarian historians think likewise of *iso-agres*? Again, there were differences as well as similarities visible to the man who walked about with open eyes. Why should peasant holdings in France so often obey some law of fragmentation while the German *Hufen* maintained a more stubborn indivisibility? And why should the Germans display a firmer social hierarchy as against the French fluidity of classes? Such questions at least threw up problems that required some explanation, whereas the study of a single society all too often disclosed only arrangements that seem natural and hence in no need of explanation.

It was the same with chronology as with geography. Bloch believed that the meaning of historical events was clarified by a study over a long period of time no less than by a study that transcended regional boundaries. When he became Professor of Economic History at the Sorbonne he had of necessity to extend his range into the modern period, and the result of this can be seen in *Les Caractères*. His concern with both modernity and the past is a standing reproach to the embattled educators and scholars of our own day. At present we suffer from the heresy that the only way to be relevant is to be contemporary. Bloch would have made short work of this abysmal confusion. He saw that the present is explained by a past that is sometimes very distant. To modernist doctrinaires he would quote Michelet: 'anyone who thinks he can stick to present actuality does not understand the actual'. On the other hand, to understand the past one needs the smell of present-day life. To mediaevalist pedants he would recall how his master, Pirenne, arrived for the first time in Stockholm and hurried off at once to see the new Town Hall, exclaiming: 'If I were an antiquarian I should have eyes only for old things, but I am a historian. That is why I love life.'

Neither was Marc Bloch bound to a doctrinal explanation of historical change.[4] He himself did not adhere to the Jewish faith of his family, though he treated it with reverence. He was influenced by Marx and Durkheim, yet he declined to allow the social group wholly to obliterate the individual man and was prepared to admit the force of spiritual ideas in social developments. In a brilliant discussion of technical innovation, for example, he argued that the decline of slavery did not simply follow from new inventions but that, on the contrary, it occurred through religious attitudes as much as through economic pressures. For he attributed slavery's decay in part to the belief of the *societas Christiana* that Christian men ought not to be enslaved; consequently servile labour became more difficult to get; and consequently the impetus came to find fresh techniques for work that had to be done.

If Bloch was impatient of boundaries and orthodoxies it may still be permissible to doubt whether he gave enough attention to political history conceived as the study of particular rulers and families. In all the pages of his *Feudal Society* he has little to say about individual lords acting as individuals, and there are no portraits drawn with the vivid sympathy that resurrects the Counts of Anjou in Professor Southern's *Making of the Middle Ages*.[5] Bloch frequently insisted that his subject-matter was not mankind but men. Yet it is hard to escape the conclusion that he meant by this more especially humble men and not their masters. The preference for the banausic which his reader grows to suspect became overt in the last, bitter days when France had been overwhelmed. French patriot and reluctant bourgeois though he was, he still felt himself in the company of mankind, but never less sympathetic to the powerful.

'And then,' he wrote to Lucien Febvre on 3rd May 1940,[6] 'you are a humanist, in the sense of the old *Homo sum*. As a mind, you are free. You are, as Michelet meant it, "a friend of the people". You have lived with the crowd. Your kids [*gosses*], like mine, have herded cows with the little peasants. When you praise the natural delicacy, tolerance and good sense of our peasants and working people underneath all the provincial varieties, you are only preaching to the converted. This is why we are great. I have known no friendships more precious than those in 1914 of a miner from the Pas-de-Calais and a café-proprietor from the Bastille quarter. They were killed, both of them – the first literally on my shoulder. Why, when they come from such stock, do our ruling classes (or those who think themselves such) show such ignorance, such limited outlook, such inhumanity of attitude? Problem, problem . . .'

This is a comment upon his own outlook. It must be confessed, finally, that a certain criticism of his method is required. Ardent though he was to overstep the boundaries of space and time and doctrine in his search for better problems, he seems sometimes too little disciplined in the structure of his own historical writing. Readers of the essays which follow may feel that his thought is digressive and parenthetical to excess. His was 'l'ésprit qui court parmi les faits comme le feu parmi les brandes'. How true was Febvre's encomium. His thought like lightning darted obliquely, and sometimes it was charged with uncontrollable knowledge. To operate at all Bloch needed to know everything – languages, linguistics, geography, law, theology, and the historical particularities of half a dozen countries. But the polymath becomes his own enemy, for even genius cannot use more than a certain number of tools at once, and if he tries to do so his creations will lack the architecture that is possible only to divinity.

This is not to cavil ungratefully. Marc Bloch was before all a teacher. Some of France's most distinguished scholars are numbered among his pupils, and beyond these ranks are a host of others who have felt his genius at a greater remove. To a new generation of students this book is directed knowing that no résumé can replace the riches it contains, and that translation will not mask or spoil *le grand rythme oratoire de son œuvre*.

NOTES

1. *Marc Bloch et Strasbourg. Souvenirs d'une grande histoire* (Publications de la Faculté des Lettres de l'Université de Strasbourg, Fasc. 103, Mémorial des années 1939-1945, 1947, pp. 171-189, et bibliographie des livres et articles fondamenteaux de Marc Bloch, pp. 190-193). Bloch himself drew up his bibliography to date in 1934 on the occasion of his candidature for the Collège de France.
   For a succinct account of Bloch's work, see Ch. E. Perrin, 'L'œuvre historique de Marc Bloch, in *Revue Historique*, Vol. 199 (1948), pp. 161-188. *Mélanges Historiques. Marc Bloch* (S.E.V.P.E.N., Bibliothèque Générale de l'école pratique des Hautes Études. Paris, 1963).
3. Apart from portions of the *Caractères*.
4. *Annales d'histoire sociale*, 1945; also J. Stengers, 'Marc Bloch et l'histoire', in *Annales*, Vol. 8 (1953), pp. 329-337.
5. R. W. Southern, *The Making of the Middle Ages* (1953), pp. 81-87.
6. Lucien Febvre, *De l'histoire au martyre: Marc Bloch 1886-1944*, in *Annales d'histoire sociale*, 1945, p. 19.

I

THE EMPIRE AND THE IDEA OF EMPIRE UNDER THE HOHENSTAUFEN[1]

I
THE IMPERIAL INSTITUTION

The State governed by the Hohenstaufen from 1138 to 1250 was called the *Empire*; the heads of this State aspired to the title of Emperor and usually bore it at least for part of their reigns. How did this political institution – the strangest known to the Middle Ages – come into being, and what in it constitutes the essentials of sovereign power?

1. Carolingian origins: the territorial formation of the Empire

At the end of the 8th and beginning of the 9th century the Frankish kingdom had subjugated and absorbed a large part of Eastern and Central Europe. On December 25th 800 its head received the imperial crown from the Pope. The German chroniclers of the 12th and 13th centuries were in the habit of summing up this event by saying that the Empire, which had previously passed from the Romans to the Greeks, was thus handed on from the Greeks to the Franks. This stating of the matter is not strictly accurate. The Greek Emperors, with their capital at Constantinople, were without any breach of tradition the heirs of the Latin-speaking Emperors whose capital city had been Rome. They continued in existence after 800, still calling themselves Emperors and holding themselves to be the legitimate successors of the Caesars. But since December 25th 800, there was once more an Emperor in the West who also claimed to be the rightful heir of Augustus and Constantine, and considered Rome to be his city and one of the principal seats of his power.

Everyone knows that the Carolingian Empire did not last as

long as the State. The treaty of Verdun in 843 divided the Empire of Louis the Pious among his three sons.

In the West, there came into being the kingdom of Charles the Bald – 'Western France', later to become simply France.

In the East, it was the kingdom of Louis, 'Eastern France'. To be precise, this kingdom comprised that part of the Empire extending north of the Alps and east of the Rhine, excluding – on the right bank of the river – Frisia, but including – on its left bank – the towns of Mainz, Worms and Speyer or Spires. Its inhabitants nearly all spoke Germanic dialects, lumped together in Carolingian times under the term *theodisca lingua* ('the language of the people': perhaps 'the language of the pagans, the *gentiles*'). Gradually it became customary to call the inhabitants of these regions by the same name as their language: *diutischiu liute*. The country was called *Diutischin lant*, nowadays *Deutschland*. The oldest examples in the vulgar tongue are from the *Annolied*, at the end of the 11th century; but evidence of its use is found in Latin transcripts from the 9th century onwards. In Latin, as a result of classical traditions and confusion with the Teutons of the 1st century B.C., they were generally called *Teutonici*, and the kingdom *Teutonicum regnum*.

Finally in the centre there was the State of Lothar, a long strip stretching from the North Sea to beyond the Tiber. The limits of this strange territory can be easily explained. Of the three sons, Lothar, the eldest, was the only one to receive (or rather to keep, for his father gave it him in his life-time) the title of Emperor; and being Emperor, he had to possess both Rome and the 'second Rome' beyond the Alps, Aachen, the real capital of the Empire since the end of Charlemagne's reign – Aachen where he could see, near the tomb of his great ancestor, the imperial palace surmounted by the bronze eagle.

The Empire in the period of the Hohenstaufen consisted, territorially speaking, of the union of the State of Louis the German and the whole of the countries that had fallen to the share of Lothar.

This union came about progressively, under the following circumstances.

The dissolution of the Carolingian Empire is commonly

dated from the year 843. Yet it must not be forgotten that, from 880 to 887, Charles the Fat, one of the sons of Louis the German, succeeded in uniting under one rule the various States that had been separated by the treaty of Verdun. This *renovatio imperii Francorum* (the actual words on Charles's seal) was extremely short-lived. Charles the Fat died on January 13th 888, after abdicating in face of an insurrection. From this moment onwards the division was already half accomplished, and was consummated after the Emperor's death.

The kingdoms of Eastern France (under a grandson of Louis the German, the bastard Arnuff), and Western France (under Eudes, Count of Paris), were reconstituted as they had been after Verdun. But what happened to the intermediate territory, whose fate was all the more uncertain because there were no longer any descendants of the Emperor Lothar in the male line?

Here, a distinction must be made between three parts – Italy, the Rhône region, and the country situated to the north of the high land separating the basin of the Saône from those of the Meuse and the Moselle. This last section had already formed a kingdom by itself from 855 to 869, under one of the sons of Lothar I, who bore the same name as his father – Lothar II. According to a custom that was common at this period, his subjects were called the men of Lothar, *Lotharingi*, from which were derived the names Lotharingia, Lothringen, Lorraine, which clung even after Lothar II's death to the countries that had formed his kingdom. Much later on the name was restricted to the infinitely smaller region that goes by the name today.

Italy, the Rhône region, and Lorraine must all be thought of separately; one after the other they were all united with Eastern France.

To take Lorraine first. No independent power was set up there in 888. Arnulf was recognised there, as he was in Germania. But neither he nor his successors were left in peaceful possession of the country. For about a century it was a constant bone of contention between the kings of the two 'Frances', Eastern and Western. These struggles only came to an end when quite unexpectedly in 987, by an intrigue originating apparently in the German court, the crown of Western France passed to the house of the Roberts, to the detriment of Charlemagne's descendants, who seemed since 936 to have made certain that it would fall to them. The new dynasty, much less attached than its rival to memories of the Carolingian past, and wielding only moderate power, ceased to concern itself with Lorraine, which now became completely absorbed in the Kingdom of Eastern France, of which it was henceforth considered to be an integral part.

Secondly, Italy.

The history of Italy is inseparable from that of the imperial name. The sovereign who found himself master of the kingdom of Italy, or, as it was also commonly called at that time, the kingdom of the Lombards, had been held since the days of Lothar I to be the prescriptive candidate for the rank of Emperor. For almost a century, the titles of King of Italy and Emperor were contested by various princes, whether related or not to the Carolingian family. In 951 the widow of one of these pretenders, Lothar of Provence, Queen Adelaide by name, being persecuted by her husband's rival, Bérenger of Ivréa, called in the help of the king of Eastern France, Otto I. Otto crossed the Alps and married Adelaide. He took the title of King of the Italians or King of the Lombards. As yet his power was very weak. But in 961 he again crossed the mountains, this time strongly establishing his authority in Italy, and entered Rome, where on February 2nd 962 he had himself crowned Emperor by the Pope. For that time onwards the kingdom of Italy and the imperial title remained indissolubly linked to the kingdom of Eastern France.

There remains the region of the Rhône.

After the collapse of 888, two kingdoms had come into being there. In the south, there was Provence, and in the north Burgundy, with 'Transjurania', that is to say the Swiss plain, forming the centre. The single kingdom that was so created was henceforward known as the kingdom of Burgundy. Much later on (at the end of the 12th century) the ancient Roman towns which were traditionally held to be the capitals of the country came to be called the kingdom of Vienne or the kingdom of A les.

There was nothing very regal about this Burgundian royalty. Great lay and ecclesiastical principalities were formed, attached to the would-be sovereign by the slenderest of links. In fact at the end of the 10th century and at the beginning of the 11th the only authority which the kings of Burgundy retained was in Transjurania. From the time of Otto I the German sovereigns exercised a kind of protectorate over them. The last of the line, Rodolph III, gave an assurance to the Emperor Henry II in 1016 that he might expect to be his heir; in 1032, before he died, he sent Henry's successor Conrad II the royal insignia. Conrad occupied the country and received definitive recognition in the year 1034.

Thus the territorial formation of the 'Empire' was complete, apart from the eastern frontiers, which are not of interest to us here.

2. *The royal election*

Let us now place ourselves in the Hohenstaufen period; and with the object of making a rather closer analysis of the political constitution of Europe, let us start with the beginning of a new reign.

The Emperor has just died: who will be his successor?

In the 10th and 11th centuries, the German monarchy, like all the monarchies of Europe, had lived under a regime that was a mixture of election and heredity. In the eyes of contemporaries, the electoral and the heredity principle, which appear to us to be contradictory, were not in the least opposed to one another. The 'people' – that is to say the great lords, lay or ecclesiastical, the only people who counted – elected their king; but his strongest title to election was the fact that he belonged to a race that was already royal. This was a survival from an age when the German tribes, who were accustomed to electing their chiefs, always chose them on principle from among the members of the same sacred families, who held high prestige, and were able by virtue of their blood to exercise command over men and affairs. Note for example the terms in which Henry II, elected in 1002 in succession to his cousin Otto III who had died childless, recalled the part played in his accession by Werner, the Bishop of Strasbourg. The passage comes from a royal proclamation. Naturally, the text was not written by the sovereign himself: the words were put into his mouth by his chancellor, and express the ideas generally accepted at the time.

'After the death of this great emperor (Otto III), mindful of a friendship dating from childhood (between the Bishop and Ourselves), and in consideration of the ties of blood and of parentage which linked us to this great Caesar, the prelate and a great many other persons resolved to trust in us; in such wise that with God's help we were unanimously elected by the peoples and the princes, and in us was vested the hereditary succession to one undivided kingdom.'[2] Here more succinctly still is the form of words contained in the Annals of Quedlimbourg, announcing the accession of Otto I, who succeeded his father in 936: 'he is elected by hereditary right to succeed to the kingdoms of his fathers'.[3]

In the time of the Hohenstaufen the position was not quite the same, in Germany or elsewhere. Changes had occurred throughout Europe, but they had taken an opposite course in different countries. In France, and in England too, though less markedly, the elective principle had vanished; the hereditary principle was firmly established, and with it respect for primogeniture. In Germany, the change was in a completely opposite direction. It reached completion at the precise period of the Hohenstaufen. The facts can speak for themselves.

In 1125 the Emperor Henry V died, leaving no issue. His nearest relatives were his nephews – his sister's sons – Frederick and Conrad Hohenstaufen. They were not elected. The magnates gave the crown to someone quite unconnected with the previous royal house – Lothar, Duke of Saxony. True, Conrad Hohenstaufen did on his side proclaim himself king in 1127, but the attempt failed, and after eight years he had to give in. In 1138 Lothar too died, leaving no son behind him. The prospective heir appeared to be his son-in-law Henry the Proud, Duke of Bavaria, head of the Guelf family. Before his death Lothar handed over to him the royal insignia. But it was not on this prince that the election fell; it was Conrad Hohenstaufen, the former rival candidate, who obtained the crown.

In 1152 Conrad died. This time royalty remained with the Hohenstaufen, and not with the son of the late king, who was held to be too young; it was Conrad's nephew, the Duke of Swabia, Frederick (Barbarossa), who was chosen. Frederick I made certain during his lifetime that the succession would pass to one of his sons. But note that it was to a younger son, who was – for reasons that are not at all clear – preferred to the elder. Henry VI – for this became his title – entered peacefully enough into possession of his heritage, but died prematurely in 1197. Then a double election took place. The Hohenstaufen's enemies chose a prince of the Guelf line, Otto IV; the Hohenstaufen's partisans rallied round a representative of this house, but they passed over the son of the previous Emperor, the youthful Frederick Roger, who was only a child, and chose instead a man who was in his prime, Henry VI's brother, Philip of Swabia. In 1208 Philip died, the victim of an assassin. But for all that Otto IV did not remain in peaceable possession. Having fallen out with Pope Innocent III, he soon saw another Hohenstaufen candidate confronting him, this same Frederick Roger, who had been previously set aside. The 'infant' Frederick triumphed, and became the Emperor Frederick II. But his was not at all a tranquil reign. Even during his lifetime groups of princes elected in succession two rival kings in opposition to him. His death in 1250 ushered in the period called the great interregnum. Not that Germany was then without a king; on the contrary, she had too many – almost always two at a time, both equally feeble, until in 1273 another unique election gave the crown to Rudolf of Hapsburg.

Here then was nothing resembling a hereditary right of succession in the Capetian sense of the word. It was rather a case of two tendencies, both clearly expressed by contemporaries, in contest with one another. The idea persisted in many minds that birth conferred certain rights. But on the other hand, the princes, fearing the hereditary principle because they were afraid of a strong monarchy, were only too ready to believe that a candidate for the throne was disqualified by the fact that he had a family link with the previous sovereign. Pope Innocent III, who was also hostile to the hereditary principle as far as Germany was concerned, once expressed this argument very clearly. Philip and Otto had just been elected simultaneously. Innocent III pronounced in favour of Otto. He explained his motives, stressing those which appeared likely to appeal particularly to the German lords. Amongst these arguments, here is the one that is our particular concern: 'If, as previously [in 1190], the son succeeded the father, and people were now to see brother immediately succeeding brother, the Empire would seem to them to be no longer elective, but hereditary.'[4] This was the extreme point of view, which did not explicitly triumph until after 1273. But let us notice that in the Hohenstaufen period, even when rights of lineage were recognised, the right of primogeniture was seldom acknowledged. Heredity – without primogeniture in a State where no partition was allowed – in an 'indivisible' kingdom, as Henry II called it – was not likely to prove very firmly based.

Now this disappearance of the hereditary principle was not only a matter of fact: it was also a matter of law. It was not the theory of the State's enemies, but rather the official doctrine, that held the monarchy to be elective, and men were very ready to glory in the fact. Two examples from the beginning of the period will suffice. In 1158 Bishop Otto of Freising, Frederick Barbarossa's uncle, wrote at the request of his imperial nephew the two books of the *Gesta Friderici*. At the beginning of Book II (*c*.1), in his account of Frederick's election, he says: 'The supreme ornament of Imperial Roman law is that, by a unique system of privilege, kings do not succeed one another by right of blood, but are made by the election of princes.' And Frederick I himself, in a manifesto dating from the beginning of his struggle with the papacy (October 1157), says: 'We hold our imperial and royal dignity from God alone' – from God, that is, and not from the Pope – 'by the election of princes'.[5]

No doubt it was all very well for sovereigns to recognise the elective character of the monarchy and even on occasion to give it considerable emphasis when it was a question of opposing the rights of princes to the claims of the papacy; but this does not mean that they were blind to its dangers. Their political sense and family affection compelled them to try to assure to their descendants the hereditary succession to the throne. In order to be successful they had at their disposal the classic procedure adopted by all monarchies finding themselves in a similar position, used by the first Capetains, used by the ancient doges of Venice – of associating their sons with the royal power even while their father was alive. This was an expedient of which they made wide use, but one which also had its dangers. Frederick II had his son Henry elected and consecrated king while he was alive; but Henry proceeded to pursue a personal policy and had to be deposed. And as well as being dangerous the procedure was not always effective: Henry VI had had his son Frederick Roger crowned and consecrated, but it was not he who succeeded him when he died. Henry VI, clearly conscious of the disadvantages latent in this association of father and son, had wanted to go one better. In 1196 he tried to obtain the princes' recognition of the hereditary nature of the succession; but his efforts were abortive, and he abandoned his plan for the time being, and in fact died before he had been able to take it up again. The double election taking place, as we have seen, at his death and the ensuing troubles were the final death-blow to the hereditary right.

Why then did the German monarchy, starting out from a position very similar to that of the French monarchy, not evolve, like its western neighbour, in the hereditary direction, but towards the electoral principle instead? It is impossible here to discuss the detailed and complex reasons which must be brought in to explain this great contrast. But it is clear enough that a whole series of events were working in the same direction.

First, there was the physiological hazard – the successive extinction, without male heirs, of the three dynasties – Carolingian, Saxon, and Salic. Sheer inescapable fact decreed that each time a royal house happened to die out, election pure and simple would come into its own.

Then there were two circumstances of a political nature which will become clearer later on. The first was the union between German royalty and the Empire. Traditionally, by virtue of ideas going back to the Roman period, and handed down in historical literature of a more or less legendary kind, the Empire was considered to be elective. *Exercitus facit imperatorem*; this ancient phrase, borrowed from Saint Jerome, became from the end of the 12th century a commonplace in political literature. The link between these ideas was clearly shown in the proclamation by which the princes, in February 1237, announced that they had just elected as king Conrad IV, the son of Frederick II, who had been associated with him in royal dignity during his lifetime. After recalling that the 'fathers' (Senators) of Rome formerly chose their kings and emperors (I need hardly say that this statement is historically incorrect) they added: 'We . . . princes occupy in this respect the place of the Roman Senate. . . .'[6]

Then there was another political circumstance—the struggle of the German sovereigns against the Popes, itself the result of the former's acquisition of the imperial dignity. Since Gregory VII's time, the Pope's classic weapon had been to raise up against a hostile king a rival king, and to this end to agitate for a new election among the princes. At the Assembly of Forchheim, at which the rival king Rudolf of Rheinfelden was elected in 1077, the papal legates being present, it was decided – if one may credit the Saxon cleric Bruno's account – that henceforward royalty should be elective. This is perhaps not an absolutely literal fact; but it is significant that a contemporary, who was well disposed towards the Pope, should already consider it a probability. We saw above in what clear terms Innocent III expressed himself in 1200 against the hereditary principle. Later on Innocent IV contrasted those kings 'whose kingdoms come to them by hereditary succession' with the Emperor 'who holds his States by free election of the German princes'. Why did the Popes adopt this attitude? First, it was a matter of policy: they had good reason to fear anything that might have strengthened the German monarchy. They were also prompted by doctrinal considerations. Election was the sole source of legitimate power in the Mediaeval Church: the bishop and the abbot had to be elected, also the Pope, and so it seemed natural to churchmen that temporal heads should be elected likewise. Later, in the 14th century, the jurist Bartole pronounced, in this same sense, that election has something more divine about it than heredity.[7] Moreover, the notion of hereditary right was traditionally linked in men's minds with that of the sanctity of certain races who were the only ones thought capable of providing effective rulers. Now the Gregorian reforms which inspired papal policy from the second half of the 11th century had consisted largely in a protest against this system of ideas and sentiments, which were judged to be semi-pagan. The Gregorians did not believe in the virtue of blood: they saw the true origin of royal power in a contrast between the sovereign and the people. Both doctrine and self-interest inclined them in the same direction. The Popes found in the German princes, who were also apprehensive of too strong a monarchy, their natural allies; and it was the opposition of the princes in 1196 that brought Henry VI's plans to grief. From his point of view the Emperor, who in practice needed the help of the princes against the Pope, and who as a matter of doctrine needed to base his power on something independent of the Papacy, fell into the habit of proclaiming himself elected by the princes: 'The princes of Germany on whom both our exaltation and our abasement depend' – these were the words that were to be used by Frederick II in protesting against his deposition by the Pope.[8]

The word election at once suggests an electoral body. Who in fact were the electors of the German king?

The Hohenstaufen period is notable for far-reaching changes in the electorate, though their nature is obscure, and they have consequently given rise to numerous controversies. I shall confine myself to a résumé of the main facts generally held to be beyond doubt.

At the beginning of our period, the king was elected by the whole body of the 'princes' (*Fürsten*); and this word prince still had a rather vague and much less restricted meaning than it would later acquire. The following bodies took part in the election: (1) the archbishops, bishops and abbots of the great royal abbeys; (2) among the laity, the Dukes and the majority of the Counts. Because of its size this electoral college functioned in a most unwieldy manner. An attempt was made to improve it in 1125, when Lothar was elected, by the prior designation of electors of the second degree, whose duty it was to make a preliminary choice among the candidates. But that did not prevent the occurrence of riots. The negotiations were in fact always prolonged. Then at a general session they proceeded with the election. But there was no written ballot. The principal persons took it in turn to put forward a name, the same one in each case, if the preliminary negotiations had been successful. The crowd's role was to respond by acclamation. Hence the importance attached to the right of having the first voice and naming the person elected – which was known as the *Kur*. Traditionally since the 11th century the *prima vox* had belonged to the Archbishop of Mainz. Who had the right to the succeeding votes? There was much speculation on this point after the double election of 1198 had called attention to the inconvenience of having no well-regulated electoral law. Drawing his inspiration from certain precedents and from the political circumstances – and even the prejudices – of his own circle (Saxony), Eike von Repgow, writing about 1230 in his *Sachsenspiegel* – the first great treatise on German law – recognises six princes as possessing a right to the *Kur* – the three Rhineland archbishops (Trier, Mainz, Cologne), and three lay lords (the Count Palatine of the Rhine, the Duke of Saxony, and the Margrave of Brandenburg); a fourth layman (the king of Bohemia) – whom Eike had expressly desired to exclude for being without German nationality, although a vassal of the Emperor, was soon added to the list. From now onwards, therefore, it included seven names, which smoothed the way for its adoption, seven being reckoned as a sacred number. It began to take on a certain official authority. According to Eike, the right of these persons lay only in being the first to vote; and even then, if the princes as a whole had reached agreement before the voting, those with the first voice were not obliged to do more than utter the name that had been previously agreed upon. These six or seven were therefore not, properly speaking, electors; but they soon became such. People ceased to consider that the other princes also possessed a vote. At the double election of 1257 (Richard Earl of Cornwall and Alphonse of Castile) the evolution was complete. It was surprisingly rapid. Without attempting to clear up all the problems posed by this almost abrupt change, we may recall that the first half of the 13th century was a period when the whole history of German society (and particularly of the nobles) was moving strongly in a hierarchical direction. The formation of a college of privileged electors ranking above the princes is in certain respects an event of the same order as the formation of a well-defined class of princes (in the new and narrow sense of the word) above the level of the Counts. When once our candidate was elected, what were to be his title and his powers?

3. Royal titles and powers: the Empire

Once elected, the prince chosen by his peers was from that moment onwards king. But so that he might appear to be invested with full royal dignity one act had to be performed, which normally followed very quickly after the election. This was a religious ceremony, the consecration, which consisted of an anointing with holy oil and a solemn investiture with the insignia of royalty. These acts conferred upon the king the impress of an almost sacred and quasi-priestly character, to which we shall have to return.

I have been speaking of kingship. Election by the princes, in fact, created a king, and not an emperor. This is a point that cannot be too strongly stressed. To become Emperor, our elected candidate needed a supplementary consecration to which we shall return later on.

He was a king, then; but king of what? After some hesitation (which does not concern us here), custom by the end of the 11th century had firmly crystallised. The candidate elected by the German princes, the king consecrated in a German church, was *Romanorum rex, Römischer König*. What did that title mean?

In the first place it meant that from the moment of his election the king ruled over all the territory called *Imperium Romanum*, that is to say Burgundy and Italy, as well as the former kingdom of Eastern France or Lorraine; no Hohenstaufen would ever be specially consecrated King of Lorraine. On the other hand it sometimes happened that when the King of the Romans passed into Italy, he had himself reconsecrated as King of the Italians or Lombards, in a church belonging to the ancient Lombard kingdom. Frederick Barbarossa was the only one of his house to add to the two royal consecrations – at Aix-la-Chapelle and Pavia – a third one at Arles, as King of Burgundy. But legally speaking these ceremonies had no force.

According to his title the King of the Romans was not an Emperor; yet he already ruled over an empire.

What were his real powers over this immense, overlarge empire? Here is another question that I cannot treat fully on this occasion. It is obvious that a distinction must be made between Germany and Lorraine (now entirely absorbed) on the one hand, and Italy and Burgundy on the other. In Germany, the royal prestige of the Hohenstaufen was still very considerable, especially in Barbarossa's time; but from then onwards it began to reveal two great weaknesses: there was no organised administration, comparable with the great bureaucracy in Angevin England, or even comparable with what was beginning to take shape at the end of the 12th century in Capetian France; and there was no concentrated royal domain, no *Ile-de-France*. Confronting the royal authority there stood the great lords, who possessed local judicial powers. Already in Barbarossa's day they were acquiring isolated privileges; more especially under Frederick II (who was almost continuously absent from Germany, pursuing his Italian and world-wide ambitions), they acquired even wider privileges. These territorial lords (*domini terrae, Landherrn*) were to succeed in obtaining from the Emperor-King some large concessions and gradually to become the real masters of the country. In Italy and in Burgundy the King of the Romans was scarcely obeyed at all – generally speaking – except when present; he very rarely visited Burgundy (except for Frederick I, who through his wife was master of Franche-Comté); in Italy he had to fight incessant wars against local powers, especially the towns. There is nothing more characteristic than the ingenuously admiring remark of Otto of Freising about Barbarossa in 1157: 'the Prince won back the lands north of the Alps; by his very presence peace was restored to the Franks, and by his absence the Italians were deprived of it'.[9]

But the title 'King of the Romans' did not denote simply a power to command which was straightway conceded to the person who wielded it; it implied also an idea of candidature or future expectations. The king who had been elected by the German princes was the future Emperor. He was the only one amongst them all who could receive the imperial dignity. Such was the current conception in Germany. The poem – the

Ligurinus – written about 1187, perhaps in Alsace, in the Cistercian Abbey of Pairis, puts these words into the mouth of one of the princes who have assembled in 1152 to elect the king :[10] 'whoever Germany has chosen as its king, to him wealthy Rome bows its head and takes him as its master'. This idea won acceptance not only among German rulers and their faithful supporters; it was almost universally recognised throughout Europe. The Popes themselves accepted it. To Gregory VII, Henry IV after election was both 'king, and by the grace of God, future Emperor'.[11] Innocent III, in March 1202, recognised that the princes possessed the right to 'elect the king who will then be promoted to the position of Emperor' (*regem in imperatorem postmodum promovendum*).[12]

But though a candidate for the Empire, the King of the Romans was not for all that already Emperor. What more was required for him to become so? A new consecration, under very strict conditions as to persons and place – much stricter than in the halcyon days of the Carolingian Empire. Only the Pope could consecrate – more precisely, have the king anointed in his presence and then personally crown him Emperor; and this ceremony could only take place in a single city – Rome – which was considered to be the capital – *caput* – both of the Roman Empire and of Christianity. There were nobles and clerics at Rome who maintained that it was only election by the Romans that created an Emperor; but no one apart from them took this archaic theory seriously. Yet it seems to have been generally admitted that no imperial consecration was valid unless attended by the acclamations of the Roman people, that is to say unless it took place in Rome itself. It might happen that a King of the Romans was prevented by circumstances from attending an imperial consecration on the banks of the Tiber; in that case he would remain all his life simply a king. Such was the lot of Conrad III, the first Hohenstaufen, and later on of King Philip (of Swabia). This is a question of title on which French writers today sometimes make mistakes, though Germans never do and never have done. Walther von der Vogelweide could speak of the imperial head – *keiserlichez houbet* – of Philip, for this head had been promised to the Empire; for did not the King of the Romans already attach to his title the imperial epithet *semper augustus*? But in Walther's eyes Philip was never anything more than *der Künec*.[13]

Normally, however, the king would become Emperor. No sooner was he elected than he set about preparing his *expeditio Romana*, his *Römerzug*. Having assembled his army, he would cross one of the alpine passes (usually the Brenner or the Septimer); and having been consecrated King of Italy on the way in a Lombardy church, he would hold a solemn diet in Northern Italy – usually in the plain of Roncaglia. Then he proceeded to Rome, where the ceremony took place – on principle in St. Peter's – according to a ritual in which every detail had significance. There were often disturbances, for the Roman people were turbulent, and were not at all fond of German knights, who for their part had no love for the Romans. But this was of little consequence. From that moment onwards the German prince would be 'the ever august 'Emperor of the Romans', *Romanorum imperator semper augustus*. By a misconception of a kind not uncommon in the Middle Ages, concerning the sense of the word *augustus* (which was thought to be derived from *augere*), the imperial chancery, when beginning to conduct its correspondence in German, would translate this by *Römischer Keiser zu allen Zeiten Merer des Richs*.

What was the content of this imperial title? To define this is the purpose of the second part of this essay.

II

THE CONCEPT OF EMPIRE

Part One

The study of political ideas and sentiments is always extremely difficult owing to various problems, of which the following are the principal ones. In the minds of men the intellect and the emotions form a well-knit whole, and ideas and feelings run into one another. In order to analyse them, however, one must examine them separately; and this act of dissection is to a large extent artificial. Moreover, a single institution like the Empire was thought of and experienced in very different ways at different periods, and even at one and the same period by different social groups; it is almost impossible in explaining the matter – and often even in research – to enter into these detailed shades of difference. And lastly, both the ideas and the sentiments are only known to us through expressions of them that still survive in texts (supplemented by sculptured monuments and ceremonies). Now the expression is often very clumsy, especially in the Middle Ages, and often falls under suspicion of being insincere through the use of conventional literary devices or because of personal or political bias. And – a still more serious fault perhaps – the texts are generally the work of professional writers, *littérateurs* or clerks belonging to the chancery. It would be childish to credit Frederick I or Frederick II with all the theories developed by their notaries, or all Germans without exception with the one-sided views of Walther von der Vogelweide or the author of the *Ligurinus*. Nevertheless it would be much more valuable for us to know the thoughts and aspirations of men of action than the conceptions or musings of a few professional stylists. In what follows I shall be obliged to make some necessary simplifications; but it is as well to warn you that some simplification is involved.

1. Historical memory; Roman & Carolingian traditions

Some of the prestige which surrounded the name of Emperor came from the historical memories that it evoked. For it would indeed be a grave mistake to think that the men of the 12th and 13th centuries were insensitive to their history. True, they had only an inaccurate knowledge of it, and in their eyes it was often confused with legend. But this history, though largely fictitious or badly understood, was food for their imaginations. For well-educated people, especially for clerks, it was handed down through lengthy chronicles of the world which were so numerous at this period. It was to Frederick Barbarossa that his uncle Bishop Otto von Freising dedicated his great *Historia de duabus civitatibus*, which was a kind of *Discourse on Universal History*. For the non-Latin-reading public, a clerk of Ratisbon – perhaps the self-same priest Conrad to whom we owe the famous German adaptation of the *Chanson de Roland* – wrote *circa* 1150 a history in German verse of more than 17,000 lines on the Empire from Augustus to Conrad III. In the 12th century the nobles, generally speaking, were cultured, and eager to read or at least listen to recitations; and even those who had no knowledge of the chronicles picked up scraps of history, from epic poems or from purely oral tradition, like that which is known to have circulated, for example, under Charlemagne. These narratives acted all the more powerfully on men's minds because the law – which was essentially customary law – and religion – which is by its nature traditional – both predisposed them to the view that the past was in itself something venerable, upon which the present ought to model itself.

The imperial monarchy was closely bound up with two great traditions: that of the Carolingians – especially Charlemagne – and that of the ancient Roman Emperors.

The Carolingian tradition always remained alive in the Empire. It is the explanation of the customary choice of place – customary, though not compulsory – for the consecration – Aix-la-Chapelle; and at Aix-la-Chapelle the very church that contained the tomb of Charlemagne. Rightly or wrongly, it was thought that the Salic dynasty, and consequently the Swabian dynasty, descended from the Salic in the female line, came down from the 'noble and ancient Carolingian seed' through the mother of Henry III, the Empress Gisèle.[14] Under Frederick Barbarossa, a very clear and concerted effort was made by the supporters of the throne to assert the importance of these great traditions. They forged a charter of Charlemagne, to this church at Aix-la-Chapelle, inserting into it one of the clearest statements in our possession about the constitutional theory of the Empire. A certain Latin poet, known by the name of *Archipoeta*, in the service of the imperial chancellor, Archbishop Rainald of Dassel, of Cologne, portrayed Frederick as 'transfixing the rebels with his avenging lance, and thus representing the conquering arm of Charles.'[15] The chancery itself delighted to reproduce at the head of many imperial decrees the redundant protocol which forms the preamble to the proclamation of Charlemagne.[16]

But there is even better evidence. Charlemagne, as we know,

was buried at Aix-la-Chapelle. Otto III, in the year 1000, had caused a search to be made for his tomb – then almost forgotten – and had opened it in order to gaze upon the marvellous remains. Here was a romantic episode which legend soon embroidered in even more romantic colours. Frederick I dared to take a particularly bold step. He added Charles to the ranks of the Church's saints. The exhumation of the relics took place, with great pomp, on December 29th 1166. Unfortunately this 'canonisation' – the actual word used in an imperial proclamation, of doubtful authenticity, it is true, but certainly drawn up by a contemporary – depended on the consent given by a Pope, Pascal III, who was opposed by the imperial party backed by most of the cardinals, and so ranks in Catholic tradition as only an anti-Pope. There is thus some doubt even today about the legitimacy of the act, and it is not quite certain whether Charlemagne is really 'Saint Charlemagne'.

We seem to have devoted a good deal of space to the Carolingian tradition. But even under Barbarossa this tradition does not appear to have been prominent; and later on it faded away perceptibly. It is not to Germany that we must turn, about the year 1200, to find a monarchy inspired by the memory of Charlemagne and concerned to revive it and make the most of it; we must turn rather to the Capetian monarchy of Philip Augustus. What was the reason for this relative weakness, and especially for the steady fading, of this aspect of historical memory in Germany? In the course of my studies I have often had cause to put this question to myself, but to this very day I have never been able to find an altogether satisfactory answer. A good deal of importance must no doubt be attached to purely literary differences. In France, it was epic literature that was responsible for the very early popularisation of the Carolingian legend. In Germany, on the other hand, there was hardly anything of this nature except a literature which palely reflected this style; its own epics were directed into other channels. True, we still have to explain why Germany did not have its own native Carolingian *geste*. I do not know whether the existence of legendary themes of a genuinely Germanic kind, forming a ready subject for poetic inspiration, would explain this rather peculiar deficiency. All we can do here is to state the facts. At the end of the 12th century, it is probable that the Charlemagne legend, as far as the mass of the people was concerned, already had something foreign and French about it; and this very circumstance must have made it seem a rather inept way of upholding a monarchy in the eyes of those to whom the Capetian monarchy, despite the excellent relationship subsisting between Philip Augustus or Saint Louis and the Hohenstaufen, appeared as a rival. Moreover, the Emperors had other precedents to invoke, which were their own, which no one could dispute, and which it was therefore only natural they should prefer – those provided by the ancient Roman Empire. In a decree of September 26th 1165, Barbarossa mentions among his 'predecessors' and alongside 'Charles' (Charlemagne) and Louis the Pious, Constantine, Justinian and Valentinian.[17]

Habits of mind going back to the humanism of the 16th century make us inclined today to imagine that there was a clear division between what we call Antiquity and what we call the Middle Ages. But the men of the 12th and 13th centuries did not view the matter at all in this light. Their thought when applied to history was generally dominated by the idea of the four empires, based upon the prophecies of Daniel. The fourth kingdom in order of time was the Roman Empire, which was to be followed by the end of the world. This had not yet happened; and so people were still living, about the year 1200, under the Roman Empire. This notion naturally took on peculiar strength in the minds of princes who called themselves *Romanorum imperatores*, and in the minds of their subjects. The *Kaiserchronik*, as I have already mentioned, began with Augustus and went straight on to the first of the Hohenstaufen, Conrad III. 'I have dealt', wrote Otto of Freising in the prologue to his *Livre des deux cités*, 'with the line of Roman Emperors . . . continuing up to the present day.'

This idea of the continuity of tradition was part of the ancient heritage of mediaeval historical writing. But in the Hohenstaufen's time it exercised a greater spell than ever over men's minds, because it was moving with the general current of ideas. We commonly speak today of 'the Renaissance of the

12th century', and this description is a fairly apt one. Not only did this century in fact see a complete transformation in the realm of ideas; but this intellectual ferment of an extremely intense and original kind, like the great upheaval of the 16th century, found its favourite food for thought in the literary models of antiquity. There was indeed a humanist movement in the 12th century and this return to the classics could not fail to exercise influence in the political sphere as well. It gave direct inspiration to two movements which were extremely different, and yet related to one another.

In the first place, in Rome itself in 1143, the population of the city rebelled against the Pope; this communal insurrection, beginning in much the same way as those of many other towns struggling against an ecclesiastical lord, soon took on the character of a quasi-archaeological effort at reconstruction, including an attempt to re-establish the Senate and the reappearance of the letters S.P.Q.R. on inscriptions. The leader of this strange enterprise was a well-educated clerk, Arnold of Brescia. The Romans sought to negotiate with the German kings, Conrad III and then Frederick I. They wanted the government of the Empire; but they wanted a truly Roman Empire in which the head would reside in the Eternal City. And they even claimed the right, if not to elect the Emperor, at least to confirm him in office. Frederick Barbarossa cared nothing for an Empire like that – Italian, popular, and anticlerical; so he helped the Papacy to suppress this Roman insurrection.

But – and here we see the second aspect of the political influence exerted by humanism – the German Sovereign and his circle were no less sensitive than Arnold of Brescia and his countrymen to the glory of the Roman past. Only they interpreted its lessons in a different way. It was the Empire, and not the Senate, that they wished to re-establish in all its ancient greatness. Some of their ideas on this subject came to them from the Italian lawyers. Italians of all periods had always had a taste for legal studies, and law had been taught in the schools. But in this sphere too, the end of the 11th century saw a revival. The great codes of Justinian, which had almost been forgotten, were rediscovered and became the subject of special teaching –

particularly in the great school at Bologna, and numerous commentaries and 'glosses' were written upon them. This renaissance of Roman law was one of the forms taken by the great Renaissance of Antiquity, and it was one of the earliest and most important in its effects. In the *Code* and the *Digest* people saw a well-ordered Empire coming to life, governed by an Emperor who was absolute. The Italian lawyers who devoted themselves to the study of the *Corpus Juris*, the so-called *glossateurs*, were for the most part devoted to the Emperors, and many joined the service of the imperial administration; some of them even lived in the household of Frederick Barbarossa during his sojourn south of the Alps.

Not surprisingly, therefore, it is a legal document which gives us the most characteristic evidence of what might be called the theory of imperial continuity in Barbarossa's time. In November 1158, at the Diet of Roncaglia, a law had been promulgated on behalf of the students.[18] It concludes with these words: 'We command that this law be inserted in the imperial constitutions under the title *ne filius pro patre*'; you must understand that the law was to be inscribed in the Justinian Code, in Book IV, section 13, following on fragments of the constitutions of Gordian and Diocletian, the latest of which was about A.D. 294. And this order, as many manuscripts attest, was carried out. There could be no clearer indication of the desire to link up the chain of legislative tradition. Moreover, quite independently of any directives from above, and simply for the convenience of readers, other Hohenstaufen constitutions were annexed by the *glossateurs* to different sections of the Code. The professors of law thus applied to these decrees issued by contemporary sovereigns the same procedure customarily used by them for the laws of Justinian, which had been issued after the Code was compiled, and so had not found a place in it. Rather than use a collection of laws gathered together separately from the main code, ways had been devised of weaving them into the very texture of the Code itself, and these were called the *Authentiques*. It is symptomatic that Frederick I and Frederick II should thus have been placed upon the same footing as Justinian. Among the Christian Emperors, this Prince and Lawgiver was the one preferred by writers, legal or otherwise, when they wished to evoke the memory of the ancient predecessors of the Hohenstaufen.

Naturally, there is also sometimes a mention of Constantine, as we have just seen above; but the references as a whole are fewer than in the Ottos' days. The fact of the matter is that he was commonly held to have been the author of the notorious *Donation*, by which the Pope was said to have been given authority over Rome and the greater part of Italy. Especially since the outbreak of the great struggle between the Papal Power and the Empire under the Salian kings, this concession was reckoned most embarrassing in the eyes of the imperialists. If they had been good historians as we understand that word today, they could easily have disputed its validity. For there can be no doubt that the celebrated document in question is purely apocryphal – an impudent forgery of the 8th century. There were in fact among the disciples of Arnold of Brescia some bold spirits who ventured to throw doubts upon its authenticity. But the critical sense was not sufficiently widespread at the time for this scepticism to meet with much support. The Hohenstaufen's most faithful partisans admitted the *Donation* as genuine, and were content to do more than cavil at it. This was Walter von der Vogelweide's attitude. According to him, when Constantine handed the Pope 'the lance, the sword and the crown', an angel was heard to proclaim: 'Misfortune, misfortune, triple misfortune.' It is not surprising that the memory of the prince who – to adopt Walter's phrase – 'had given this poison to Christianity', was not gladly recalled.

Moreover, the Christian Emperors were not the only ones whom people delighted to call to mind. In the eyes of *Archipoeta*, Barbarossa was not only another Charlemagne, he was also the new Augustus. Under Frederick II these authentically classical and almost pagan traditions were very clearly expressed in the realm of art. Like the Caesars of antiquity, the Emperor had his own statue erected, dressed in the chlamys, on a triumphal arch at the entrance to Capua. And in obvious imitation of the ancient Roman coinage, his effigy, crowned with laurel, figured on the fine gold pieces that he struck from 1231 onwards at Brindisi and Messina – the 'Augustales'.

The classical tradition did not furnish the Empire with forms of literary or plastic expression only; it underlay certain claims of a much more realistic kind. Before long we shall be studying the practical content of the idea of Empire; but we must first say a word about another element in the idea of imperial prestige – the sacred character of the sovereign.

2. *The Emperor as a sacred person; messianism*

The idea of royalty as something sacred, which was common to the whole of the Middle Ages, did not simply apply to the imperial monarchy. It went back much further than that. The dynasties of the ancient *Germania* had been invested with a hereditary religious character. Later on, in the Carolingian period, the Church had to some extent authenticated this concept by christianising it. The rite of unction was then borrowed from the Old Testament. From now onwards the rite of unction with holy oil would, in the eyes of the majority of his subjects, give the king a quasi-supernatural character. Now unction was not confined to the Emperors; the kings of France and England – to mention only two – also had a right to it. But the full consequences of the sacred anointing of the sovereign were nowhere better exploited than in the Empire. It was a German, Guy of Osnabrück, who said: 'The king must be deemed a person apart from the ordinary run of men; for, having been anointed with sacred oil, he assumes priestly qualities.'[19] But Guy of Osnabrück was writing these words in 1084 or 1085, under Henry IV, at a time when the vigorous attack led by the Gregorian reformers against royalty was at its height, and was provoking a most vigorous response from the imperialists. Under the Hohenstaufen controversy on this point died down, and the protagonists took up less clearly defined positions. The Gregorians, anxious to reduce royalty to a condition of simple temporal power and kings to a position of simple loyal Christians, were in part successful. No doubt the old notion of the sacred character of royalty did not disappear from men's minds. The Canonist Rufinus, writing in Barbarossa's reign, knew that in order to justify the oath of loyalty to the Emperor taken by bishops (a priest could not in principle swear fealty to a layman), it must be stated that the Emperor 'consecrated by holy unction is not altogether a layman'.[20] We shall see in a few moments even clearer proof of the latent persistence of this idea; but when it found expression, it was now usually only in rather attenuated forms. According to the ancient ritual of consecration the future Emperor used to receive the priestly robes from the Pope; and the official documents described this part of the solemn rite in words which contain the idea put forward above by Guy of Osnabrück: 'Here the Pope makes him a cleric (*Ibique facit eum clericum*)'. Under the Hohenstaufen, the ceremony of investing with robes still survived, but it had a weaker significance, the King of the Romans being deemed to be admitted to the number of the canons of St. Peter. This was a distinct downgrading, for in the Middle Ages one could be a canon without having been admitted to Holy Orders. The rest of the ritual is marked by a very curious tendency. Since it was essential to recognise that the Emperor belonged to some specific Christian rank above that of a simple layman, and as there was some reluctance to put him on a level with the priests, an attempt was made to place him on a par with the deacons. Neither the status of canon nor that of deacon carried much prestige as far as the imperial monarchy was concerned.

Yet by the time of Frederick Barbarossa, Henry VI or Frederick II, we have reached the moment when the fullest use was made of the words 'consecrated' or even 'holy' as applied to the imperial majesty in the Emperor's palace, in his laws and proclamations, and in the Empire itself. The phrase *Sacrum Imperium* – later rendered as *Heiliges Reich* or Holy Empire, dates from this period. More than this: these relatively human terms of 'sacred' or 'holy' were sometimes replaced by the almost blasphemous one 'divine': '*Deus es, de prole deorum*', says the writer Godefroy of Viterbo (an Italian, but coming from a family of German origin), when addressing Henry VI.[21] And Frederick II himself wrote to his son: *O Caesarei sanguinis divina proles*. But the origin of these fulsome expressions is not to be sought in any very profound depth of feeling; it is entirely a literary matter. The chancery clerks or writers borrowed from the vocabulary of the Later Empire, from the *Corpus Juris Civilis* itself. One must always make allowance when interpreting the documents of this period, for a certain intentional archaism and pedantry of language. Innumerable charters call the Counts 'consuls'; and Barbarossa's chancery would from time to time style the archbishops *archiflamines*.[22] These words such as sacred, holy, divine, were thus a kind of tradition; though not a tradition entirely devoid of meaning. They sought to express a very lofty conception of the imperial dignity, whose value in practice will become apparent later on; but they were in any case the language of educated people, and they expressed the ideas of a fairly restricted circle.

On the other hand speculations about the end of the world, when applied to the imperial monarchy, caused a tremendous stirring of the soul. This is a very important point, and a very strange one, worth dwelling on for a moment.

The people of the Middle Ages thought much about the end of the world. They were ready to believe that it was quite near, and with the help of signs in the Sacred Books they often reflected on the conditions in which the Last Judgment would take place. Of course, it was to be preceded by the coming and the triumph of Antichrist. The general course of events – according to sources that are not our immediate concern – had been sketched out at the end of the 11th century by a Burgundian monk, Adso de Montiérender, in a treatise entitled *De Ortu et Tempore Antichristi*, which created a great stir. There would come a king of the Franks who would unite the whole Roman Empire under his rule. Once he had gained the victory he would betake himself to Jerusalem, where he would lay down his crown and sceptre on the Mount of Olives. Then the Antichrist would appear. Naturally enough, in an Empire reconstituted by the German kings, the last and glorious Emperor was thought of in terms of one of these sovereigns; and there was constant speculation as to whether it might not be the particular prince of the moment who was destined to fulfil this wondrous role. The persistence of these speculations in Barbarossa's time is attested in various documents – including a play in Latin verse, probably composed in the Bavarian monastery of Tegernsee, the *Ludus de Antichristo*.[23] In this play we see the Roman Emperor (*Imperator Romanus*) winning successive victories over the kings of France, Greece, Jerusalem and the pagan King of Babylon, then laying down the imperial crown upon the altar at Jerusalem, though still remaining king of Germany (*rex Teutonicorum*). The Antichrist comes on the scene, and though he is powerless to triumph over the arms of the German king, he wins him over by faked miracles. Following the appearance and martyrdom of the prophets Enoch and Elijah, the Antichrist reigns until the trumpets suddenly sound, Antichrist collapses, and everyone sings *Laudem dicite Deo nostro*. In a short while I shall return to several passages in this strange document, which expresses, beneath the traditional theological imagery, a strong faith in the imperial supremacy.

In Frederick II's time, thoughts of the Antichrist, which were more intense than ever, took a singular turn. More or less everywhere in Europe, but particularly in Italy, the end of the 12th and the beginning of the 13th century witnessed an intense religious ferment. The orthodox Church of the period was threatened simultaneously by a great mystical heresy – that of the Vaudois – and by a sect that was almost devoid of Christianity, but full of asceticism and inclined above all to mystical discoveries – the Cathari. The Papacy reacted to this peril by organising a crusade, and then by the Inquisition. Moreover in 1209 – the year when Otto IV was crowned Emperor – the Franciscans began their great preaching mission. Full of dangers as it was for Church discipline, it was only kept within the bosom of the Church by the deep respect of St. Francis for the priesthood on the one hand, and by the broad-mindedness and skill shown by the Curia on the other. And even then it was not to be without some heretical offshoots. More than ever men's thoughts were turning to the beyond and to the end of the world, to the figure of Antichrist, which was orthodox enough – yes, even to a new kind of messianism, which was much less so. A Cistercian abbot in Calabria, Joachim of Flore, who died in 1202, announced that after the reign of the Father (the Old Law) and the Son, a third kingdom would come, the kingdom of the Holy Spirit, in which the faithful would understand the *Eternal Gospel* in its spiritual meaning. Joachim did not think he was making any breach with the traditional faith. But his disciples, who were recruited especially from Franciscan convents, were to go much further than he had, for they expected that the third age – close at hand, in their opinion – would see the ruin of the established Church.

It was here in Italy, agitated by these mystical hopes and fears, that the destiny of the Empire under Frederick II was decided. The war between the imperial party and the papal party, which constantly set one town against another, and even different parties within a town, put the whole country in disarray. As the disturbance spread, it made men all the more inclined to reflect upon the future. Prophecies were rife. Frederick himself was a strange personality who greatly exercised the imaginations of his contemporaries as he exercises the imaginations of many Germans to this day. Brought up in Italy, and quite foreign in manners and outlook to all things German – he could probably not even speak the language – he was nevertheless immensely cultured, in Greek and Arabic no less than in Latin. He surrounded himself with an oriental luxury that struck and often scandalised the crowd. He was curious about philosophy and about observing natural phenomena; he was probably a mystic in his own peculiar way, a way that was apparently not particularly orthodox; for his lofty intelligence – so it seems – had been attracted by the Averroist philosophy. Finally, as was only fitting, he was deeply impressed with the grandeur of his own role, and was politically ruthless. Men's opinions of him tended to veer according to their views of prophets and messianism. For the servants of the Papacy, for Pope Gregory IX and even for Innocent IV, Frederick was, if not the Antichrist (for as theologians they knew that he did not exhibit all the marks of the Antichrist), at any rate his forerunner, *infelix prenuntius Antichristi*, as Innocent IV expressed it,[24] 'the beast coming up out of the sea', who was described in grand phrases lifted from the Apocalypse. The faithful supporters of the Emperor, on the other hand, naturally drew on very different pictures. One of them, a German Dominican, Brother Arnold, thought that he had actually discovered the Antichrist. There could be no doubt about it – he was Innocent IV! And above all they were unanimous in holding a positively messianic conception of what might be called the historical mission of their prince.

After all, there is not such a great distance between Antichrist and Messiah – not much more than a simple inversion of the point of view! The same words could be used on either side. *Inmutator saeculi* – he who will change the face of the centuries: it was in these terms that a publicist from the papal party, Albert de Behaim, described Frederick II, *typicus prenuntius Antichristi*.[25] Well there is certainly more than one way of 'changing the centuries'. The faithful adherents of Frederick II also believed that profound changes were imminent and were confident that they would be brought about by their master, but in the form of a golden age with which men's minds had become familiar through the musings of the Joachites. A prophecy that was widespread enough to have reached the English chronicler Matthew Paris[26] proclaimed these glorious days in a style that was intentionally obscure. 'Those who walked in darkness will return to light; and the things which were separated and scattered abroad will be consolidated. A large cloud will begin to rain because a changer of the world is born (*quia natus est inmutator saeculi*). This word '*inmutator*', charged as it was with mystic meaning, clung to Frederick II. Matthew Paris himself notes[27] as he follows the Emperor's death: 'About this time there died the greatest of the princes of the earth, Frederick, the marvel of the world and the miraculous transformer of the times (*stupor mundi et inmutator mirabilis*).

But to return to the prophecy that has just been quoted. One particular phrase deserves attention: 'A large cloud will begin to rain.' It is clearly an echo of a celebrated verse in Isaiah.[28] The verse itself, almost literally reproduced (*quem nubes pluerunt justum et super eum coeli desuper roraverant*), occurs in an anonymous passage that also applies it to the Emperor, and this time not simply in an allusive fashion, but in the most explicit manner. The Emperor is named, and there is attached to his name a very characteristic epithet: 'Frederick the Holy.'[29] Now everyone at that time knew that the Church traditionally looked upon this prophetic passage as a proclamation of the coming of the Christ. Among Frederick's entourage, however sacrilegious it may seem to us, the reference was a perfectly conscious one. It can even be found in the Emperor's decrees, which were drawn up by his chancery; for example, a letter to his son Conrad, in which he tells him of his successes against the Pope:[30] 'The pontiffs and the pharisees had gathered together against the Lord Christ; the prince of sedition, filled with headlong pride, had risen up against the prince of the Romans, to fight against him by word and by deed; but behold the Lord of hosts has brought down the pride of the prince of the priests . . .'; and in a letter to the town of Iesi, his native place, 'resplendent with his cradle', he twice calls it his 'Bethlehem'.[31]

Such expressions seemed much less blasphemous to the men of the 13th century than they would to the most pious of our contemporaries. Men's minds at that period were accustomed to a symbolical view of the universe; everyone knew that a human being can be a 'type' of Christ, without ceasing to be a simple human being. It is a well-known fact that the disciples of St. Francis – or at least the most advanced among them – laid great stress upon this idea of the perfect imitation of Jesus: 'It is well that we should remember in the first place that Francis, our blessed master, conformed in all his actions to the pattern of Christ' – these are the opening words both of the *Actus b. Francisci et sociorum ejus* and the *Little Flowers of St. Francis*.[32] But it was no slight matter for an Emperor to be held up as an image of the Saviour. One can hardly refrain from seeing in this audacious concept one of the extreme forms in which the ancient but still lively notion of the sacred character of royalty reappeared under the influence of Italian mysticism of the 13th century; and it was of course to a large extent similar ideas and similar hopes that explain the posthumous legend of Frederick II, which I do not propose to deal with here.

III

THE CONCEPT OF EMPIRE

Part Two

3. *The temporal power of the Emperors; universal monarchy*

What contribution was made to the Swabian Emperors by the

heritage of Charlemagne, and further back still, by that of Justinian and Augustus?

In the first place, they received a lesson in absolutism. From Barbarossa's time onwards, the servants of the Emperor supplied a multitude of formulae affirming, in theory, the omnipotence of the prince, who was raised by his rank above the laws: *pro lege voluntas principis esse solet*, as the author of the *Ligurinus* puts it.[33] True, these were commonplaces borrowed from Roman Law, which were constantly in the mouths of lawyers at all the European courts of this period, but without any very precise meaning being attached to them; but in imperial circles these banalities were repeated more often than elsewhere, and perhaps with more emphasis. As for Frederick II, he found in his patrimony a new example of absolutism, nearer at hand and more vivid than that offered by the Rome of the Caesars to the admirers of the past. For, as well as being Emperor, he was the King of Sicily, and as such the heir and upholder of a monarchy which was Norman in origin, and peculiarly strong and despotic in character. His counsellors, mostly taken from among the Sicilian bureaucracy, held the highest ideas of sovereign power and inspired Frederick with the same views. The sacred qualities with which, as we know, contemporaries endowed the Emperor, formed the basis of the most extreme claims. Whoever disobeyed his master – even if the recalcitrant person were the Pope himself – committed sacrilege.

Within the frontiers of the Empire proper the Emperor was equally a king. His power over these territories (apart from the city of Rome, to which we shall return) had after all nothing specifically imperial about it. But the fact to note is that the frontiers of the Empire, in the restricted sense of the term, were by no means the limits of the Emperor's aspirations. As the successor of the masters of the ancient world, he, like them, was *dominus mundi*, an expression that frequently occurs in the writings of his supporters. The very moderate Otto of Freising writes in his chronicle:[34] 'The imperial authority, in which is vested responsibility for the supreme government [*patrocinium*] of the whole universe'. And Barbarossa himself[35] says: 'and we, who by the grace of the divine mercy, hold the helm both of the City [Rome] and of the World'. And in clearer terms still an imperial clerk, at the Council of Pavia in 1159, used these words of the Emperor: 'the Prince of princes, who holds the Empire and the diadem of universal monarchy'.[36] This idea of universal dominion was not only justified by historical precedents; it also satisfied the need for writing in the temporal sphere as well as in the spiritual, for which the best minds of the age were searching. 'One God, one Pope, one Emperor' – this phrase occurs in this exact form in a decree of Barbarossa.[37]

In practice, what ambitions were comprised in this worldwide *patrocinium*? The claims which the German Emperors more than once asserted against their competitors for the Empire and for the Roman succession, the *basileis* of Byzantium, cannot really be considered as more than a series of rather theatrical gestures; for it was only in the *Ludus de Antichristo* that the *Imperator Romanorum* subjugated the King of the Greeks! Much more serious were the claims of the Empire upon the kingdoms of the West, formerly an integral part of the ancient Roman Empire, or upon the new kingdoms set up to the north and east of Germany, on Scandinavian or Slavonic territory. Not that the Emperor dreamt of annexing these lands; but he clearly considered himself superior to their rulers, who were nothing more than plain kings.

In order to catch the full flavour, and up to a certain point to realise these visions of far-spreading dominion, we must place ourselves in the reigns of Frederick I and Henry VI. A great deal of their strength was drawn from the renaissance of classical learning, particularly the renaissance of Roman law. An Italian jurist, Huguccio of Pisa, wrote in his commentary on the decretals of Gratian:[38] 'It is by Roman law alone that the Romans and the subjects of the Roman Empire are guided and governed. What of the French and other people beyond the Alps? Are they bound by Roman laws, and should they live according to them?' The reply comes: '*Most certainly, for they are and are meant to be subject to the Roman Empire.*' This line of thought, which was widespread among the Romanists during the period of Philip Augustus and his immediate successors, imbued the royal government of France, which was very jealous of its independence, with a lively mistrust of any teaching of Roman Law. And literature as well as legal works proclaimed the rights of the Emperor to universal dominion. The *Ludus de Antichristo* contained scenes depicting the future victories of the Empire, notably over France. We should notice, moreover, that the author of the *Ludus*, in pursuance of the well-known tendencies of Hohenstaufen policy, clearly felt no particular dislike for the Capetian dynasty. The *rex Francorum* is a valiant man; he only gives up his independence after a struggle, and when he has been defeated he makes his submission in tolerably noble terms. On the other hand the King of the Greeks goes down without a struggle before the Emperor. These two princes take up the same attitude when faced by the Antichrist: a threat is enough to win over the King of the Greeks; but the King of France only gives way when rich presents are offered to him. There is a perceptible shade of difference between the two. But in what uncompromising terms the imperial supremacy is proclaimed, based upon historical tradition and upon Roman Law! The Emperor says to the ambassadors whom he sends to the King of France in order to demand his submission:

'As it is written in the chronicles of the historians, the whole world was formerly the domain of the Romans, but the work of courageous men of the past is now destroyed by the degeneracy of their successors. . . . They have been responsible for the decay of that power which is now being recovered by our Most Puissant Majesty. Let all kings, then, now pay to the Roman Empire those tributes that were decreed of old.'

Whereupon the ambassadors reply to the king: 'We know full well that His Majesty in his wisdom must submit himself to *Roman Law*.'

But this was not merely the language of literary men or scholars. The Emperor's counsellors – and even the Emperor himself – speak in very similar terms. The Anglo-French writer John of Salisbury waxes indignant because Barbarossa's chancellor, the famous Rainald of Dassel, has addressed the King of France not as *rex*, but as *regulus*.[39] More clearly still the Emperor at the Diet of Dole, recalling the fact that he has invited to his court the kings of France, England and Denmark, to take counsel with them about the schism then dividing the Papacy, calls these sovereigns *provinciarum reges*, that is to say the kings of provinces of the Empire.[40] This supremacy even found expression in the insignia. Walter von der Vogelweide, who, as a good court poet, was very attentive to this kind of symbolism, contrasts the *zirkel* – the simple circle of gold – belonging to royalty with the more complicated shape, on an octagonal base, of the imperial crown.

Were these nothing more than empty words? Not entirely. For on several occasions the Emperor succeeded in getting his authority recognised by the northern kings and by the Slav kings or princes, and that in a form altogether foreign to Roman Law – claiming homage from vassals and feudal lords alike. The idea of universal dominion came from Rome, but it was embodied in rites that were the expression of contemporary society; and in the same way homage was quite often the expression of Papal theocracy. The Emperor would have been equally ready to demand homage of the kings of the West – of France and England: in the *Ludus* he requires it and actually obtains it from the King of France. The Capetians always knew how to defend their independence; but the care taken by writers in their service, especially since Philip Augustus's time, to affirm it, and the reaction against Roman Law referred to above; the exploitation in a French sense of the Carolingian legend; the theory – incidentally, a little later in date – about the king being 'Emperor in his own kingdom' – all these go to prove that the French Court had become aware of the danger and considered it to be by no means insignificant. Circumstances did not permit the English kings any such steady successes. In 1155 Henry II wrote to Barbarossa in humble terms which have not as yet perhaps been sufficiently explained:[41] 'We offer you our kingdom and all the lands under our dominion, we hand them over to your power, so that you may dispose of them as seems good to you, and so that your imperial will may be accomplished in all things.' In 1193 Richard Cœur de Lion, who had by chance fallen into the hands of Henry VI, paid him homage.

All this however did not produce any very tangible practical results. Under Frederick II, the imperial government's attitude changed slightly. It did not of course give up the claim to universal sovereignty – witness (amongst others) the preamble to the Great Charter of the Teutonic Order, in which the religious and crusading mission of the supreme power is so clearly set forth: 'God has established Our Empire above all the kings of the earth and extended Our dominion over diverse climes in order that We may set Ourselves to magnify his name down the centuries and to spread the faith among the Gentiles; for thus did the Holy Roman Empire of old prepare the way for the preaching of the Gospel. . . .'[42] But the imperial court in general was much less inclined than in the past to indulge in these grandiose dreams. The fact is that the Emperor was at this time engaged in an inexorable struggle with the Papacy. He would have liked to rally against it all sovereigns – and even lay lords – whom he considered to be threatened in the same way as himself by the encroachments of the spiritual power. It would have been unwise to scare away possible allies by any untimely declarations, all the more so because the Popes, who also looked for support from the kings, did not fail to represent themselves in that quarter as the adversaries of imperial ambition. 'What [said Innocent IV] is the main cause of the hatred shown by Frederick for the Catholic Church? The reason is this: he casts an ambitious eye on other kingdoms which he would fain subdue to his own power; and in the path he finds this Church whose duty it is, with maternal solicitude, to protect the rights and defend the liberties of Christian kings, who are her spiritual sons.' In the imperial manifestoes, the theme of world dominion gives way before that of the solidarity of kings. It goes without saying that this did not mean the death of the idea; and it would not be very difficult to follow its various manifestations in periods much nearer to our own.

4. The power over Rome and over the Church

In their Roman and Carolingian heritage, the German sovereigns not only found material for some rather vague dreams of universal monarchy; it also inspired them with two quite definite ambitions, seemingly of very different extent and yet closely bound up with one another – to exercise power over Rome, and power over the Papacy.

Properly speaking, Rome was not part of the Kingdom of

Italy, which was the heir of the former Lombard kingdom that had never been able to subjugate the papal city. The rights which the German sovereign managed to assert over it came from his position as Emperor or as King of the Romans. It appeared quite obvious to the imperialists that Rome, being in principle the capital of the Empire, must of necessity belong to it. 'By the will of God,' the chronicler Rahewin[43] represents Frederick Barbarossa as saying, 'I am called, and I verily am, the Roman Emperor; and I should therefore only possess the semblance of dominion, I should only bear a worthless title, a name without substance, if power over the city of Rome were to fall from my grasp.' But in the city itself there were two powers opposing the Emperor: a *de facto* power, the Roman nobility (for in Italy and generally speaking in the Mediterranean countries, in contrast with Northern and Central Europe, a large number of nobles lived in the towns, and were an influential urban class); and above all a power which, as well as being *de facto*, could rely upon *de jure* arguments – namely the papal power. The Popes supported their claims by an apocryphal document, the *Donation* of Constantine, and by more authentic decrees, requiring somewhat careful interpretation, however, which emanated from the Carolingian and Saxon kings. The legal situation of Rome and of the papal territory in general was, in short, extremely ill-defined. Hardly anyone disputed the fact that the Emperor possessed a rather vague supremacy.[44] But he had in fact considerable difficulty in exercising any effective authority, and hardly succeeded in doing so until he had subjected the local nobility and become in addition master of the Papacy itself.

The struggle between the Emperors and the Popes fills the entire Hohenstaufen period. It is impossible to give an account of it in a few words. But it is necessary to show how it was a direct consequence of the imperial idea. Not that the frequent dissensions between lay sovereigns and Popes during the Middle Ages were in any way confined to the Empire. They existed among all the Catholic States. In particular, when Gregory VII and his immediate successors asserted their claim to deprive the lay princes of the right to nominate the bishops and abbots, this 'Investiture dispute' outside the Empire – in

France and in England – became an extremely lively issue. But only in the case of the Emperor did it rapidly degenerate into an inexorable war of far-reaching significance, which lasted for centuries. Under Frederick II in particular it gave contemporaries the impression that the struggle could only come to an end with the crushing defeat of one or other of the two adversaries. Why was there this contrast? The reason is to be found in the different nature and varying importance of the interests at stake.

The French and English kings defended their rights against the Curia; they wanted to remain masters of their own clergy; they rejected all papal interference in their States. But they had no thought of subjugating the Papacy itself (leaving aside the Avignon Papacy, which came later). Between the Emperor and the Pope, however, the stakes were quite different: the Emperor thought he had rights over the Holy See; the Pope thought he had rights over the Empire; and both parties claimed to have rights over Rome.

What was the imperial point of view? In 1152 the papal election resulted in two candidates: the imperialist cardinals elected Victor IV, and the others Alexander III. The Emperor was quick to recognise Victor. At the Diet of Dole in 1162 Rainald of Dassel, the imperial chancellor, was indignant because the kings of France and of England did not rally round his master's candidate. To show the absurdity of their behaviour, he had recourse to an argument which he obviously thought effective, for he repeated it in three languages – Latin, French and German: 'If in any city of the kingdom some disagreement should arise concerning the episcopal dignity, and if Caesar should intervene to put an end to it by his own decision, there is no doubt at all that the prince would consider such an act a great insult; yet here they are trying to interfere in the same manner in Rome.'[45] The argument ran like this: the Pope is Bishop of Rome; now Rome is a city of the Empire, the imperial city of all cities; therefore just as the election of the Bishop of Paris, for example, is subject to the consent, and may require the arbitration, of the King of France, or the election of the Bishop of London is, under similar conditions, subject to the King of England, so the election of the Pope concerns the

Emperor, and the Emperor alone. Rainald did not tell the full story. Certainly, it was not only by virtue of his temporal sovereignty over Rome, but also by reason of his being entrusted with the *patrocinium* of the whole Christian world, that the Emperor thought he had a right to exercise over the Pope – the spiritual head of the world – the same protective supremacy that all kings, in their capacity as sacred persons, claimed over the Churches of their respective States. This was moreover very clearly expressed in the imperial proclamation of October 28th 1159, relating to the double election: 'The Roman Empire . . . must keep watch over the wellbeing of the whole world.'[46] Historically speaking, this was not an altogether invalid argument. It could fall back upon ancient precedents and even documents in which the imperial rights over the papal nomination had been recognised. The Saxon Emperors, the second Salian Emperor, Henry III, had made and unmade Popes; by their intervention they had snatched the Papacy from the yoke of the Roman factions; they had restored its moral dignity. The great misunderstanding, which broke out under Henry IV, arose from the fact that the Emperors did not and could not understand that the Papacy as reformed by their predecessors wanted henceforward to be independent, and having recovered its spiritual prestige was capable from now on of carrying along with it a large part of the clergy of Europe, and even of Germany.

Under Frederick II, when the struggle reached its climax, the imperial party found a new weapon in the doctrine of evangelical poverty, a very ancient doctrine, which at that period agitated many minds. It was really a protest by pious people against the worldliness of the Church. In 1227 Henry II wrote to Henry III of England:[47] 'It was on poverty and simplicity that the Early Church was founded.' And in a manifesto of 1246:[48] 'It was always our intention to see that clerics of all ranks, and in particular the foremost of them, should be brought to such a condition, and to the end of time maintained in the same, whereby they would resemble the fathers of the primitive Church, leading an apostolic life and imitating the humility of Our Lord. Those clerics were accustomed to see the angels, they abounded in miracles, they healed the sick, they raised the dead; and it was by their holiness, and not by force of arms, that they subdued kings and princes.' This evangelical outlook best suited the temporal interests of the secular power; for the clergy, deprived of their territorial possessions, would cease to be a danger to the State. At the same time the Emperor, perhaps an only half-sincere apostle of the return to pure Christianity (for who can claim to be able to plumb the secret depths of this complex personality?), was flattering the aspirations of certain devout groups and rallying round himself some useful support. He was playing his role as *immutator saeculi*.

And what was the Pope's point of view? One essential aspect of it is very clearly expressed in an often repeated phrase borrowed from the Epistle to the Hebrews (vii): 'For without all contradiction the less is blessed of the better'; meaning that the Pope, who was alone capable of making an Emperor by the rite of unction, should have some voice in his selection, and in consequence – so ran Innocent III's contention – in the election of the King of the Romans, who was by birth the prospective candidate for the Empire. On the other hand the Pope, St. Peter's successor, divinely commissioned to exercise control over Christian morality, has the power to summon all sinners before his judgment-seat. The heir of the Caesars, no less than the humblest of his subjects, is answerable to his jurisdiction. Here, too, there was a precedent: it was the Pope who, in Charlemagne's day, 'transferred' the Empire of the Greeks to the Franks. And this precedent was at the same time a threat; for what the Pope once gave, had he not still the power to take away? The vote of the princes was not enough to create a king, the Emperor-to-be; the Pope's consent was also necessary, at least in a contested election. By virtue of his power 'to bind and to loose', the Pope had the right to depose a heretical Emperor, or one who was morally unworthy. During interregna, it was he who kept order in the Empire. Between these opposing sets of principles, war was inevitable. And in these tragic circumstances the Empire, as the Hohenstaufen had conceived it, succumbed.

5. *The imperial idea and German patriotism*

Until now I have only considered the imperial idea in – so to speak – its international aspect. But the Emperor was also, by universal consent, sovereign over Germany; and from 962 to 1257 he was in fact always of German extraction. The title *Saint-Empire romain de nation germanique* (*Heiliges Römisches Reich Deutscher Nation*) did not appear till later – in the 15th century; but it was true before it actually came into use. This prerogative was calculated to foster patriotic pride; and this was certainly the effect it had in the Hohenstaufen period. It will be enough to produce a few examples to attest the fact. Otto of Freising[49] makes Frederick I say, in answer to the Romans who attempt to present him with the Empire as a gift from Rome: 'I am the lawful master. Let him who would wrest the club from the hands of Hercules come and do so – if he can. . . . The hand of the Franks, who are also called Germans [*Francorum sive Teutonicorum*], has not yet lost its vigour.' 'The Rhine, by a turn of the wheel of fortune, now governs the Tiber,' says the author of the *Ligurinus*.[50] In the *Ludus de Antichristo*, as we have seen, the Emperor, having laid down the crown, keeps the title of King of the 'Teutons'; and into the mouth of Antichrist the poet, whose imperialist sentiments are already known to us, puts a flamboyant eulogy of the Germans' military virtues. Other peoples were very plainly aware that the Empire, in spite of its aspirations towards universalism, was an essentially German thing. That was one of the reasons given by John of Salisbury for rejecting Barbarossa's pretensions over the papal election: 'Who made the Germans judges of the nations? Who gave those brutal and impetuous men such authority that at their own sweet will they can set up a prince above the heads of the sons of men?'[51] Protests of this kind, recognising the national character of the Empire, could not but have the effect – even among the Germans themselves – of strengthening these sentiments. In his manifesto of March 16th 1240, Frederick II addressed himself to Germany, personified in the best rhetorical manner: 'Arise, unconquerable Germania, arise, you German peoples! Defend this Empire of ours which, in spite of the jealousy of other nations, has brought us to the highest of dignities and to the sovereignty of the world.'[52] Frederick II, who was himself hardly German, was no doubt quite innocent of any such feelings; but he knew how to play upon the emotions.

At various times during the Middle Ages it was a great subject for debate among German writers whether their sovereigns had been right or wrong to pursue these vast imperial ambitions, instead of confining themselves to the more modest task of national unification, as it was achieved for example by the kings of France. In the years from 1859 to 1862, when Germany was still seeking unity, a lively polemical controversy on this point arose between a Protestant historian on the one side, with a *Kleindeutsch* tendency, Heinrich von Sybel, and a Catholic historian on the other, Julius Ficker, who favoured Austria. The former maintained that 'the Empire... had constantly prejudiced the interests of the nation'; the latter, on the contrary, exalted the grandeur of the imperial idea. In the Empire as reborn in 1871, this controversy died down. Although 'little Germany', Prussian Germany, so dear to Sybel's heart, triumphed, the great majority of historians were obviously inclined to support Ficker's thesis, for contemporary *Weltpolitik* had aroused a fellow-feeling for the mediaeval *Weltherrschaft*. But the end of this *Weltpolitik* was not a particularly happy one either; and in 1927 Georg von Below took up once more the ancient quarrel, and placed himself under Sybel's banner. These value-judgments upon the past are only of interest as symptoms of tendencies at work in the present. A more important task would be to attempt an analysis of the influence, exercised by the imperial concept, on the general trend of thought in Germany after 1250, for after all it has never been forgotten. In ways which have varied according to the period, history and literature have always kept its memory green. It might not be impossible even today to trace its effects in certain undercurrents of German patriotism which reveal a fundamental will to power.

NOTES

1. These lectures were delivered at Strasbourg in the course of the academic year 1927–1928 to students preparing for the *agrégation* in German. *Revue des Cours et Conférences*, 1929, Vol. 60, pp. 481–494, 577–589, and 759–768.
2. *Diplomata reg. et imp.*, Vol. III, no. 34.
3. SS, Vol. III, p. 54.
4. *Registrum super negotio imperii*, no. 29; Krammer, *Quellen zur Geschichte der deutschen Königswahl*, Vol. I, p. 50.
5. Rahewin, *Gesta*, III, 11.
6. *Constitutiones*, II, no. 329.
7. *De regimine civitatis*, 23.
8. *Constitutiones*, Vol. II, no. 262, p. 365.
9. 51.
10. I, 11. 252ff.
11. *Registrum*, I, 20; edit. E. Caspar, p. 33.
12. *Constitutiones*, II, no. 398, c. 3.
13. There are hardly any exceptions to this rule except in the case of certain letters of Conrad III, Frederick I (before his imperial consecration), and letters written by their supporters to the Greek emperors. It is easy to see why, in such cases, the Kings of the Romans should consider it good policy to anticipate their title of future Emperor (Otto of Freising, *Gesta*, 25; Jaffe, *Bibliotheca*, Vol. 1, letters 243, 245, 410, 411).
14. Otto of Freising, *Chron.* VI, 32.
15. J. Grimm, *Kleinere Schriften*, Vol. III, p. 68.
16. Wattenbach, in *Archiv. für Kunde österreichischer Geschichtsquellen*, Vol. XIV, 1855, p. 21.
17. *Constitutiones*, I, no. 227, c. 3.
18. *Ibid.*, I, no. 178.
19. *Libelli de lite*, Vol. I, p. 467.
20. *Summa Decret.*, XXII, qu. 5, c. 22.
21. SS., Vol. XXII, p. 39, 1. 197.
22. Böhmer, *Acta imperii*, no. 124.
23. Éditions Wilhelm Meyer, *SB. der Bayer. Akad.*, *Phil. Kl*, 1882, or *Ges. Abh*, I, and F. Wilhelm, *Münchener Texte*, H. 1.
24. *Epistolae saec. XIII e regestis pontificum*, Vol. II, no. 456.
25. Edit. Höfler, pp. 61 and 68.
26. *Chronica majora*, edit. Luard, Vol. III, p. 550.
27. *Ibid.*, Vol. V, p. 190.
28. 45, 8.
29. Huilliard-Bréholles, *Étude sur la vie . . . de Pierre de la Vigne*, p. 425.
30. Huilliard-Bréholles, Vol. V, 2, p. 1003.
31. *Constitutiones*, II, no. 219.
32. For the expression of analogous ideas in the 14th and 15th centuries,

see J. Huizinga, *The Waning of the Middle Ages*, 2nd ed. pp. 141–2, 223, 224.
33. VIII, v. 540.
34. VII, 34.
35. *Constitutiones*, I, no. 161.
36. *Ibid.*, I, no. 187, p. 258.
37. *Ibid.*, Vol. I, no. 182.
38. C. 12, D. I.
39. Migne, *P.L.*, Vol. CXCIX, col. 200.
40. *Saxo Grammaticus*, LXIV, edit. A. Holder, p. 539.
41. It is true that the letter is only known to us through the German writer Rahewin (*Gesta* III, 7). As far as I know its authenticity has not up till now been called in question: is it above all suspicion?
42. *Preussisches Urkundenbach*, no. 56.
43. IV, 35.
44. The title of 'patrician of the Romans', which the Emperors had sometimes added to the imperial title in order to express their power over Roma, was no longer in use under the Hohenstaufen.
45. *Saxo Grammaticus*, Vol. XIV, edit. A. Holder, p. 539.
46. *Constitutiones*, I, no. 182.
47. Huillard-Bréholles, Vol. III, p. 50.
48. *Ibid.*, Vol. VI, p. 393.
49. *Gesta*, II, 30.
50. I, 1. 254.
51. Migne, *P.L.*, Vol. CXCIX, Col. 39.
52. *Constitutiones*, Vol. II, no. 244, p. 312.

2

A CONTRIBUTION TOWARDS A COMPARATIVE HISTORY OF EUROPEAN SOCIETIES[1]

I

I should like first of all to forestall a possible misunderstanding and spare myself unnecessary ridicule. I am not a 'discoverer' of a new panacea. The comparative method has great possibilities; I consider that an improved and more general use of this method in historical study is one of the most urgent tasks for the present day. But the method has its limitations, for there is no such thing as a talisman of knowledge. But it is already a well-tried method, which has long since proved its value. There have already been many voices to recommend its application to the history of political, economic and legal institutions.[2] Nevertheless it is obvious that the majority of historians are not yet fundamentally converted to it. They make polite gestures of assent, then go back to their work without effecting the slightest change in their habits. Why is this? It is no doubt because they have been too easily persuaded that 'comparative history' is a chapter of the philosophy of history or of general sociology, and these are disciplines which the historian – according to his cast of mind – either reveres or greets with a sceptical smile, but in general takes good care not to practise; for what he requires of a method is that it should be a tool, in ordinary use, easy to manipulate, and yielding positive results. Now that is exactly what the comparative method is – but I doubt whether up till now it has been sufficiently shown to be such. It can and it should enter the world of detailed research. Its future – perhaps even the future of our discipline – depends on its doing so. At this point I should like to define the nature and the possible applications of this excellent tool, to show by means of some examples the chief services that it may be expected to render, and finally to suggest some practical methods of making it easier to use.

Addressing a group of mediaevalists, I shall take my examples preferably from the period usually called – whether rightly or wrongly – the Middle Ages. But it goes without saying that – *mutatis mutandis* – the observations I am about to make would apply equally well to the European societies that we call modern. And I shall also allow myself sometimes to refer to the latter.

II

The term 'comparative history', common enough today, has undergone the fate of almost all common words: it has changed its meaning. Even if we leave aside all obviously wrong usages, an ambiguity still remains. People studying the humanities are constantly grouping together under the expression 'the comparative method' two widely different intellectual processes. The linguists seem to have been the only ones to have concerned themselves with making a careful distinction between them.[3] Let us attempt an accurate definition from the historian's own point of view.

First, what do we mean in our field of study by comparison? No doubt about it, we mean this: to choose from one or several social situations, two or more phenomena which appear at first sight to offer certain analogies between them; then to trace their line of evolution, to note the likenesses and the differences, and as far as possible explain them. Thus two conditions are necessary to make a comparison, historically speaking, possible: there must be a certain similarity between the facts observed – an obvious point – and a certain dissimilarity between the situations in which they have arisen. For example, if I am studying the manorial system in the Limousin, I shall be continually impelled to consider setting side by side information drawn from other manors; in common or garden language, I shall be comparing them. But I shall not consider myself to be engaged in what is technically called 'comparative' history, for I shall be taking the different objects studied from a crosssection of a single society in which, looked at as a whole, there is a considerable degree of unity. In practice, it has become customary to reserve the term 'comparative history' almost entirely for the comparative examination of phenomena that have taken place on different sides of a State, or national, frontier. Political or national contrasts are, indeed, always the ones that strike the mind most immediately. But, as we shall see, this is really a gross simplification. Let us confine ourselves to the idea of differences in environment – an idea that is both more flexible and more accurate.

Thus understood, the process of comparison is common to all aspects of the method. But it is capable of two completely different uses – different in principle and in result – according to the field of study envisaged.

Let us now consider the first case. The historian selects some societies so widely separated in time and space that any analogies observed between them with respect to such and such phenomena can obviously not be explained either by mutual influence or by a common origin. The commonest type of example, since the distant days when Father Lafitan S.J. invited his readers to compare 'the customs of the American savages' with those of 'primitive times',[4] consists of an examination of Mediterranean civilisations – Hellenic or Roman – alongside contemporary 'primitive' societies. In the early days of the Roman Empire, only a short distance from Rome and on the delightful shores of Lake Némi, a rite was enacted which stands out by reason of its strange cruelty in the midst of the customs of a relatively well-policed society. Whoever aspired to become the priest of the little temple of Diana could do so under one condition only – he must kill the officiant whose place he coveted. 'If we can show that a barbarous custom like that of the priesthood of Némi has existed elsewhere; if we can detect the motives which led to its institution; and if we can prove that these motives have operated widely, universally, in human society, producing in varied circumstances a variety of institutions specifically different but generically alike; if we can show, lastly, that these very motives were at work in classical antiquity; then we may fairly infer that at a remoter age the same motives gave birth to the priesthood of Némi.'[5] This was the starting-point for the immense enquiry undertaken by Frazer in *The Golden Bough*, a pre-eminent example of a well-illustrated and instructive piece of research entirely based on the collection of facts from the four corners of the world. The comparative method as thus interpreted has rendered immense services of every kind, more particularly to the ancient history of the Mediterranean region. A humanist education had accustomed us to picture Rome and Greece as too like ourselves; but the comparative method in the hands of ethnographers has restored to us with a kind of mental shock this sense of the difference, the exotic element, which is the indispensable condition for a balanced understanding of the past. The other benefits have been rather more general ones, such as the possibility of filling in certain gaps in documentation by means of hypotheses based upon analogy; the opening up of new avenues of research suggested by the comparative method; above all, the explanation of a great many survivals that have up to now been incomprehensible. I am thinking here of customs which have survived and become crystallised after the original psychological environment that gave them birth has disappeared, customs which would seem inexplicably strange if the examination of other similar cases in other civilisations did not make it possible to reconstruct precisely this vanished situation, as in the ritual murder at Lake Némi.[6] In short, this long-range comparative method is essentially a matter of interpolating a graph. It postulates, and always reverts in conclusion to the fundamental unity of the human mind, or, alternatively, the monotony and astonishing poverty of the intellectual resources at man's disposal throughout the course of history. This was particularly true of primitive times, when, as Sir James Frazer puts it, 'the human race in all its early crudity was building up its philosophy of life'.

But there is another use for the comparative method. This is to make a parallel study of societies that are at once neighbouring and contemporary, exercising a constant mutual influence, exposed throughout their development to the action of the same broad causes just because they are close and contemporaneous, and owing their existence in part at least to a common origin. In history proper, this is the equivalent of the historical study of languages (for example, Indo-European languages); whereas comparative history in the broad sense would more or less correspond to linguistics in general. In both history and language, it appears true that of these two comparative methods the one with the more limited horizon is also the richer in results. Because it is more capable of rigorous classification, and more critical about the objects it compares, it may hope to reach conclusions of fact that are less hypothetical and much more precise.[7] This at any rate is what I hope to be able to show; for it is certainly this method that I intend to elaborate. I propose to compare the various European societies —especially in Eastern and Central Europe – societies that are contemporary, that live close to one another, and that go back if not to one common origin, at any rate to several.

III

But before phenomena can be interpreted, they must be discovered. And this preliminary step will reveal in the first place the usefulness of the comparative method. But – it may be asked – is it really necessary to go to such trouble to 'discover' historical facts? They are and can only be known through documents: in order to bring them to light, isn't it enough to read texts and monuments? Yes, but one must know how to read them. A document is a witness; and like most witnesses, it does not say much except under cross-examination. The real difficulty lies in putting the right questions. That is where comparisons can be of such valuable help to the historian, who is always in the position of the magistrate hearing the case.

This is what frequently happens. In a given society, a phenomenon has occurred over such a wide field and has had so many and such obvious consequences that the historian – short of being blind – can hardly fail to be struck by it. This is particularly so in the political sphere, where extended effects are ordinarily the easiest to detect in our source-material. Let us now consider a neighbouring society. It may well be that analogous events have arisen in it, and that the effects have been just about the same in extent and power. But either because of inadequate documents, or because the political and social structure of that society is different, the result of these events is less immediately perceptible. Not that they have been any less serious: but their effect has been produced in depth, like those obscure bodily diseases which do not immediately reveal a series of well-defined symptoms, and therefore go on undiscovered for years. When at last they do show up, they are still almost impossible to recognise because the observer cannot connect the superficial effects with an original cause that arose such a long time ago. Is that simply a theoretical hypothesis? To show that it is nothing of the kind, I am led to take an example from my own researches. I am sorry to have to take the stage in person; but research-workers do not normally take the trouble to record their tentative efforts, and literature does not supply any case which I could substitute for my own personal experience.[8]

If in the agrarian history of Europe there is one really striking transformation, it is the one that took place in the greater part of England, from about the beginning of the 15th century up to the early years of the 19th – namely the great enclosure movement, which in its twofold form (enclosure of the commons, and enclosure of the arable) may be defined basically as a movement leading to the disappearance of communal obligations and the growth of individualism in agriculture. Let us here consider only the enclosures of arable. We start out with a system by which the arable land, as soon as the harvest was finished, was turned over to common grazing. Then it would be sown again and bear another harvest, repeating the rhythm of cultivation and obeying the rules laid down in the interests of the community. We find, at the end of the transformation, all land held strictly in severalty. Everything about this great metamorphosis catches and holds our attention: the polemics to which it gave rise in the course of its history; the relative ease of access to most of the documents (Acts of Parliament and official enquiries) bearing upon them; its links with political history, in which the growing influence of Parliament, where the great landowners were predominant, had the counter-effect of entrenching the gentry more firmly in power; its possible relationships with the two most immediately obvious facts of English Economic History – I mean colonial expansion and the industrial revolution, for both of which it probably prepared the way. (This has been doubted, but for our purpose it is enough that it should be a matter of discussion); and finally the way in which it not only extended its influence into the field of social development, always a difficult subject to uncover, but also affected the most obvious features of the landscape, causing hedges to spring up throughout the English countryside where it was formerly open as far as the eye could see. And so no history of England, however elementary, will fail to include some account of the enclosures.

But on turning to a history of France – even, alas, an economic history – we shall not find the slightest allusion to movements of this kind. And yet there certainly have been such movements. We are beginning nowadays, thanks particularly to the labours of Henri Sée, to be aware of their existence, though we are very far from being able to appreciate their extent, and further still from any clear perception of the points of similarity and of divergence between these developments in French and in English society. But let us leave on one side this last topic, for when the comparative method is properly used, our first task is not to discuss the significance of contrasts but to discover the facts. It is most remarkable that up to the present the disappearance of communal obligations in France has hardly been noted except at periods and in places where – as in England – the phenomenon was recorded in official documents, and where it was thus readily noticeable – namely in the 'enclosure awards' of the 18th century and the preceding or subsequent official enquiries. The same transformation, however, took place in another part of France, where it has not so far – to the best of my knowledge – been noticed, namely in Provence: and it began in a relatively remote period, the 15th, 16th and 17th centuries. In Provence, it was most probably a much more profound and thorough-going change than in most of the more northerly regions where the same facts have been studied again and again; but it had the misfortune to occur at a time when economic life – especially rural life – was hardly of any interest to writers or administrators. Moreover, the change did not bring about any visible modification of the countryside, since the disappearance of communal obligations did not entail the construction of hedges, and it was therefore easy for it to pass unnoticed.

Were the repercussions in Provence the same as those in England? For the moment, I must confess ignorance on this point. Moreover, I am very far from believing that all the characteristics of the English movement were reproduced on the shores of the Mediterranean. On the contrary, I am struck by the fact that conditions in the south were peculiar owing to the very different system of land tenure when compared with the north. (It did not, as in England, give rise to a redistribution of the 'strips', to 'consolidation'. Special customs such as transhumance account for social conditions that are without parallel in the English countryside. I am thinking particularly of the antagonism between the big graziers, the large-scale breeders of stock and the other classes of the population.

It is none the less extremely interesting to note in a Mediterranean country a phenomenon, with its own special characteristics, which might have seemed, up till now, to be found mainly in higher latitudes. Moreover, it is not very difficult to see the process at work in Provence; a closer examination reveals the existence of a fair number of documents enabling its course to be followed, such as county orders, communal discussions, and lawsuits whose lengthy and roundabout proceedings bear eloquent testimony to the seriousness of the interests at stake. But there is a real need to search out these documents and compare them with each other. If I have been able to do this, it is certainly not because I am particularly familiar with these local documents, far from it – I know them, and always shall, much less well than the scholars whose ordinary field of study has been the history of Provence. They are the only people who can really work the vein: all I can do here is to point out its existence. I have only one advantage over them, a quite impersonal one; I happen to have read works on English enclosures or on similar rural revolutions in other European countries, and I have tried to draw some inspiration from them. In short, I have used that most effective of all magician's wands – the comparative method.

IV

Now let us pass on to interpretation.

The most obvious service we can hope for from a careful comparison between facts drawn from different and neighbouring societies is to enable us to discern the mutual influences exercised by these groups. Careful enquiry would no doubt reveal among mediaeval societies the direction of some borrowings which have so far been insufficiently investigated. Here is one example, which I put forward simply as a working hypothesis.

The Carolingian monarchy, when compared with that of the Merovingians which immediately preceded it, shows some completely original characteristics. The Merovingians in their relations with the Church had never been anything but simple laymen. But Pepin and his descendants were anointed with holy oil at their coronation and so marked with its sacred character. The Merovingians, sharing the beliefs of their contemporaries, had in turn dominated, enriched, and exploited the Church; they had never been much concerned with backing its precepts with the force at the disposal of the State. But the Carolingians behaved quite differently. Although they did not in their times of power fail to domineer over the clergy and use their property for the benefit of their own policies, they nevertheless clearly considered themselves in duty bound to establish the law of God. Their legislation was essentially religious and tinged with morality. When I read in a newspaper some time ago a decree promulgated by the Wahabite emir of the Nedj, I was struck by its points of resemblance to the pietist literature of the Capitularies. There is not much difference between the great courts assembled round the king or the emperor and the assembly of the Councils. And lastly, the protective relationships under the Merovingians, already such a prominent force in society, had only occupied a marginal position in the law, which traditionally took no cognisance of them. The Carolingians, on the other hand, recognised these links and gave them sanction. They defined and set limits to the cases in which commended man might be allowed to leave his lord. They tried to use these personal relationships to consolidate the public peace, which was at once the most cherished and the most fleeting object of their dogged ambition. 'Let each overlord exercise a coercive action upon those who are set under him, so that they may become more and more obedient and submissive to the imperial mandates and precepts.'[9] This phrase from a Capitulary of 810 is an expressive short summary of the imperial social policy. No doubt a thorough search in the Gaul of the Merovingians would reveal the germs of any one of these features. It is none the less true that, when one considers Gaul only, the Carolingian state seems to have come into being *ex nihilo*. But let us look beyond the Pyrenees. In barbarian Europe from the 7th century onwards kings could be observed receiving 'most holy unction',[10] as one of them, Ervig, calls it. This was among the Visigoth kings; a monarchy that was entirely religious, preoccupied with ensuring by State action that the orders of the Church were carried out. Or consider Spain, where Councils were almost indistinguishable from political assemblies; or the laws of the Visigoth sovereigns, which had been replaced very early on, in order to assure some measure of control, by the ties of feudal lord and vassal[11] upon which personalities the military organisation tended to be founded.[12] Naturally, it is not difficult to discover, along with these analogies, a number of differences. The chief one is that the first Carolingians governed the Church, instead of being governed by the Church like the Gothic princes of the 7th century. The likenesses remain however extremely striking. Is it only a matter of seeing them simply as the product of similar causes, acting on both sides in the same direction – causes which one would then have to define? Or – remembering that the facts about the Visigoths are of course earlier than those about the Franks – are we to believe that a certain conception of royalty and its proper role, certain ideas concerning the constitution of a feudal society, and of its use by the State, appearing first in Spain and having become embodied in its legislative documents, were later consciously taken up by the entourage of the Frankish kings and the kings themselves? To win the right to answer this question, a detailed enquiry would clearly be required, which I could not enter upon here. Its principal object would be to discover by what channels the influence of the Visigoths was able to penetrate into Gaul. There are some universally recognised facts which seem to be of the kind that would make this hypothesis fairly probable. It is indisputable that there was during the century following the Arabic conquest a Spanish *diaspora* in the Frankish kingdom. The fugitives *de partibus Hispaniae*, whom Charlemagne and Louis the Pious settled in Septimania (i.e. southern Gaul), were to a large extent people of humble station; but they also included some from the upper classes (*majores et potentiores*) and some priests, that is to say, people who were familiar with the political and religious customs of the country they had been forced to leave.[13] Some of the Spaniards who took refuge in Gaul had brilliant careers in the Church: such men as Claude of Turin and Agobard of Lyons, who preached on the unified legislation which he had seen in his native country; and especially Theodulfe of Orleans, who was the first to arrive and without doubt the most influential of them all. Finally, there was the Spanish collection of conciliar documents, which exerted an undeniable effect on Carolingian canon law, though its extent has not so far been accurately estimated. Let us again stress the point that I am not claiming to reach any decisions. But I hope you will admit that this is a problem deserving attention. And it is not the only one of its kind.[14]

v

'Historical resemblances,' said Renan with regard to Jesus and the Essenes, 'do not always imply connections.' This is certainly true. Many similarities, when closely examined, prove not to be explicable in terms of imitation. I would freely admit that these are the most interesting ones to observe, for they allow us to take a real step forward in the exciting search for causes. This is where the comparative method seems capable of rendering the most conspicuous service to historians by setting them on the road that may lead to the discovery of real causes. Moreover – and perhaps most important of all – it can benefit them in a more modest but very necessary way by preventing them from following certain paths that are merely blind alleys.

Everyone knows what is meant by the Estates General or Provincial in 14th and 15th century France. (I use these epithets in their ordinary and approximate sense as a matter of convenience, without of course failing to be aware that the Estates General and Provincial were somewhat indeterminate bodies, that a truly 'general' Estates was practically never summoned, and finally that provincial representation was by no means fixed over a considerable period.) In the course of the last few years[15] a number of monographs have been written on the Estates Provincial, especially those of the great feudal principalities. They represent an effort on the part of scholars that is all the more praiseworthy, seeing that almost everywhere, especially for the earlier period, the documents are appallingly scanty and barren of information. These monographs have cleared up a number of important points in a most interesting manner. But from the very start almost all their authors have come up against a difficulty they had no means of overcoming, the nature of which they sometimes did not even recognise – I mean the problem of 'origins'. I am quite ready to use this expression as ordinarily employed by historians; but though current, it is ambiguous. It tends to confuse two intellectual operations that are different in essence and unequal in scope. On the one hand there is research into the oldest institutions (ducal or hundred courts, for example), out of which the Estates seem simply to have developed. This is a perfectly legitimate and necessary enquiry. But there remains the second procedure – namely research into the reasons that could explain why, at a given moment, these traditional institutions took on a new lease of life and a new significance, why they became transformed into Estates; that is into assemblies endowed with political and financial duties, who were conscious of possessing, over against the sovereign and his council, a certain power, subordinate perhaps, yet none the less distinct, which was the ultimate expression, through infinitely variable means, of the different social forces in the country. To bring the seed to light is not the same thing as to show the causes for its germination. Might we then hope to discover these causes if for instance we live in Artois (so far as the estates of Artois are concerned) or in Brittany (if it is a question of the Breton Estates), or even if we are content to take a general look at the kingdom of France? Certainly not. This procedure would simply land us in a maze of little local facts, to which we should be inclined to attribute a value that they certainly never possessed; and we should inevitably miss the essential point. For a general phenomenon can only be produced by equally general causes; and if there is such a thing as a phenomenon occurring throughout Europe, this – which I have called by its French name, the formation of the Estates – is undoubtedly a case in point.

At varying moments – all, however, very close to one another in time – *Estates* may be observed springing up throughout France; but in Germany too, in the territorial principalities, there were the *Stände* (the two words are curiously alike in meaning), in Spain the *Cortes*, in Italy the *Parliamenti*. Even in the English Parliament, which was born in a vastly different political environment, development was often subject to a trend of ideas and a series of needs analogous to those which led to the formation of what the Germans call the *Ständestaat*. Please do not misunderstand me. I fully recognise the immense value of local monographs, and I do not in the least suggest that their authors should step outside the framework of their proper studies and follow one another in a search for the solution to this large-scale European problem that I have just referred to. On the contrary, we beg them to realise that they could not, each one working on his own, find a solution to it. The chief service they can do us is to uncover the different political and social phenomena in their respective provinces which preceded or accompanied the appearance of the Estates or the *Stände*, and which would therefore seem to have some provisional claim to be numbered among its possible causes. In this enquiry, they would do well to pay some attention to the results obtained in other regions – to engage in fact in a little comparative history. The overall comparison would have to come later. Without preliminary local research it would be useless; but it alone will be able to select from the tangle of conceivable causes those which exercised a general effect – the only real ones.

It would not, I feel sure, be difficult to give further examples. To select one among many, I should say without a doubt that when the German historians studied the formation of the imperial 'territories' (the little States that were formed in the course of the 12th and 13th centuries in the interior of the Empire and gradually acquired, to their own advantage, the lions' share of public power), they too often allowed themselves to slip into a habit of looking upon this phenomenon as specifically Germanic. But how can it really be separated from the consolidation of the feudal principalities in France? Here is another illustration of the circumspection which the comparative method ought to engender in historians who are too inclined to see the causes of local social transformations as exclusively local: the development of the manor in the closing centuries of the Middle Ages and at the beginning of modern times. The lords of the manor, when their revenue was threatened by the fall in the value of their money rents, became for the first time sharply aware of the impoverishment which had for a long while been eating piecemeal into their fortunes.[16] In every country they were concerned to ward off this danger. With this end in view they used various means in various places, which proved more or less effective. They increased certain casual profits where the amount was not rigorously fixed by custom (the English 'fines'); they substituted, wherever the law allowed it, a rent in kind for a money rent, proportional to the harvest (hence the great extension of the *métayage** system in France); they brutally dispossessed their tenants, incidentally using methods that differed greatly according to the locality (England, Eastern Germany). This was in principle a general effort; but there were extreme variations in the methods used, and their success. Here then comparison invites us to note extremely marked divergences as between one national setting and another – which we shall see below to be one of its chief points of interest. But it forces us at the same time to see in the original impulse that gave birth to such a variety of results a European phenomenon, for which only European causes could be responsible. To try to explain the formation of the *Gutsherrschaft* in Mecklenburg or Pomerania, or the accumulation of land by the English squire, solely with

* *Métayage*, the system of leasing land in return for a rent in kind.

the help of facts gathered from Mecklenburg, Pomerania and England, and not found elsewhere, would be to waste one's time in a rather futile intellectual pursuit.[17]

VI

But let us beware of a misunderstanding from which the comparative method has only too frequently suffered. Too often people have believed or affected to believe that its only aim is to search for similarities. They are only too ready to accuse it of being satisfied with forced analogies, and even of inventing them on occasion by arbitrarily postulating some necessary parallelism between the various developments. There is no point in examining whether these reproaches have sometimes seemed justified, for it is only too certain that the method, if practised thus, would be no more than a sorry caricature. On the contrary, the comparative method, rightly conceived, should involve specially lively interest in the perception of differences, whether original or resulting from divergent developments from the same starting-point. Not long ago, at the beginning of a work intended to 'mark the specific elements in the development of the Germanic languages as compared with the other Indo-Germanic languages', Meillet put forward as one of the essential tasks for comparative linguistics a sustained attempt to 'show the originality of the different languages'.[18] In the same way comparative history has a duty to bring out the 'originality' of the different societies. Is it superfluous to remark that there is hardly any more delicate operation than this, or any that more imperatively calls for methodical comparisons? If one is to determine, not only in a general way, that two objects are not alike, but also – an infinitely more difficult but much more interesting task – by what precise characteristics they are distinguishable, the first step must obviously be to examine them one by one.

First of all, it is essential to clear the ground of false similarities, which are often merely homonymous. And some of them can be very insidious.

How often has English villeinage been treated as the equivalent of the French *servage* in the 13th, 14th, and 15th centuries. No doubt a rather cursory examination of them both could easily produce some points of resemblance. Both serfs and villeins were considered by jurists and by public opinion to be without 'freedom', and were described in certain Latin documents as *servi*. (English writers, when expressing themselves in French, did not hesitate to use *serf* as synonymous with *villein*.) Because of this absence of 'freedom' and this servile name, learned persons have been very ready to equate them with the Roman slaves. But this is a superficial analogy: the concept of 'unfreedom' has varied greatly in content according to the period and the environment. Villeinage is in fact a specifically English institution. As Vinogradoff has shown in a work that has become a classic,[19] it drew its original characteristics from the very special political circumstances in which it was born.

As early as the second half of the 12th century, much earlier, that is, than their neighbours in France, the kings of England succeeded in getting the authority of their courts of justice recognised over the whole country. But this precocious development had its disadvantages. The state of society as then constituted meant that the judges came up against a frontier which they were not able to cross until the very end of the Middle Ages. They had to make sure never to intervene between feudal lords and those who held land from them in 'villeinage', i.e. on payment of certain dues and especially labour services, both fixed by custom of the 'manor'. The status of these tenants varied considerably according to their origins. Some – the villeins properly speaking – were reckoned free, because they were simply dependent upon their lord by reason of their tenure, by the fact that they belonged to the *villa*; the others – *servi, nativi* – were tied to their master by personal and hereditary bonds, considered at this period to be a mark of servitude. But all of them, whatever their traditional status, were passed by when it was a question of royal jurisdiction. In their relationship with their lords (and only in these) they were completely outside the scope of the king's courts, and so of the law applied and elaborated by them, the *Common Law* of the realm. The result was that in the course of the 13th century they amalgamated, on the basis of this common incapacity – the most glaring and disadvantageous one conceivable – in spite of the original differences between them, and formed themselves into a single class. The lawyers had some difficulty in defining this new group, composed as it was of such diverse elements. But they very soon reached agreement, and they agreed on a formula which reserved the name of 'freeman' for those alone among the king's subjects whom his courts were willing to protect against all others. This was a new notion of liberty.[20] The one-time villein, that is, the tenant pure and simple – if I may so call him – ceased to be numbered among the *liberi homines* and was confused with the hereditary *servus* or *nativus*, because like him he was without access to royal justice. These two words *servus* and *villein* came to be treated as synonymous. This had taken place by about the year 1300. At the same time certain obligations of an essentially servile nature – notably marriage dues – which should in principle have fallen only upon the descendants of the former *servi*, were gradually extended – at least in many of the manors – to all villeins (in the new sense of the word). This kind of contagion, common enough in mediaeval societies, was here able to spread with particular ease. The assimilation of one class to the other was no doubt quite wrong: but how could its victims have made any effective protest, since by definition they were unable to take their grievance before any other body but the lord's court, that is to say before the very person who profited by the abuse? And before long it was admitted that villeinage, like the former servitude, was hereditary. This was a movement in keeping with the general tendencies of the time. But here, it was still further accentuated by a special circumstance. From time to time it happened that a person of high standing acquired a holding in villeinage. Of course the land, although it had changed hands, remained subject to all the charges and disabilities that had formerly adhered to it, and which the new tenant must have been aware of – in particular the lack of protection of his possessory rights by the royal courts *vis-à-vis* his lord. But the holder himself – a great man in society, maybe – could not possibly have been reduced unceremoniously to the ranks of the unfree. The way out was to reintroduce a distinction between the condition of the land and the condition of the man, and to agree that no one but the descendants – all the descendants – of the original tenants should be classed as villeins. A new and lowly caste had been created. It was defined in law in terms of a principle readily formulated by the legal theorists, namely that the villein is a serf or slave (*servus*) in relation to his lord; that is to say no man, not even the king, may come between him and his lord. But there was nothing like this in France. There, royal justice was much slower in developing, and its progress took a quite different course. There were no great legislative enactments like those of Henry II in England. There was no strict classification of the means of action open to plaintiffs before the royal courts (like the English 'writs'). It was by a series of incursions, often hardly premeditated, taking place earlier at one place, many years later at another, strengthened now by one precedent, then by another, that the king's men gained power over the country step by step. But their victories, just because of their leisureliness, and – to start with at any rate – because they were not guided by any theoretical plan, were more far-reaching in their effect. In France as in England, the lord's jurisdiction, which was an amalgam of powers with very diverse origins, covered widely differing groups of dependants – military vassals, citizens, freeholders and serfs. But the French monarchy treated the lord's jurisdiction as an indivisible whole. The royal courts allowed the *seigneur* to continue to try such and such a kind of case, or took it away from him; they either insisted, or did not insist, on the right of appeal; but in so doing they made no kind of distinction between the dependants of the lord. So it came to pass that gradually the royal judge began to slip in between the *seigneur* and his tenant. Hence no reason arose for assimilating the freeholder to the serf, who was called a villein in France, too. The two classes of men would go on existing side by side up to the end. The French serf at the beginning of the 12th century, the *servus* or *nativus*, and the English *theow* of the same period, had belonged to very similar legal classes, which it is quite permissible to treat as two branches of one single institution. Then villeinage came into existence. There was no longer any parallel. The French serf of the 14th century and the English serf or villein of the same period belonged to two totally dissimilar classes. Is it worth even comparing them? It certainly is: but the point will now be to mark the contrasts between them, which will bring out a striking antithesis between the respective developments of the two nations.[21]

Let us pursue this comparison in still greater detail. It was not always easy in the English manor of the 13th and 14th centuries to distinguish with certainty, amidst the manifold variety of property rights, which holdings should be classed as tenancies in villeinage, and so carefully put in a class apart from the equally large medley of tenures for which the epithet 'free' was reserved. Yet it was absolutely necessary to agree upon certain more or less fixed criteria; for it was necessary to be able to determine which were the lands – and hence, at least in origin, the tenants – whom royal justice could not protect, because rights of jurisdiction had been conferred upon the lord of the manor. In their efforts to discover these criteria, the lawyers sometimes reckoned to find them in the nature of the services attached to the land. They worked out a concept of servile labour.[22] It was agreed to treat as symptomatic of this all compulsory labour on the land whenever it implied the obligation to perform a large number of days' work, and above all whenever there was any element of uncertainty – either in the number of days due or the kind of work to be done, both of these being left to the arbitrary will of the lord. And it was generally admitted that the obligation to serve as the headman of the village (the *reeve*, not unlike the *staroste* with whom Russian novels have familiarised us) should likewise be considered as a taint upon the freedom of those who were forced by their terms of tenure, willy-nilly, to undertake this heavy burden. In establishing these norms the English lawyers and judges were not inventing anything. They were simply drawing upon a fund of collective experience which had been worked out in a more or less confused fashion for a long time by mediaeval society, on the continent as well as in England.

The idea that agricultural work in itself was in some way incompatible with freedom is in keeping with very ancient tendencies of the human mind. In the barbarian age it was embodied in the expression *opera servilia* often used to designate this kind of work. The idea that the *servus* differed from the freeholder because of the indeterminate character of the compulsory labour demanded of him, arising from the original contrast between the slave and the Roman *colonus*, was a very powerful one in Gaul and Italy during Carolingian days. It never completely disappeared. In France under the Capetian kings, was it not quite customary to give the label 'franchises' to the privileges which, while not removing the peasants' obligations, set limits to them and especially fixed them?

As for the obligation to perform for the lord some particular specialised service that he might see fit to impose, in addition to the general burden of compulsory labour, a burden which in England consisted in filling the office of *reeve*, this was considered in many places in Germany to fall always upon unfree persons. In France, this notion, although less generally admitted, has nevertheless left some traces, particularly in the documents of the 12th century.[23] But in France – to which I confine myself here – these ideas as a whole were never embodied in any precise legal formulations, though one of them by itself – the emphasis on the degrading character of agricultural occupations – was, it is true, used in the 13th century to trace a clearer line of demarcation between the classes than had existed in the past. But it did not, as in England, serve to fix the frontier between the free and the non-free; it was rather used as one of the distinguishing features between the nobleman, who was allowed to 'demean himself' – manual work being considered as, in a sense, derogatory – and the great multitude of non-nobles, which always – and now increasingly – included people whom no one would have dreamt of excluding from the category of the 'free'. But was there never any temptation in France, too, to define the unfree in terms of the particular services that they were bound to render? There are certainly some indications that people were not averse to making this kind of claim. At Gonesse, near Paris, about the beginning of the 13th century, certain tenants were considered by their neighbours as serfs because of the special forced labour incumbent upon them, particularly the task of escorting prisoners, which was thought to be a base service. But the tenants had no difficulty in getting the king to recognise that, legally speaking, there was no question but what they were free.[24] In their efforts to define a serf no lawyer or French law-court had recourse to any criterion based upon services rendered. Here then we come face to face with one of the most suggestive aspects of this contrast between two related societies.

Both of them exhibited analogous tendencies; but in one of them these remained vague and amorphous, and had no official backing, disappearing among the medley of ideas and feelings that constitute public opinion. In the other, they blossomed forth and were embodied in legal institutions of a very hard-and-fast kind.

It will be as well to dwell a little longer on the history of classes in mediaeval society. There is no study better calculated to disclose deep disharmonies within such societies – so deep, in truth, that we can hardly explain them at all and must, for the moment at any rate, be content to note them.

First, let us go back to Western and Central Europe about the 10th and 11th centuries. The idea that birth sets an immeasurable gulf between one man and another, a notion common to almost all periods, was certainly not absent from men's minds. In 987, in order to justify the exclusion of Charles of Lorraine, candidate for the throne of France and the legitimate heir of the Carolingians, Archbishop Auberon – or, if you prefer it, the historian Richer, attributing to the prelate a speech that was perhaps a composite work, but was certainly in keeping with the ideas of the time – invoked the marriage contracted by the claimant to the throne with someone beneath his rank belonging to the vassal class.[25] And what son of a knight would have allowed himself to be considered on a par with the son of a serf or even a villein? But we must not deceive ourselves; rights, based upon inheritance, had little power at this period. Society was not so much a gradation of castes distinguished from one another by blood, but rather a somewhat confused tangle of groups based upon relationships of dependence. These ties of protection and obedience were the strongest that could be conceived. Even in the case of Charles of Lorraine, let us carefully note the turn taken spontaneously by Auberon's argument. There is no doubt that the bishop first reproaches the Carolingian prince with having contracted a mesalliance in the strict sense of the word: 'He has married a woman not his equal from the ranks of the vassals.' But he immediately adds – remembering that this person's father had saved the dukes of France: 'How the great duke [Hugh Capet] would suffer to know that the Queen had been chosen from among *his own vassals!*' This at once shifts the matter on to the personal plane. The servile condition itself was the only thing considered strictly hereditary: but even so it was not in practice strictly incompatible with the status of knighthood. As for the rights of freemen, they were dependent upon differences of locality, varieties of contractual relationships, the individual's social rank, as such, and not upon birth. Then came the 12th and 13th centuries. A silent but decisive modification took place in the ideas and legal outlook of the time. The strength of the personal bond was relaxed: homage tended, though very slowly, to become a solemn but rather empty form; the French serf, the *'homme de corps'*, was from now on thought of much less as his lord's 'man' than as the member of a despised class. On all sides classes based upon heredity were forming, each with its own legal rules. But what differences there were in the richness of this development![26] In England, villeinage was firmly established; but this was almost the only real class. Between free men, the law made no distinctions at all. In France, the lowest degree was serfdom, the members of which class would not henceforward be eligible for knighthood; at the top came the nobility, gradually differentiated from the rest of society by a series of special rights (sometimes simply survivals of ancient custom) relating to private law, criminal law and fiscal law. And lastly in Germany, from the 13th century onwards, the hierarchical idea developed with unparalleled vigour. The serf-knights, who had been eliminated in France by the crystallisation of class feeling, became in Germany the nucleus of a very well-defined social category. In the south of Germany there were even two such classes. The nobility on the one side, and the servile masses on the other, became broken up into a series of ranks graded one above the other; the nobles were not all equal in birth (*ebenbürtig*) or possessed the *connubium*. And jurists, working things out as they went, constructed the celebrated theory of the *Heerschild* in order to regulate the classification of the upper levels of society. They pictured a kind of ladder, each class having its own fixed place on one of the rungs. No one belonging to any one of these groups could, without loss of caste, accept a fief from a man lower down the scale.

Neighbouring and contemporary societies; in all cases a development in the same direction, stressing the hierarchical and the hereditary tendencies; but the progress and results of this development reveal such pronounced differences of degree that they are almost equivalent to a difference in kind, and in any case are marked by antitheses characteristic of their respective environments: this is the situation as revealed by the example I have briefly outlined to you. There were other contradictions, simpler to grasp if not to explain, flowing from another kind of divergence between these societies: in one society, the persistence, and in the neighbouring one the extinction, of institutions originally common to them both.

In the Carolingian period, over the territory that was later to be France, and over what was destined to become Germany, by far the larger share of that portion of the soil reserved for tenants was divided into tenements (as they were usually called in Romance countries), or Hufen (which was the Germanic term, usually rendered by the Latin *mansus*). Quite often there were several families of farmers settled on the same tenement. But in the eyes of the lord it did not therefore cease to be viewed as a unity. There were dues and services that bore upon the whole tenement in its entirety – or rather, on its fragmented parts – on the plots of ground or buildings which it comprised. In principle, it was not permissible ever to subdivide any of these agrarian units. Now let us turn to France round about the year 1200. Hardly anywhere is there any further mention of the peasant tenement as a unit of assessment; where the word does survive in the Romance form of *meix* or *mas*, it is in the quite different sense of a house or centre from which the surrounding country is worked.[27] Those who drew up charters no longer assessed the extent of *seigneuries* in terms of the number of tenements they contained. The *censiers*, or lists of dues levied by the lord, were no longer content, as before, with enumerating the holdings: they set about it either by considering each separate piece of ground in great detail, or at least each tenant.

There were no more holdings composed of a fixed amount of land. Fields, vineyards and gardens could all be split up quite independently of one another between hereditary holders and various newcomers who had acquired them. In Germany on the other hand the *Hufe*, which was still not allowed to be subdivided, continued in the majority of manors to form the basis for the levying of rents or services. It, too, was destined in the end to disappear, though only slowly, and often earlier in name than in fact; for up to the end of the feudal period, the German lords sought to preserve by various means the principle of indivisibility of holdings. No parallel efforts were made, it would seem, by their French counterparts. The contrast certainly appears to be an extremely ancient one, seeing that the gradual crumbling away of the peasant tenement in the western part of the Frankish Empire is observable as early as the reign of Charles the Bald.[28] I am not even going to attempt to examine the reasons for this here. But I think you will admit that any French or German agrarian history omitting to consider this question would be neglecting an essential part of its task. If we took into account one country only, the demise of the peasant tenement here and its survival in the other country would appear to be one of those quite natural phenomena that did not need to be explained. Only comparison shows that there is a real problem here, and this in itself is a step forward: for is there a greater danger in any branch of science than the temptation to think that everything happens 'quite naturally'?

VII

Although one of the essential tasks in comparative linguistics today is the tracing of the original characteristics of the various languages, it is nonetheless true that its first efforts have been directed rather towards another objective – the determination of kinship among the languages, and the search for mother-tongues. One of the most impressive successes of the comparative method has been the delimitation of the Indo-European group, the reconstruction – no doubt hypothetical, yet based on well-founded conjecture – of the basic forms of the original

'Indo-European' language. The history of social organisation is in this respect a much more difficult problem. The fact is that a language presents a much more unified and easily definable framework than any system of institutions: hence the relative simplicity of the problem of linguistic affiliations. 'Up to now,' writes Meillet, 'no case has been discovered giving cause for the belief that the morphological system of a given language is the result of the intermingling of the morphologies of two distinct languages. In all cases so far observed, a language presents a continuous tradition', whether this tradition be 'of the current type – the transmission of the language from the adults to the children' – or whether it arises 'from a change of language'. But let us suppose that at a given moment examples are discovered of this phenomenon so far unknown – 'real mixtures' between languages. When that happens (I am still quoting M. Meillet) 'linguistics will have to devise new methods'.[29] Now the historian of societies finds that the facts themselves impose upon him this formidable hypothesis of 'mixtures', which, if realised in the linguistic field, would be such a disturbing influence in that humane science which is rightly most self-confident. The fact that French has been deeply influenced in its vocabulary and no doubt also in its phonetics by the Germanic languages is of little consequence: there was also some transformation, involuntary and as often as not unconscious, in the Latin language as spoken in Roman Gaul. The descendants of the Teutons who adopted the Romance dialects virtually changed over from one language to the other. But who would venture to represent French mediaeval society as a transformation pure and simple of Gallo-Roman society? Comparative history can reveal to us interactions between human societies which were previously unknown; but, when confronted with societies so far considered as lacking any ancestry in common, it would be foolish to expect to discover detached fragments, broken off long ago from the original mother-society whose existence was previously unsuspected; to seek for them would be to nurse a hope destined almost always to be disappointed.

In certain exceptional cases, however, comparison may reveal among societies with very different histories a series of extremely ancient relationships. It would obviously be absurdly rash to jump to the conclusion that these were directly interrelated; but it would seem reasonable to take them as evidence that in a very remote past there was a certain community of make-up in civilisation as a whole. The idea of making use of the study of agrarian customs to reconstruct the ethnic map of Europe before the time of written documents is one that occurred long ago to a variety of research workers. No one can fail to recognise Meitzen's great contribution, but it is generally admitted today that it ended in bankruptcy. Without entering into the details of this failure, we may perhaps indicate the essential faults in method which must be held responsible for it: (1) Meitzen confused the study of different categories of fact, when a more correct method would have begun to distinguish such things as the pattern of settlement and the lay-out; (2) he postulated a 'primitive' character for a number of phenomena observed in historical times, and often quite recent times, forgetting that they might well have been the result of relatively recent changes; (3) be paid too exclusive attention to examining facts of a material nature, at the expense of social customs which were reflected in the facts; (4) he only took for his ethnic elements those groups that were historically attested Celts, Teutons, Slavs, etc.—who were all newcomers to their habitats, thus refusing *a priori* to admit that any part had been played by the nameless mass of people previously established on the land – the 'substratum', to use the linguist's term – though there is no indication that they were destroyed by the invaders, nor that they had been obliged to abandon the whole of their previous customs and way of life. There is an important lesson to be learned from these mistakes: it is not that one should give up the enquiry, but rather pursue it in a more critical spirit and by more prudent methods. Straight away, it is essential to note certain facts. Land in fragmented parcels, in long narrow fields without enclosures, covered enormous tracts of Europe: England, Northern and Central France, almost the whole of Germany, and no doubt also a large part of Poland and Russia. This was in contradistinction to other very different forms of land arrangement: the almost square fields of Southern France, and the enclosed fields in the eastern parts of France and England. In short, the agrarian map of Europe is completely at variance with its political and linguistic map. It is perhaps earlier than either of these last two. This is at least a possible conjecture. For the moment, our task is to collect the facts rather than to explain them. To confine ourselves for the moment to the very striking extension, across societies apparently separated in every other way, of the first type of land-system referred to above (long open strips in scattered ownership) it is only too clear *a priori* that it will be our duty to try out a variety of explanations one after the other. We must consider as possible ones not only a kinship among primitive civilisations, but also the hypothesis of borrowings, and the spread of certain technical processes about a primitive centre. But one thing is certain: we shall never arrive at a complete understanding of the English open field system, the German *Gewanndorf*, or the French *champs ouverts*, by examining England, Germany or France alone.

It becomes equally clear moreover—and this is perhaps the clearest and most cogent lesson to be drawn from comparative history—that it is high time to set about breaking down the outmoded topographical compartments within which we seek to confine social realities, for they are not large enough to hold the material we try to cram into them. A certain worthy scholar some time ago wrote a whole book on *Les Templiers en Eure-et-Loir*.[30] We can but smile at such ingenuousness. But can any of us who are historians be quite sure that we are not constantly guilty of the same failing? To be sure, it is hardly correct practice to transpose the *départements* into the Middle Ages. But how often have the frontiers of existing States not been treated as a convenient framework for such and such a study of the legal or economic institutions of the past? There are two errors here. First, anachronism, and that of the most obvious kind. It must be some sort of blind faith in a vague historical predestination that has led people to attribute to these mere lines on a map some definite meaning, some pre-natal existence – if I may so call it – before the precise moment when the complicated interplay of wars and treaties actually fixed them. Then there is a more fundamental error too, which still persists even when one uses what appears to be a more exact method of selecting the facts for research according to contemporary political, administrative, or national divisions; for where has it ever happened that social phenomena, in any period, have obligingly and with one accord stopped their development at the same boundaries, these being precisely the same as those of political rule or nationality? It is a universally acknowledged fact that the line of demarcation, or, if you prefer it, the marginal zone between those who spoke the *langue d'oil* and those who spoke the *langue d'oc*, or the boundary of the *langue d'oil* on the Germanic side, does not correspond to any State frontier or great feudal estate. The same is true of many other facts in the history of civilisation. If you study the French towns of the Middle Ages when the urban renaissance is taking place, you will be trying to comprehend in one sweep two objects almost totally dissimilar in every way, except in name. The ancient Mediterranean towns on the one hand, the traditional centres of the life of the plains, the *oppida* inhabited from time immemorial by the great men, the lords, the 'knights'; on the other, the towns in the rest of France, inhabited above all by merchants, who re-created them. What arbitrary cut with the scissors would justify us in separating this latter urban type from the analogous types of the German Rhineland? Or when the historian has began by studying the *seigneurie* to the north of the Loire, and then turns to the documents of Languedoc, does he not often feel further removed from his own country than when he is looking at documents from Hainault or even the Moselle?

Whatever particular aspect of European social life is being studied, and at whatever period, the student must find his own geographical framework, fixed not from outside but from within, if he wishes to escape from a world of artificiality. This will be a difficult piece of research, needing a great deal of circumspection and much feeling of one's way; but to refuse to undertake it would be an open admission of mental laziness.

VIII

How are we to set about this in practical terms?

It goes without saying that the comparison will be valueless unless based on the study of facts gleaned from detailed, critical, and reliable documentary research. It is no less evident that human frailty makes it useless to dream of first-hand research in geographical or chronological fields that are too vast. Moreover, it seems inevitable that comparative history properly speaking should always be reserved for a small section of historians. It would perhaps seem to be time to think of organising it and in particular giving it some place in the teaching of the universities.[31] All the same, we must not hide from ourselves the fact that since research in many fields is still at a rather backward stage, comparative study can itself only expect to make slow progress. It is always the same old story: it requires years of analysis before there is material for one day's synthesis.[32] This maxim is too often quoted without adding the necessary corrective; 'analysis' can only be transformed into 'synthesis' if it has had the latter in view from the beginning and has been deliberately designed to serve that purpose.

The authors of monographs must be once again reminded that it is their duty to read the literature previously published on subjects analogous to theirs, and not only that bearing upon their own region – which they all do read – not only that concerning immediately neighbouring regions – which they nearly all do read – but also (something too often neglected) that dealing with more distant societies, separated by differences of political constitution or nationality from those they are studying. I will even venture to add: not only general text-books, but also if possible detailed monographs, of a parallel kind to the ones they are themselves undertaking, which will generally be found much more lively and satisfying than extensive summaries. In the course of reading they will find material for their questionnaires, and, maybe, some guiding hypotheses suitable for directing their researches until such time as their own progress will clearly show them as they go whether these provisional guides need correcting or abandoning. They will learn not to attach too much importance to local pseudo-causes; at the same time they will learn to become sensitive to specific differences.

This invitation to scholars to pursue this preliminary enquiry by means of books does not mean that they are being invited to follow an easy path. I will not go into the details of the material inconveniences that confront them, but there is no harm in recalling the fact that they are by no means inconsiderable. Bibliographical information is difficult to collect, and the books themselves more difficult still to come by. A good international library loan system, developed and extended to certain great countries who have up till now jealously kept their riches to themselves, would do more for the future of comparative history than a great deal of good advice. But the principal obstacle is an intellectual one; it concerns fixed habits of work; but even these, no doubt, are not impossible to reform.

The linguist who has made a special study of a particular language and wants to gather some information about the general characteristics of another language does not usually meet with much difficulty. The grammar he consults sets out the facts classified in a manner not very different from the one he himself uses and explains them in formulae more or less parallel with the ones he is familiar with. But how much less happily placed the historian is! If, for example, he is familiar with French society and wishes to place one aspect of it side by side with something analogous that a neighbouring society – let us say Germany – has to offer, he turns over the pages of some works devoted to the latter, only to find himself – even if they are the most elementary text-books – having to grope his way all of a sudden in what seems to be a new world. Is it simply the difference of language? Not precisely, for in principle there is no reason why two scientific vocabularies should not correspond pretty exactly as between one language and another. The natural sciences provide many examples of such agreement. The difficulty is that as between the German and the French work most of the words simply do not correspond. How is one to translate into French the German *Hörige*, or into German the French *tenancier*? One can see some possible translations, but these are mostly periphrases (one might translate *Hörigen* as those who depended on the *seigneurie*) or approximations (*Zinsleute* would only do for *tenanciers en censive*, a particular case of a more general idea);[33] and very often – as in the translation suggested for *Hörigen* – these expressions are only moderately common, and do not occur in the books. It would be understandable if this absence of parallelism could be explained by a too obstinate faithfulness to popular mediaeval usage preserved by both languages, whose divergences were a historical fact that had simply to be accepted. But this is far from being the case. The majority of these dissonant terms are entirely the creation of the historians; or at any rate they are the people who have given both precision and extension to the sense in which these terms are used. Rightly or wrongly, and more or less unconsciously, we have elaborated technical vocabularies. Each national school has constructed its own without taking any notice of its neighbour. European history has thus become a veritable Babel. Hence the formidable dangers that lie in wait for inexperienced research-workers – and after all, do not; all experts deserve this epithet once they are outside their own domain? I was once in touch with a worker who was studying, in a one-time Teutonic country, some common land used by several villages together, that is to say what the German books, at any rate of a certain period, call a *Mark*.[34] I had the greatest difficulty in persuading him that analogous practices existed – and sometimes still exist – outside Germany, in numberless countries, and notably in France; for French books have no special word for this kind of common land.

But this discordance in vocabulary is hardly more than the expression of a deeper disharmony. On all sides we have French, German, Italian, English studies going on; but hardly ever are they asking the same questions. I quoted just now an example of these perpetual cross-purposes on the subject of agrarian changes. It would not be very difficult to produce others equally eloquent of the situation: 'the administrative class', for example, has been up to now a completely neglected subject, in France and in England, in descriptions of mediaeval society; or legal rights, which have been discussed in the various countries under completely different schemes of classification. A historian may well be led to wonder whether a certain institution or fact in his own national past is to be found elsewhere too, and if so, with what modifications due to checks in development or greater expansion; but it is more often than not impossible for him to satisfy this legitimate curiosity. When he finds nothing on the subject in the books he consults, he may well wonder whether their silence is to be explained by the silence of the facts themselves, or by the state of oblivion into which a great problem has been allowed to fall.

This congress will, I think, be much concerned with reconciliation between nations by means of history. Do not be alarmed: I am not going to attempt any impromptu treatment of this most delicate of all themes. Comparative history as I see it is a purely scientific discipline, orientated towards knowledge and not towards practical results. But what would you say about attempting a reconciliation of our terminologies and our questionnaires? Let us address ourselves in the first place to the authors of general text-books, for they hold the first place of importance as informers and guides. We will not ask them for the moment to abandon the national framework in which their work is ordinarily done. It is clearly an artificial one, but it is still imposed by practical needs. Only gradually will the pursuit of knowledge adapt itself on this point to a position more in keeping with the true facts. But we appeal to them here and now not to forget that they will be read beyond their national frontiers. We beg them, as we have already besought the authors of monographs, to base their plan, the treatment of the problems they raise, even the terms they use, on the knowledge gleaned from work carried out in other countries. In this way, through mutual good will, a common scientific language in the highest sense – a collection of symbols and a system of classification – will progressively come into being. Comparative history will thus become easier to understand and to serve, and will inspire local studies with its own spirit – those local studies without which it is powerless, but which can themselves only come to fruition with its help. In a word, let us stop talking about the history of one nation and then of another without attempting to understand them – a course which leads to no understanding. A dialogue between deaf men, in which each one answers the other's questions all wrong, is an ancient comic device on the stage, getting an easy laugh from an audience which is always ready to be amused; but it is not really to be recommended as a serious intellectual exercise.

NOTES

1. *Revue de Synthèse Historique*, Dec. 1928. This article reproduces an address given in the previous August at Oslo, to the International Congress of Historical Sciences (mediaeval section). I have not aimed at more than filling out the argument where the very limited time at my disposal had necessitated certain last-moment cuts.
2. Without making any pretension to drawing up a general bibliography, which would be out of place here, I would just mention the address given by Henri Pirenne to the Fifth International Congress of Historical Sciences (*Report*, pp. 17–32), which is all the more significant because it embodies the thoughts of a historian whose fame rests upon a national work; also in the *Revue de Synthèse* the articles by Louis Davillé (Vol. 27, 1913), conceived in a different spirit from the present work, and an article by Henri Sée (Vol. 36, 1923; reprinted in *Science et philosophie de l'histoire*, 1928); also Henri Beer's reflections (Vol. 35, 1923, p. 11). As positive contributions to comparative history let us recall, in the field of political history, the remarkable article by Ch. V. Langlois, 'The comparative history of England and France during the Middle Ages', in *The English Historical Review*, 1900; and on a rather different topic some very revealing pages in *Les Villes du Moyen Age*, by H. Pirenne.
3. See especially A. Meillet, *La méthode comparative en linguistique historique*, 1925, to which I owe the general idea of development in the two kinds of approach.
4. *Moeurs des sauvages Américains comparées aux moeurs des premiers temps*, Paris, 1724; on the work itself, cf. Gilbert Chinard, *L'Amérique et le rêve exotique dans la littérature française au XVIIe et XVIIIe siècles*, 1913, pp. 315ff.
5. J. Frazer, *The Golden Bough*, 3rd edit. Vol. I, p. 10. The example chosen by Meillet (op.cit) is different, drawn from researches on animal stories.
6. But naturally the mere fact of 'survival' is not enough; other things have to be taken into account. An interesting fact which must be explained is why the rite or institution survived despite its apparent failure to fit into its new environment.

7. The study of primitive civilisations is today turning quite clearly towards a more exact classification of the societies to be compared. There is no reason at all why the second type of method I am trying to classify here should not apply to these societies just as much as to others. Moreover, it is obvious that certain of the advantages of a comparative history with limited horizons, as outlined below – where I discuss suggestions for research, and caution in attributing everything to pseudo or local causes – are equally applicable to the other method. The two aspects of the method have certain features in common; but this does not mean that they do not need to be carefully distinguished. The study of sacred kingship in Europe provides a very clear example both of the immense value and of the limitations of comparative ethnography. Though it alone is able to put us on the right road to the correct psychological explanation of the phenomenon, it has been shown by experience to be altogether unfitted for the task of drawing out its real meaning. That at any rate is what I attempted to show in *Les Rois Thaumaturges*, especially pp. 53 and 59.
8. In what follows – and later on in dealing with the theories of Meitzen – I am anticipating the results of a work on agrarian systems in which I have been for long engaged, whose conclusions were presented to another section of the congress. Compare *Les Caractères originaux de l'histoire rurale française*, 1951, p. 262.
9. Cap. no. 64, cl. 17 (edit. Boretius): 'Ut unusquisque suos iuniores distringat ut melius ac melius obediant et consentiant mandatis et praeceptis imperialibus.'
10. The twelfth Council of Toledo (681), in a letter from King Ervig, *Mansi*, Vol. XI, col. 1025.
11. In the collection of documents of Sanchez-Albornoz, *Les Behetrias*, in *Annario di historia del derecho español*, Vol. 1, 1924, notes on pp. 183, 184, 185. M. Sanchez-Albornoz's study gives the most reliable and complete explanation of the Visigoth *patrocinium*. Particularly to be noted is the passage in the *Codex Euricianus*, CCX, which originally applied to the *buccellarius* (private soldier), and reappears in the *Lex Reccessvindiana*, V, 3, 1, with the word *buccellarius* substituted for a rather looser term: *et quem in patrocinio habuerit*.
12. The laws of Ervig (680–687), in the collection *Lex Visig.*, IX, 2, 9, ed. Zeumer, p. 378. cf. Sanchez-Albornoz, loc. cit., p. 194.
13. *Maiores et potentiores*: Cap. no. 133 (Vol. 1, p. 263, 1.26), Prêtres: *Diplomata Karolin.*, Vol. 1, no. 217; *Hist. de Languedoc*, Vol. 2, col. 1, 228. See E. Cauvet, *Étude historique sur l'établissement des Espagnols dans la Septimanie*, 1898, and Imbart de la Tour, *Les colonies agricoles et l'occupation des terres désertes à l'epoque carolingienne*, in *Questions d'histoire sociale et religieuse*, 1907.
14. Sustained as it was by borrowings from elsewhere, the Carolingian monarchy in its turn was copied by others. Its influence on the Anglo-Saxon monarchies does not seem to have been sufficiently studied. Helen Cam's useful essay, *Local Government in Francia and England. A*

comparison of the local administration and jurisdiction of the Carolingian Empire with that of the West Saxon kingdom, 1912, is far from exhausting the subject.

15. Cf. H. Prentout, *Les États provinciaux en France*, in *Bulletin of the International Committee of historical sciences*, July 1928 (*Scientific reports presented to the sixth international congress of historical sciences*).

16. Alain Chartier, in his *Quadriloge invectif*, composed in 1422, puts into the mouth of the knight the following words (ed. E. Droz, *Les Classiques français du Moyen Age*, p. 30): 'the common people have this advantage, that their purse is like a cistern that has collected and continues to collect all the waters and showers provided by all the wealth of this kingdom . . . *for the fall in the value of money has lessened the amount that they have to pay us in dues and rents*, and the monstrous rise in the price of food and of labour for which they are responsible has enabled them to collect and build up their substance by reason of what they collect and amass day by day.' I do not think I have come across an older passage where this observation is as clearly stated. But it would be well worth while pursuing this line of research. For – though this is too often forgotten – the important point here is not so much the moment when the phenomenon began to exist (one would have to go a long way back to find the starting-point), but rather the moment when it began to be noticed. As long as the *seigneurs* did not realise that their dues were diminishing, they obviously would not seek for the means of repairing their loss. We have good reason to know at the present time that the depreciation of a currency while the nominal value remains the same can easily remain unnoticed for quite a long time by the people affected. Once again we see that an economic problem turns out to be a psychological problem.

17. The necessity for comparative studies, which are alone capable of dispelling the mirage of mistaken local causes, has been well demonstrated in a book by A. Brun, remarkable in spite of some deficiencies: *Recherches historiques sur l'introduction du français dans les provinces du Midi*, 1923 (cf. L. Febvre in the *Revue de Synthèse*, Vol. 38, 1924, pp. 37ff). Brun, as is well known, has proved that French did not begin to win its way in the south of France before the middle of the 15th century. Here in his own words are the reasons why, having first decided to restrict himself to a summary examination of the relevant documents, he then decided to extend his researches over the whole of southern France, instead of exploring one region only with extreme thoroughness, as so many scholars would no doubt have advised him to do. 'It would perhaps have been preferable to restrict the problem to a single province and to exhaust the mass of documents available there. Yes – from the point of view of strict method this would have been the preferable course; but in fact this could have led to serious errors of interpretation. For example, having chosen Provence, and noting that French was in this region an innovation of the 16th century, one would have jumped to the conclusion that it had followed upon the

reunion of 1481–1486 – which is approximately correct. But would one have noticed that the deeper cause of this event was not the reunion itself, but the special circumstances in which it took place in the 15th century, at a turning-point in our history, and that Provence was sharing in a common and simultaneous development taking place in all the regions of southern France? A local enquiry would have suggested a local explanation, and the general characteristics of the phenomenon – the only important ones – would have escaped notice' (p. xii). The point could not be better expressed. The results of Brun's researches are in themselves an emphatic plea for the method I am here concerned to defend.

18. *Caractères généraux des langues germaniques*, 1917, p. vii.
19. *Villeinage in England*, 1892. Naturally the literature is considerable. To tell the truth, there are few works dealing with the subject as a whole, even in English (see however Pollock and Maitland, *The History of English Law*, 2nd ed, I, pp. 356ff and 412ff.) There are fewer still in French. This will I hope provide some excuse for the schematic way in which I have had to develop my argument.
20. New – or perhaps renewed. In the days when slavery proper existed, the slave had clearly had no other court of appeal against his master than the master himself. The free man depended on the law-courts of the tribe, either popular or royal. The progress of seignorial jurisdiction – less complete in England than on the continent – the development of a new form of personal and heritable attachment, which placed the individual among the unfree, had blurred the old conception and deprived it of its legal value, though probably without removing it altogether from men's minds. The renaissance of a national judicial system revived it. Mediaeval law, adapting its forms to the evolution of the facts, thus often found itself dipping into an ancient fund of popular representative institutions belonging to the more or less distant and forgotten past. We shall come across a striking example of this later on, when discussing the villein's services.
21. There is another and more subtle kind of misleading similarity when two institutions in two different societies seem to be designed for similar ends; but analysis shows these ends to be completely antithetical, and reveals that these institutions have arisen in response to absolutely opposite needs. An example of this would be the mediaeval and modern testamentary will on the one hand and the Roman will on the other, The former represents the 'triumph' of individualism over 'old family communism', the latter represents the exact opposite – it is an instrument designed to favour the omnipotence of the *pater familias*, taking its origin therefore not from any 'tendency towards individualisation' but on the contrary from a tremendous 'concentration of the family'. I take this example from a review by Durkheim (*Année sociologique*, Vol. 5, p. 375), one of the most finished pieces of methodology that he has produced.
22. There was moreover some ambiguity about the expression 'servitium'

in English legal language – or rather, in mediaeval language in general – used as the equivalent of 'due' as well as of service properly speaking. I am here using the term only in the restricted sense.
23. I have referred to certain documents in *Revue historique du droit*, 1928, pp. 49, 50.
24. On this matter cf. my article in *Mélanges d'histoire du Moyen Age offerts à M. Ferdinand Lot*, 1925, pp. 55ff., where I was incidentally at fault in neglecting to compare the facts with those in England.
25. Book IV, Ch. 11.
26. Cf. Marc Bloch, *Un problème d'histoire comparée: la ministerialité en France et en Allemagne*, in *Revue historique de droit français et étranger*, 1928, especially pp. 86ff, and *infra*, pp. 503–528, and particularly pp. 525 and 526.
27. This was moreover the original meaning (the relationship between *mansus* and *manese* is obvious). The tenure had been called after the house, 'mother of the field', as the Scandinavian documents express it. The derived sense had taken on a technical meaning, which disappeared along with the institution that it designated. The first sense of the word survived or was resuscitated. Naturally one can discover here and there some survivals of the 'manse' in the ancient sense of the word, as a unit of taxation, late examples which bear witness both to the past state of affairs and to the general revolution which only a few *seigneuries*, here and there, managed to escape.
28. *Cap*. no. 273, ch. 30 (vol. 2, p. 323). One is tempted to put alongside this document the information already provided by Gregory of Tours (*Hist. franc.* X, 7), about the splitting up of *possessiones*, the basis of the general Romano-Frankish system of taxation; but this is not the place to go into the relationships between the Frankish manse and the Roman *caput* – an extremely intricate question.
29. *La méthode comparative en linguistique historique*, pp. 82, 83.
30. Ch. Métais, *Les Templiers en Eure-et-Loir*, 1896. Examples of this kind of anachronism are less rare than one would imagine. In the same *département* I could refer to: Henry Lehr, *La Réforme et les églises réformées dans le département actuel d'Eure-et-Loir* (1523–1912), 1912. In a neighbouring region, Abbé Denis, *Lectures sur l'histoire de l'agricultur dans le département de Seine-et-Marne*, 1830 (the greater part of the volume deals with the period before the Revolution).
31. I think I should here add a further problem peculiar to the French universities, and therefore not suitable for enlarging upon at Oslo. Our higher education is hamstrung by the requirements of the *licence*, and still more so, in the main faculties, by the syllabus for the *agrégation*, which reaches the teachers ready made from the hands of the responsible authority, namely the *jury*. Neither of these, it is true, is limited to the history of France; they almost always include some questions on foreign history; but, for reasons of practical convenience, and quite legitimate ones, these questions are regularly presented in a national framework. The result is that the teacher may well be inclined to give his lessons or direct his pupils' studies along the lines

of English or German institutions, for example; if he is not to neglect the infinitely important interests of the pupils committed to his charge, he can only under very exceptional circumstances reserve a place in his teaching for certain problems that positively demand to be treated today along comparative lines, such as the system of lord and vassal in Western Europe, the development of urban societies, and the agrarian revolution. Teaching and research being in the nature of the case closely bound up with one another, and both having much to gain by mutual support, one can see how damaging this situation is to our studies.

32. The exact wording is: 'Pour un jour de synthèse il faut des années d'analyse' (Fustel de Coulanges, *La Gaule romaine*, ed. C. Jullian, p. xiii, 1875 preface). Cf. the reflections of M. Henri Berr, *Bulletin du centre international de Synthèse*, June 1928, p. 28.

33. Naturally one could put something like 'Inhaber der Leihegüter' – but who would use an expression like that? *Hörige*, moreover, does not quite represent *tenancier*: the meaning is more general. In Spanish, as I was able to satisfy myself when working on a translation, there is literally no word equivalent to '*tenure*'.

34. Today there can be absolutely no doubt that the word never really bore this narrowly specialised meaning, but should be considered, like *Allmende*, as equivalent to *communal*. Cf. G. v. Below, *Allmende und Markgenossenschaft*, in *Vierteljahrschr. für Sozial-und Wirtschaftsgesch.*, 1903.

3
A PROBLEM IN COMPARATIVE HISTORY THE ADMINISTRATIVE CLASSES IN FRANCE AND IN GERMANY[1]

I

There is almost always something disappointing about reading two histories one after the other – however excellent they may be – dealing on the one hand with the institutions of mediaeval France, and on the other with those of Germany during the same period. You seem to be looking on at a desultory dialogue in which neither of the speakers ever gives an answer exactly meeting the requirements of his partner. One of the two books points to a problem and solves it in a certain way. But when you turn to the second book you find most of the time that the problem is not even mentioned. Yet the two societies originally – and for a good reason – had a great many points in common, and their development offers undeniable parallels. No doubt, numerous differences existed from the start, and they seem to have gone on becoming more marked in the course of the ages. But how is it going to be possible to throw light upon these particular differences if the same questions are not being asked in both studies?[2]

If there is one institution better suited than any other to bring out the deep likenesses and divergences between these two great mediaeval civilisations by setting them side by side, it is surely the one that historians call the administrative classes. Though the term has long been famous in German scholarship, it would have been quite fruitless until quite recently to look for any mention of the subject in even the most classical French works. But today this silence has been broken, and the credit goes to the Belgian historians, who are constrained and privileged by the past history of their country to keep constantly in view both France and the Empire. As early as 1911 Pirenne was inviting us to consider whether 'an

ADMINISTRATIVE CLASSES: FRANCE AND GERMANY 83

administrative class' has ever 'existed in France'.³ More recently, one of his pupils, Ganshof, has studied the lord's servants (*ministeriales*) both in a French fief – Flanders – and in the imperial principalities of Lower Lorraine.⁴ His book not only contains a considerable quantity of information, brought together and scrutinised with immense care, but it also constitutes an attempted interpretation of the greatest possible interest.⁵ Following in his footsteps, and taking advantage of his personal researches, I should like to show here what this serious problem of comparative history really involves.

I shall in the first instance have recourse to the French facts, but from the start shall make full use as occasion demands of any light that can be thrown on them by comparison with other countries. This will then be followed by a methodical comparison with Germany.

II

The manors (*seigneuries*) during the High Middle Ages in Capetian France comprised a whole staff of officials and servants – using these words together because of the impossibility of choosing between them. The language of the period did not distinguish between these two ideas; the commonest of the Latin terms – *ministerialis* – the French *sergent*, the Provençal *sirvent*, and the German *Dienstmann* are used indifferently in both senses, meaning in fact one and the same thing.⁶ Administrative officials, those concerned with justice, servants proper, artisans whose business it was to supply the needs of the lord and his household, were all lumped together in the same category, not only in popular usage, but in legal documents too, and often enjoyed the same privileges. About 1050 the Comte de Poitiers, dispensing all those in the employment of the monks of Saint-Jean-d'Angély from military service – except in the case of expeditions led by the Count himself – enumerates them in a random fashion, thus: 'their bailiffs, overseers, shoemakers, skinners, millers, gardeners and all their own servants [*sergents*], those who hold office under them, perform their duties [*ministeria*] and carry out tasks for them, either by hereditary right, or because the monks have chosen of their own free will men of no matter what estate from among those of the township, who are nearly all dependent upon them.'[7]

In the ordinary way the lord would recruit these indispensable helpers from among his own men. He did not always consider himself bound to consult the feelings of those whom he honoured by summoning them to his service. The document just quoted certainly seems to recognise that the monks of Saint-Jean had a right to exercise constraint. In June 1248, the charter of liberties of Saint-Germain-Laval prescribed that the lord could not take from among the men within his franchise more than six servants 'and then only if they are willing';[8] a clear proof that in the past the consent of the persons concerned had not always been required. The serfs in particular, more closely bound to their master than the other subject persons, would easily have seemed to him to be entirely at his beck and call. The monks of Saint-Père de Chartres, at the beginning of the 12th century, were accustomed to give wine to their servants, whether freemen or serfs. One year, when William I (1101–1129) was abbot, there was no wine in the cellars. Rather than buy in wine from outside, the monks, arguing on the basis of a tradition that had always been observed, according to them, in lean times, preferred to stop the distribution of wine. The *sergents*, feeling themselves injured, brought an action against them; but the judges (we do not know what court they belonged to) entered judgment against the plaintiffs – 'mainly for this reason [says the document drawn up on this occasion in the monastery], that several of the servants were our bondmen, and it was lawful for us in case of need to expect them to perform our tasks on any conditions we chose to impose'.[9] All the same this institution of compulsory service in the household, which was quite widespread in Germany, never seems to have undergone any extensive development in France. A large part of the staff necessary on the manors seems to have been provided for them early on simply by inheritance. There, as elsewhere, it was the generally prevailing custom at this period for an office to become vested in one family, and to be handed down from father to son; but furthermore, as we shall see in a moment, the custom of creating tenancies in return for services rendered, and on condition of such services, compelled the heirs, if they did not wish to lose the land, to take over the regular sequence of services performed by the deceased. For the rest, the lords of manors seem in general not to have had much difficulty in finding the manpower they needed without having recourse to any oppressive action. The fact is that such service received very appreciable rewards. Moreover, it would always have been necessary to give the servants a subsistence allowance, whether they were volunteers or impressed. In what form did they receive the price of their work?

In the first place, it took the form of certain exemptions from dues, particularly and almost everywhere from tallage. This was the privilege which, when transferred later on to royal officials and applied to the royal taxes, was to constitute one of the most precious benefits offered by the monarchy to its servants. More than one institution of the State is thus rooted in the institutions of the manor. But these negative favours were not enough. For a long time the offering of a money wage was more or less incompatible with the general economic conditions of the period. It was hardly ever resorted to except when it was a matter of hiring some extra workmen for a short-term project, such as extra farm work in the busy seasons.[10] For more regular employments, there were two systems in use. Either the lord of the manor undertook to provide his men with their keep, supplying them with food. (A judgment of the Court of Eude de Blois excluded from the overseer's jurisdiction, and from all financial obligation to him, the servants of Saint-Martin de Tours, whether they were freemen or serfs who had been freed, whether they worked in the monastery itself or outside it, since they were 'fed, clothed, and looked after' by the monks.)[11] Or the lord could make over to them some land from which they could feed themselves, or else an income derived from land. In this last case the land or income from land (mediaeval law made no distinction between the two, but placed the income arising from land, and the land itself, in the category of real estate), was considered to be in exchange not, like the unfree tenement, involving the payment of dues accompanied by forced labour at certain periods, but essentially in exchange for a regular service. In current usage, this was called a 'fief'.[12] At the height of the Middle Ages, Latinists used the word *beneficium* in the same sense, having gradually given a specialised meaning to this ancient word which was already used in vulgar Latin – through an initial semantic limitation which did not rule out other meanings – to denote payment for labour, whatever its form might be.[13] As the word *beneficium* had belonged to the vocabulary of classical Latin, writers and lawyers, when anxious to maintain a precise terminology, continued for a long time to prefer it to Latin transcriptions of 'fief'. The opposition between the system of fiefs and the system of maintenance in the master's household (prebend) was an ancient one. The capitulary *de villis* already distinguished among the royal grooms those who received prebend (*praebenda*) from their lord the king, and those who held manors from him as fiefs.[14] It goes without saying that the two systems were capable of being blended. In all periods it was quite common to see servants of enfeoffed vassals taking part more or less regularly in distributions of food or clothes; this was such a common event that it does not need any supporting references here.[15] After all, nothing could have been simpler or more logical than this dual arrangement.

Nevertheless the word 'fief' has been the source of many ambiguities in the course of literary history. It has been thought to designate from the start, not every tenure with an obligation of service, but, according to the custom prevailing over at any rate a large part of the feudal world towards the end of the Middle Ages, only those tenures with an obligation to render some special knightly service. The 'fief', thus reduced to its knightly form, has been looked upon as a species of real estate exclusively reserved for the nobility. Hence there has arisen a whole host of otiose questions about the right of the lord's servants to hold fiefs, and worse still, the idea that the possession of a fief by a lord's servant was a sign that he had risen to a higher social rank. Summing up the 'classical' German theory, and – it would appear – making it his own,[16] Ganshof writes (pp. 43–44): 'the lesser servants... the launderers, the cooks, the messengers, the gardeners, the carpenters, etc., did not receive fiefs'. But a rapid glance through diplomatic documents is enough to unearth fiefs among those occupying administrative posts – provosts, overseers, reeves, doyens – whose existence nobody questions, a respectable number of fiefs among the carpenters[17] and cooks (I mean those who actually did the cooking, not those high officials who were simply responsible for the service of the food at table).[18] To these might be added without difficulty fiefs among the slaters,[19] painters,[20] goldsmiths,[21] blacksmiths,[22] fishermen,[23] even surgeons whose special duty it was to bleed their masters;[24] and all of this is taken from French or Rhineland documents, going back in most cases to the 12th or even the 11th century. In another place (p. 342) Ganshof says: 'It was not customary for noble vassals to receive their keep [prebend].' This is to forget the whole crowd of vassals, very numerous in primitive times, who were not enfeoffed. Look at Norman England, for example. The tenants-in-chief were all obliged to put at the disposal of the royal army a fixed number of horsemen. But this did not oblige them to turn these into fiefs; they could if they so desired keep them under their own wing, providing them with food and shelter; and many, especially in early days, preferred this solution of the matter.[25] Even when they had been enfeoffed, vassals were not above soliciting or claiming on occasions, either for themselves or the younger sons of their house, the hospitality of the lord's household. Among the advantages which were recognised as late as 1139 as belonging to the lords of Saint-Anatholy by the abbey of Saint-Sernin at Toulouse, from whom they held their fief, was the privilege of having either a canon of their lineage or a knight – also of their lineage – 'living with the abbot'.[26] The prebend and the fief were but two different methods of rewarding work, and not the distinctive marks of two social grades, one above the other. By the same token, how could one imagine the existence in the 11th and even in the 12th century of a tenure specifically tied to the nobility, since there did not yet exist such a body, in the exact sense of the word, that is to say a hereditary caste endowed with precise legal privileges?

Certain German historians, having recognised the existence

of these fiefs belonging to the lord's servants, have nevertheless refused to recognise them as 'genuine' (*echte*): you can have as many fiefs as you like, they have said in effect – for the documentary evidence of their existence can hardly be disputed – but they are of an inferior sort, their lower status being marked by the fact that their holders do not owe homage. Although in accordance with the interpretations of certain lawyers going back to the first half of the 13th century, this distinction, even as far as it concerns Germany, hardly appears to gain much support from the documents of the 11th and 12th centuries.[27] In France it is thoroughly contradicted by the facts at almost any period. The trouble is always anachronism. Ignoring chronology, people will insist on projecting back into the most distant past an idea of class which only emerged extremely slowly. Even the word homage kept an extremely general meaning over a very long period: it was used of any dependent relationship of any kind whatsoever – for to be dependent on someone more powerful than oneself, what was that in mediaeval parlance but to call oneself 'his man'? – and then, consequently, of any symbolical expression of this dependence, for example the ceremony of the rope (*rites de la corde*) or the offering of money, by which the status of serf was acknowledged.[28] But the learned persons who deny that the lord's servants owed homage are clearly thinking of a more particular and precise meaning of the term, namely a vassal's homage rendered by the kiss and the taking of hands. Even in this sense homage was not anything specifically confined to the nobility, any more than was the fief – and for a long time fief and homage were not necessarily linked. In the early ages of vassalage many poor people had received this status. In the 12th century, by virtue of a custom from thenceforward considered an ancient one, the Count of Flanders used to receive, together with the homage of those of his fief, the homage of the citizens from his towns.[29] The performance of homage to the new lord by his citizens and his tenants one by one remained traditionally in force up to the end of the Middle Ages, especially in the South.[30] At the beginning of the 13th century, when the right to sub-let land was still ill-defined, it sometimes happened that homage was imposed on farmers or tenants.³¹ But furthermore: in certain places, the ordinary ceremonies acknowledging servile status were replaced by those elsewhere reserved for the homage of a vassal³² – the joining of hands and the kiss. In the same way, but in the other direction, homage by a vassal, particularly when the lord was the Church, or rather a saint, towards whom humility was laudable, sometimes took on the forms properly belonging to servitude, such as payment of chevage (poll tax) to St. Denis by the kings of France, or to St. Thomas by the Kings of England,³³ or to St. Gall by Conrad I of Germany;³⁴ or the homage paid by the Count of Toulouse to St. Vincent de Viviers with a chain round his neck.³⁵ The early confusion between bond service and vassalage, on which Guilhiermoz has so rightly insisted, lingered long in human memories. That being so, was it surprising that certain lord's servants should have been subjected to homage proper? Or that they should have had to submit to it even when they were serfs? – the position of the mayor of the Canons of Orleans, who paid them liege homage in 1176.³⁶ But not all of them owed it. In the case of a good many of them, a simple oath of fidelity was considered sufficient. We shall never know the detailed reasons for this difference. The most we can gather is that homage was required especially from those who held the most important offices; in the case of the minor posts, the faithfulness of their holders seemed for the most part to be guaranteed by the very fact of their humble station. It was also required preferably – though with some exceptions, one of which I have just referred to – from free-born *sergents*, the serfs being already tied to their masters by the strongest of bonds. Naturally any precedent in the Middle Ages tended to create a right, and custom gradually came to attach the duty of homage to certain offices. At Corbie, about the year 1200, the majority of the mayors, along with a forester and two moneyers, were obliged to pay homage, sometimes – and more often than not – in the form of liege homage, sometimes without this reinforcement; but there was no such obligation resting upon the others. A little later we meet the same varied practice at Saint-Corneille de Compiègne and on the Bishop of Chartres' lands, where in 1280 the porter, the gardener and the carpenter all paid liege homage,³⁷ just like certain barons, the vidame, for example, and like certain mayors and provosts.

I have had to dwell rather lengthily upon this thorny question of the *sergents'* fief. I could on the other hand almost completely pass over in silence the parallel matter raised concerning the freeholds (allods) held by the *ministeriales*, for I am not aware of any facts in France bearing upon this theme, perhaps for the simple reason that they have escaped my notice. While however documents from Lotharingia have led Ganshof to examine this problem repeatedly (see especially pp. 291 ff.), I may perhaps be allowed to put in a word as well. The only real difficulty appears to me to lie in the terminology. Precision of language in mediaeval legal documents was a result of the spread among notaries of more exact legal knowledge. This is as much as to say that before the 13th century they hardly paid any attention to accuracy. Before this period they would cheerfully use now one word and now another in the same sense. Not all words, however, suffered equally from this ambiguity; those with a vigorous popular life – like fief – were more or less fixed in sense by popular usage; but others denoting less common institutions, less in keeping with the general spirit of custom, carried a great variety of possible meaning. Such was the case with the word *allod*. Its precise technical meaning, frequently defined in contemporary documents, and finally the only meaning to hold the field, is well enough known – namely, land exempt from any kind of dues or seignorial services. But alongside this meaning, the older sense of 'hereditary possession' seems to have survived. Above all, as Ganshof has very ingeniously shown, there was a readiness to treat as an allod any holding carved out of an allodial lordship, a piece of ground which, whilst really being an allod, was in truth only liable to dues and services – that is, a fief – in relation to the person who worked it.[38]

But there is nothing surprising about the fact, which is very widely attested in Germany, that genuine allods in the full sense of the word – land situated, amid the general medley of seignorial rights, in a position of simplicity and isolation that was quite peculiar – should have been held by the *ministeriales*;

even if these people were serfs, for the existence of allods in the hands of those of humble station, and more especially in the hands of serfs, is well attested.[39] Whatever the penetrative power of the seignorial system may have been, there were certain islands here and there which altogether escaped its impact, just as in the economic system today, capitalism, even where it has invaded industry most thoroughly, has still not succeeded in killing the small craftsman. Only when the allod happened to come into the hands of a serf, it necessarily lost by that very fact something of its strict autonomy; for the serf, by reason of the fact that the lord 'of his body' in certain cases inherited from him, and could, in any event, levy a charge on the whole of his goods, was incapable of disposing of his possessions – even in favour of parties who, according to the laws of property, were dependent on other lords or were not dependent upon anyone – without this consent creating eventually a right.[40] In Hainault, where allods were fairly numerous, feudal custom, fixed in 1200 by Count Baldwin VI, laid down a perfectly clear ruling: 'the serf can under no circumstances alienate his allod or change it into a fief without his lord's consent'.[41] The same principle applied in Germany.[42] The allod, as such, did not constitute a tenancy: it was on the proprietor, and not on the ground, that this incapacity rested.

Among the crowd of *sergents*, undifferentiated as they must have been in early times, differences must nevertheless have fairly quickly made themselves felt. They were all bound to their lord of similar ties; but they were not alike in manner of life, in fortune, or in power. It was not long before public opinion had marked out certain degrees among them. A notice at the beginning of the 12th century tells us of a certain skinner in the service of the monks of St. Père de Chartres, who managed to become a cellarer, that he had chosen '*ad maiora conscendere*'.[43] Over the heads of the craftsmen, servants and employees engaged in minor administrative and legal tasks there began to grow up a class of people on whom their duties conferred a handsome income, a certain position and – this, I think, was the heart of the matter – power over other men. On the one hand, there were certain officers of the seignorial court, who, though originally appointed to fairly lowly tasks in the house and often at table, had soon ceased to carry them out in person, except from time to time at great festivals, and had transformed themselves into superintendents, constituting themselves counsellors to their master, and often sitting as judges in his court;[44] on the other hand there were the officials entrusted with the administration of the various lands, the *maires* (or lord's stewards) to use the word most widely current in France. Generally, the custom has been to stress the first group; and there can be no doubt that in the great *seigneuries* the holders of court offices succeeded more completely and more quickly than their colleagues in other employments in raising themselves to the most enviable ranks of the feudal world. But this was only on the large estates, and even there this central staff was not very large. On the other hand the *maires* or lord's stewards were extremely numerous. I am inclined to think that the most important part they played was in forming a noble class from the ranks of the *ministeriales*. At any rate this seems to me to be the case in most of the regions of France; but Flanders, on Ganshof's showing, was a curious exception.

The stewards in the village were powerful people in their little circle. They directed the cultivation of the domain, levied the dues, presided over the fixing of boundaries and investitures, and often meted out justice. The ancient cartularies are full of their names, full of their disputes with their masters too, and of their attempts to assert their independence. Charlemagne was already expressing his distrust of them in recommending that they should never be selected in the royal *villae* as members of the *potentiores*.[45] At the beginning of the 12th century, the steward of the monks of Saint-Benoît, at Fleury, succeeded in getting himself recognised as the king's man (probably his serf) and in the same breath persuading the other *sergents* at the abbey and the stewards of the other *villae* to do him fealty and homage, whereby he threw off the seignorial yoke and, moreover, substituted his own authority over his fellows. The king had to intervene in person to set matters right.[46] About the same time, the steward of the Abbey of St-Père de Chartres à la Pommeraye, in dispute with a clerical official – the *chevecier* – to whom the village belonged, set fire

ADMINISTRATIVE CLASSES: FRANCE AND GERMANY 93

to the monks' houses and pillaged their cowsheds.[47] The monastic writers are constantly groaning about the 'rapacity' and 'perfidy' of these evil servants.[48] The poets, on the other hand, delighted to sketch the portraits of faithful stewards, such as the one who led Percival's mother into the desert, or that 'good steward who ran to succour Gansi when he was mortally wounded, and who, making a somewhat premature gesture of veneration' – for the worthy veteran had not quite given up the ghost – cut off his lord's arm in order to preserve it as a relic.[49] In the 13th century certain stewards possessed a seal, the characteristic sign of high rank, others a fortified house.[50] The members of stewards' families constantly intermarried,[51] unless their wealth enabled them to aim higher still, like Aleaume, provost and steward of St. Denis à Maisoncelles, who, although a serf, won the hand of Mistress Agnes about the year 1230, the daughter of the knight Etienne' Jouvin. The enormous fine of 500 livres in the currency of Provins imposed on him by the monks on the occasion of this prohibited marriage outside the manor gives some idea of the extent of his fortune.[52]

Towards the end of the 13th century, what were the respective situations in France of the *seigneurs* and their chief servants, stewards, or officers at court?

Almost everywhere, the *sergents* had succeeded in making theirs a hereditary office, quite often in law and nearly always in practice. It would sometimes happen that when a *seigneur* conferred the office of steward upon a new candidate, he had it stated in a written deed that the office was not alienable and could never be inherited; but on taking a closer look we frequently observe that the beneficiary of this concession, benevolent as its intention was, turned out to be none other than the son or heir of the ex-mayor. In 1225 – to quote a single case among many – Colin, the son of the late steward of Choisy, claimed the stewardship as belonging to him by right of inheritance from the Abbot of Sainte-Geneviève of Paris, and failed to obtain it. Thinking better of it, he then appealed to the abbot's 'pity'; and the latter, satisfied with this show of 'humility', granted the coveted dignity to the suppliant – for his life only. The deed specifies that the heirs of Colin shall have no right to the paternal office of servant; but Colin's own example shows that custom was stronger than any written stipulations.[53] The abbot of Saint-Germain-des-Prés, Thibaut (1154–22nd July 1162), had forbidden under pain of anathema the transmission of the steward's office to the son of the then holder. His successor, Hugo V, needed a papal bull to have this prohibition removed, and the son whom Thibaut had wished to exclude nevertheless became the steward of the monks.[54]

The hereditary condition applied of course not only to the function but also to the fief with which it was rewarded. But on this point the *seigneurs* as a general rule continued to avoid the very serious danger that threatened from the stewards, more than from any of the *sergents*, namely the gradual tendency for the stewards to merge their fief – that is, the land held in return for their services – with the *seigneurie* they were trusted to administer, in the same way that the Counts had usurped so many counties at the King's expense, and the clerics so many Church lands which it was their business to protect. Even a case like that of the steward of Souplainville, as early as the middle of the 12th century, who had managed to appropriate not indeed the whole, but at least a good half of the village and its rights, remained a quite exceptional one, explicable only in terms of the weakness of the lord of those parts, the small Chapter of Saint-Cloud.[55] The *seigneurs* managed to preserve their property as a whole, though they were sometimes obliged to detach a few *seigneuries* now and again for some high-ranking officers at their court, and for the benefit of the stewards a large slice of land and a bonus on the dues collected by their efforts. Sometimes the steward was endowed on a scale that allowed him to establish his own tenancies, and even – like certain of the stewards of Saint-Vrast d'Arras, Saint-Benoît-sur-Loire and Saint-Père de Chartres – his own vassals (*vavasseurs*, that is to say sub-vassals, in relation to the monastery); in this fashion he himself became a small-scale *seigneur*.[56] The stewards in certain places had such good standing that it often seemed to knights, citizens and even other more exalted persons that it would be a good investment to buy them out (for their property, hereditary in the first place, had soon become something that could be bought and sold). In 1316 the Viscount of Lomagne, a nephew of Clement V and very anxious to grow rich, did not consider it beneath him to acquire one of these stewardly properties at St. Benoît-sur-Loire.[57]

Did these servants, who had gradually become people of some importance, continue to exercise their original functions? The majority of court officers ended, no doubt, by hardly keeping anything more of their original state than an empty name attached to their fief, such as those at Saint-Denis-en-France, where there were at the end of the 12th century surviving fiefs belonging to the marshal, the butler, the cook and the chamberlain, hardly distinguishable by the attachment of any specialised service from any common-or-garden vassal's estate.[58] At Saint-Trond in Lower Lorraine, everyone – including the jack-of-all-trades who made keys, repaired window panes and bled the monks' bodies when required – was attempting as early as 1136 to transform his tenure, encumbered with these modest services, into a 'free military fief'. On this occasion he was not successful; but his descendants were probably more fortunate.[59] This movement towards emancipation met with some opposition, especially to start with, from the *seigneurs*; but in the long run they seem to have accepted it readily enough, and sometimes even favoured it by reducing their *sergent's* fiefs or prebend rights.[60] They did in fact reap some quite solid advantages from the process. True, they were then obliged to recruit a new domestic staff, and consequently to set up either new fiefs or prebends and so incur new expenses, or – according to a new and more flexible system that was beginning to take hold – spend a certain sum of money each year in wages. The small part of their income which they thus had to sacrifice was compensated by the assurance of docile service which they had a right to expect over the generations from servants who had started at the bottom of the ladder. In 1231 Matthew Auger, chamberlain at Saint-Denis – we don't know how exactly this dignity had come his way: the documents simply show it passing by sale from person to person – anxious, no doubt, to acquire free board and lodging in the monastery, had the idea of claiming that he was actually practising his calling: he wished to dine at the abbot's table and sleep 'in his presence'. The refusal came from the monks' side. When the matter was submitted to arbitration, a decision was given in the monks' favour. Matthew was accepted as chamberlain, but his functions were reduced to that of mounted attendance; and even then the abbot, in spite of the claims of this too eager bodyguard, was constrained to assert his right to choose at his pleasure between either a personal escort and the simple provision of a horse.[61] As for the stewards, they were still to be seen in many villages at the end of the 13th century fulfilling their ancient role of levying dues and keeping a watchful eye on the lord's demesne. Elsewhere, however, their duties were being systematically redeemed by the great ecclesiastical establishments, sometimes at the price of granting their freedom. But in particular, and almost everywhere, their functions as land agents ceased to have any significance because the *seigneurs* were developing the practice of leasing their demesne and their rights – a custom that was to continue as a rule up to the end of the seignorial regime. It would be worth while finding out whether many of the stewards themselves figured among these lessees.[62]

The great ambition of all the more distinguished *ministeriales* had always been to live the kind of life which throughout the ages was considered noble – the life of a warrior, a 'knight', fully armed, the kind of life led by those who held military fiefs. The *sergents*, because of their close dependence on their masters, were generally bound to serve in time of war – an obligation which was the most useful and honourable of all in a society that was perpetually in a state of unrest. For some of them, such as the horsemen and the couriers (*caballarii*),[63] this obligation constituted the essential part of their duties; but it was generally in addition to the technical demands laid upon them by their various duties. The most important of them served on horseback, as a mounted escort, in command of small bands, armed from head to foot. Already in Charlemagne's days slaves possessing *ministeria* were by this very fact authorised to have horses, a shield, a lance, a sword and a dagger.[64] Everywhere the class of lord's servants (*ministeriales*) were of a naturally war-like disposition. On June 3rd 1083 the Papal City was delivered into the hands of the Emperor

Henry IV by the bold initiative of two persons belonging to the Archbishop of Milan's retinue, one of them a gentleman of the bedchamber and the other a baker, both of them, according to Landulphe, 'accustomed to combat and familiar with deeds of daring'. As a reward, they were dubbed knights.[65] The *seigneurs*, reckoning these servants as more amenable than vassals, were very ready to assign them important posts in the army. And this was not only true of the officers at court. Stewards too went to war. Amongst the obligations of the steward of Saint-Mesmin de Mecy à Nemois at the end of the 12th century was that of riding with the abbot.[66] At Bonneval, when the men of the place went on expeditions under the orders of the Count of Chartres, those who held the small offices did not stir hand or foot. The steward on the other hand, at the head of the contingent provided by the village, carried the standard of his masters the monks.[67]

Used as they were to wearing the sword, and occupying a brilliant place in the host, the most important of the *sergents* could hardly have avoided bearing themselves everywhere like warriors and considering themselves the equals of the military vassals. The adoption of knightly weapons and costume and habits – including a strong liking for hunting – figures among the abuses of which the monastic chroniclers at Saint-Benoît-sur-Loire,[68] Beaulieu,[69] at Saint-Gall in Alemannia,[70] most bitterly complained from the 10th to the 12th centuries – abuses which the heads of the ecclesiastical communities were trying to suppress with the utmost vigour. But the pressure on this point was almost irresistible.

Ganshof has clearly shown that the law was bound to follow in the footsteps of custom. Little by little society formed itself into a hierarchy. The putting on of knightly armour and the dubbing of a knight which had become a regular ceremony was in principle reserved for the sons of knights. The nobility formed themselves into a legal class which included all who, whether they had in fact received knighthood or no, possessed the hereditary right to receive it. This movement, which has as yet been very little studied, took place more or less throughout Europe during the first half of the 13th century. The new class then found that it included, along with the ancient possessors of *seigneuries*, a large number of *sergent* families – officers at court, most of whom were no longer distinguishable by their occupations from the vassals as a whole; this class included stewards too, not all of them, to be sure,[71] but those with fortunes which often comprised real *seigneuries* on a small scale and whose traditional manner of life, and alliances with families of undoubted noble status, placed them in the class of persons whom nobody could refuse to call knights. One has only to look through the bundles of documents in a region like the Île-de-France to come across large numbers of stewards bearing this title in the second half of the 13th century, a title to be interpreted from that time onwards in its fullest sense. Sometimes it is possible to follow quite closely the progress of a particular family, and watch it consolidating its social position more and more firmly. Take for example the steward of the lay *seigneurs* at Luzarches, Eude, in 1176. He was a rich man, for he was able to give the abbey of Hérivaux, on the occasion of his wife's birthday, an annual income of a *setier** of corn and four acres of land; but there is no indication that he claimed to be anything more than a *sergent*. But his son Hugo styled himself from that time onwards a knight. He succeeded his father as mayor, in 1183 at the latest. He owned not only fields but also quit-rents and tithes. He had several children, the eldest of whom, Clement, also became steward (before 1220). He, too, was a knight, possessing quit-rents, a mill, and some woodland; his brothers held their share of an enfeoffed inheritance from him, according to the system of inheritance which was practised among the nobility; his wife was 'Dame Mary, the steward's lady'. The second son, Bartholomew, adopted the name of squire (*écuyer*); in July 1220 he was in Albigeois. The third, Renaud, took holy orders and became a canon and cantor at Guise. We know nothing about the fourth son, Beaudouin, except that his daughter 'the noble lady Constance' married a knight.[72] Titles, the law of succession, the ties of kinship, careers open to the younger sons, the source of wealth – all these are pointers to nobility. Of how many other families could we not probably make similar observations if only we had more information![73] It can scarcely be doubted

* A *setier* – about a gallon.

that the small country gentry, who held such an important place in provincial life during the last centuries of the Middle Ages, and in modern times, are to be traced back to a large extent to *sergent* ancestors. This nobility based upon office, but seignorial office, rose in the social scale before the *noblesse de robe*. This latter class rose from the ranks of royal officials, a class whose fortunes during the period of the French monarchy have been so often recounted.

III

I have avoided so far any mention of a particularly delicate point in the history of the *ministeriales* – the original servile condition of many of them. Something must be said in conclusion about this aspect of the problem.

They were not all serfs. German authors have noted that free men entered the administrative class at a relatively late date (12th to 13th centuries); some of them have even spoken of mass entries, which must surely be an exaggeration. The expression, suggesting as it does the idea of entry into a well-defined class, cannot, as we shall see, apply as such to France. But there can be no manner of doubt that in France at all times men who had not been born in serfdom took on seignorial responsibilities. There was nothing in this condition to prevent them from preserving their freedom. At St. Martin de Tours, about the beginning of the 11th century, the monastery's officials holding prebends, employed on inside and outside work, numbered among their ranks, along with the freedmen (non-free persons whose status was almost that of a serf), some humble people.[74] At Saint-Père de Chartres, in the first years of the following century, the abbey's servants included along with the knights a tailor, a baker, a cook and an attendant in the infirmary; the former were, it appears, for the most part 'bound by the ties of servitude'; the latter, it seems, were free.[75] About 1134 the Chapter in Paris entrusted its mayoral office at Rozoy to a certain Raoul *ut libero homini*.[76] Ganshof, who has so meticulously tracked down so many seignorial officers in Flanders and in Lorraine, seems to me to have been too easily persuaded, in many cases, of their servile status. Often, in the absence of any precise indications as to the indubitable marks of servitude, it would have been better to have admitted ignorance in the matter. The words *ministerialis*, indicating simply a function, *familia* (mesnie), which may mean, as well as a group of serfs, the whole entourage of a household, servants of all grades and even vassals, prove nothing.[77] Nor does the alienation by his master of such and such a serf prove anything; for according to the ideas and language of the time, to sell or give a man was simply to cede the rights attaching to him; and the expression was used as much of a vassal as of a serf.[78] The arrangement of the signatures at the bottom of Lorraine Charters, ordinarily arranged in order of precedence, is nevertheless a matter of considerable doubt; was it not quite possible for the names of freemen and serfs to be indiscriminately jumbled together in the same section if they all belonged to the same entourage?

:Truth to tell, Ganshof has perhaps only been so ready to accept these rather fragile proofs because his thinking has been dominated by a single postulate, and that only half-consciously. He would admit readily enough, if I follow his argument, that between the Carolingian period and the great liberation movements of the 12th and 13th centuries the only free men were the 'nobles', or – more precisely –. the military vassals and those who possessed allodial lordships; the whole of the rest of society would have been sunk in servitude. I cannot here discuss this theory in detail, a theory that has been again and again, and rightly, attacked. It seems to me to be based above all on insufficient verbal analysis. The language of the Middle Ages made terribly ambiguous use of the word *liber*. Sometimes it was applied to the state of a man who was not a serf (nor in any analogous condition, such as a freedman); sometimes it was used more vaguely to describe any relative relaxation in the seignorial power. This second meaning is capable of an infinite number of subtle shades: in this sense there could scarcely be any individual who could not be called more free than so-and-so among his neighbours; and no one, on the other hand (with the possible exception of an allodial lord, who was dispensed from all requirements of homage), could have passed as absolutely free. The first meaning is the only one corresponding to a clear legal conception, and it was the one adopted by the jurists as soon as they came into existence. If we are to keep our argument clear, this is the meaning we must hold to. Now it seems to be an undeniable fact that there were at all periods, even among the humblest, men who, although bound down by their tenure to various dues and services owing to their lord, were none the less not thereby attached to their master by the personal and hereditary bonds of serfdom. In a perfect feudal and vassalic society, there would only have been two types of land – either fiefs or unfree tenements – and only two types of men – vassals or serfs; but this ideal state of perfection was never realised, and so there were always some allods (freeholds) and some free villeins.[79]

There can however be no doubt that a large number of *ministeriales* were of servile birth. Those *judices* of Beaulieu whom the monks claimed to prevent from wearing swords[80] were serfs. Aleaume, provost mayor of Maisoncelles, who paid so dearly for the honour of a too brilliant marriage,[81] was also a serf. And most of those intractable stewards, of whose quarrels with their masters we read in the documents, were serfs, and expressly named as such. Serfs too, by all appearances, were those *milites ignobiles*, who composed, along with the 'noble' knights, at the end of the 11th century, the court of the *seigneur* of Talmont.[82] One has only to look through the cartularies of the 13th century to come across countless numbers of manumissions of *sergents*, who, if they could be set free, must formerly have been serfs, both they and their ancestors who had likewise been *sergents*. And there was even more to it still: for certain *seigneurs* were disposed to lay down servitude – which they saw as a guarantee of dependence – as a necessary condition for the holding of certain offices.[83] How can we reconcile this original absence of liberty with the elevation of so many of these people into the noble class?

Society in the 10th, 11th and 12th centuries – I have already made the point, but it needs constant reiteration – was not a hierarchy of classes; it was rather an agglomeration or jumble of personal groupings, serfs or vassals, dependent on lords who in their turn were attached to other analogous groups. There was not such a thing, strictly speaking, as a nobility, but only men living in noble style; no such thing as hereditary knights, but only horsemen turned out in fine style and serving in the wars. Any powerful man who was well armed and not engaged in any pursuit deemed to be despicable could be called a knight and accoutred as such. To be sure, the serf is marked by a certain note of inferiority. The bond that ties him to his lord is a hereditary one, whereas that which ties the vassal is not hereditary in the eyes of the law.[84] It was probably this native dependence from the first days of his life, which weighed upon the servile body, attaching itself – as Guy Coquille says – 'to his very flesh and bones', and excluding every element of choice in subjection, that contemporaries thought of in the first place when they spoke of being deprived of 'liberty'. Such a man was forced by his family status to submit to humiliating hardships. He could not in general bear witness against free men. The Church inexorably refused to admit him to holy orders. Moreover those who had a nice sense of social distinctions did not allow him to ape the ways of the knight. The chronicler of Saint-Benoît-sur-Loire calls a certain serf-knight a 'spurious miles'.[85] It must also be observed that what the poets, interpreting the opinions of the upper classes in their country houses, denounced as scandalous, was not precisely the dubbing of a serf as knight; it was rather in a more general way the dubbing of the 'villein', the peasant defined not in terms of personal status (for one could be a 'villein' though free), but in terms of his profession and that of his ancestors. 'O Lord!' runs the complaint in *Girard de Roussillon*, 'how ill-rewarded is the worthy warrior who makes a knight of the *villein's* son, and then raises him to be his seneschal and his councillor.'[86] The style of life seemed to count for more than the legal condition. That was why their servile origin did not prevent many *sergents* from pushing their way forward to knighthood at the same time that they were acquiring fortunes, of the seignorial type.

Understandably enough, they then only asked to have the stain of their birth forgotten, from which so many painful incapacities and so much contempt had arisen. It is not surprising either that they so often succeeded. As I have tried to show elsewhere, it was sometimes difficult to prove servitude.[87] The payment of poll tax (*chevage*) was the most certain indication of it; but in many regions it gradually ceased to be regularly levied. Not all *seigneurs* were intelligent enough to realise that in spite of its small yield – still further diminished by the fall in the value of money – it would have been in their own interest to insist on it strictly because it furnished them with a legal weapon of the most substantial kind in their disputes with rebellious serfs.[88] At the time when Garnier de Mailly (d.1050 or 1051) was governing the abbey of Saint-Etienne de Dijon, a steward of the Viscount, who was also a serf of the monks, claimed the right to pay this humiliating contribution clandestinely, when no one was looking; but Garnier forced him to place it upon the altar in the sight of all. Writing rather more than a century later, the monk who reports this episode adds: 'I will not give the name of this man for fear of offending his descendants, who are resplendent today in all the brilliance of knighthood.'[89] Surely these brilliant warriors must have altogether ceased to lay their mite upon the altar of Saint-Etienne.

Knights of servile blood who wanted to climb too high must have come up against the dangerous rivalry of the members of the old vassal lineages, all those who, as the *Couronnement de Louis* puts it, did not accept the fact that a king could make a counsellor out of 'a steward or surveyor's son'.[90] They risked being roughly reminded of their hereditary antecedents. Ganshof, following Galbert de Bruges, has traced the greatness and the fall of the family of the Flemish Lord (*châtelain*) Érembaud. The misadventures of the gentleman of the bedchamber Ertaud, at the court of the Count of Champagne, Henry the Liberal, though of a less tragic kind, provided material for a narrative that Joinville doubtless borrowed from the traditions of the nobles of Champagne, a theme that the preachers for their part found it easy to develop.[91]

But other *ministeriales*, serfs by birth and more modest in their ambitions, succeeded without much difficulty in getting themselves recognised as belonging to the social rank of knight. Some, perhaps most, of them gradually escaped from the actual condition of serfdom. Others, in spite of their new dignities, remained bound down by it. They formed the greater part of those serf-knights spoken of here and there in our documents.[92]

Then, as the result of a slow transformation, long prepared for in the customs of the time, the idea of class, which had up till then been rather vague, came into full vigour. Serviture was less and less thought of as a personal bond and more and more as a mark of inferior social position. Knighthood and serfdom became decidedly incompatible: 'serfs, male and female, are not capable of nobility' will become a maxim of Common Law.[93] It was an accomplished fact from the beginning of the 13th century in France, and in England.[94] According to a famous decision by the Parliament of Paris under Saint Louis, the lord who dubs his serf a knight is to be considered, whether he will or no, as setting him free.[95] What happened then to the serf-knight? There were still a few of them at rare intervals in the first half of the century. But the majority of them, or of their descendants, appear to have risen out of serfdom. Some of them did it honestly, by being enfranchised—sometimes on condition that they gave up the offices they held under their lord.[96] Many no doubt effected the change by simple prescription. As for the succession of *sergents* who had acquired riches and power without however being able so far to achieve knighthood – they seem to have been in evidence particularly on the lands of some great Church lords who kept a very tight hold upon their staff – the great movement towards freedom which was then growing throughout almost the whole of France allowed them to get rid of the stain of servitude by a money payment before they continued their social climb. Very often we can watch the steward buying his manumission several years before the rest of the village. A part of the lesser nobility of the days to come was to be drawn not only from former *sergents*, but also from one-time serfs.

IV

We possess a French translation carried out in the 14th century of the German custumal known today as the 'Mirror of Swabia'. The author had a good knowledge of both languages and their

ADMINISTRATIVE CLASSES: FRANCE AND GERMANY 105

equivalent terms. He rendered *lehn*, for example, quite correctly by the French *fief*. Yet there was one word that embarrassed him – the word *dienstmann*. Sometimes he attempted an approximate translation – *vavassour* – which doubtless called up in his mind, as in the literary documents, an idea of the lesser nobility; or, in a longer but more correct rendering, 'highly placed persons who have not been set free'; sometimes – and much more often – he is simply content to transcribe the original.[97] It is clear that he realised the German *dienstmann* to have no exact legal equivalent in France. This humble writer had a good notion of comparative history.[98]

The evolution of the administrative class in French would be fairly well characterised by saying that the chief seignorial officers formed a powerful social class, consolidated by the heritability obligations and fiefs – an important point distinguishing them from what would today be a mere collection of officials – and later on attained noble status in large numbers; but they never formed a legally defined class. The picture would appear to be the same in its broad outlines in England and in Italy.[99] We know through Ganshof's work that Flanders, barring one strange peculiarity in the position of the stewards, did not deviate from the normal French type. In the principalities of Lorraine, in spite of the influence of German institutions, the class of *ministeriales* never achieved more than an embryonic legal status. Germany, on the other hand, starting from a very similar point, developed quite differently. Quite early on in the large estates one can see the *ministeriales* being recognised as a group apart, possessing precise privileges and inspired by a vigorous *esprit de corps*. This was true to such an extent that it soon became necessary to put down in writing the customs appropriate to these little societies (for the first time, as far as we know, at Bamberg between 1057 and 1065). But as early as 1020 we find a mention on the estates belonging to the Chapter of Saint-Adalbert of Aachen of the 'law' about *sergents*, still most probably in a purely oral state, but already thought of as something well defined.[100] They had their own law-courts at a time when their colleagues in France appear to have been still amenable to the ordinary seignorial courts. In the 12th and in the 13th centuries a *jus ministeriale* grew up everywhere, varying in its details in the different lordships, as the author of the *Sachsenspiegel* (III, 42, 2) rightly noticed, yet everywhere distinguished by a characteristic dualism: on the one hand, there were obligations of a servile nature, corresponding to the origin of most of the *dienstleute*, but falling even upon freemen who had entered this class; on the other hand there were duties essentially belonging to the nobility. In France, when the nobility became a class with rigorously-drawn frontiers, the *sergents*, who had formerly been both knights and serfs, were obliged either to cease being serfs or to renounce knighthood. In Germany the *dienstleute*, serf-knights, formed a distinct class within the ranks of the nobility, accepted by custom as such, and by the law-books and the imperial constitutions. The law of Southern Germany, by an additional refinement, divided it into further sub-classes.[101] In the end, it is true, it became merged with the lesser nobility, but only rather late in the day; and in the south this did not happen till towards the end of the Middle Ages. Elsewhere, on the Lower Rhine, there was a further complication; beneath the knightly ministerial class those of the *ministeriales* who had, without reaching the noble class, nevertheless won their freedom, also formed themselves in the 14th and 15th centuries into a clearly-defined class, entered by a deliberate and often ceremonial procedure.[102] Everywhere the households of the lord's servants and officials had given birth to legal categories.

How are we to explain such a sharp contrast between the two countries?

Ganshof seems to consider this a simple matter of difference in dates. 'In France,' he says (p. 376), 'where the development of the whole of society in a feudal direction took place more rapidly, the *ministeriales* ... were from the course of the 11th century onwards absorbed into the nobility.' I do not really know what is meant by this 'feudal type': the epithet is such an elastic one that historians ought strictly to refrain from using it without defining it. Above all I do not see that the class of nobility was already formed in France by the 11th century, nor, in a general way, much earlier than in Germany. The turning-point in this development was when the knightly class became a hereditary caste. Did this really happen before

1100? I doubt whether Ganshof could produce proof of this.

Mlle Zeglin, more strangely still, has claimed to be able to explain 'the absence of an administrative class' in France by the institution of 'liege loyalty'.[103] The lords, she maintains, would not have needed the *ministeriales* because they had been able to collect around themselves a close-knit group of 'liegemen'. But what was a liegeman? The word, which evoked the idea of a very close dependence,[104] had two very distinct meanings in the 12th and 13th centuries. On the one hand it was a designation, in many places, for a serf;[105] on the other hand it was used for a category of vassals, from whom one of their lords required a particularly strict homage which bound them to him more than to any other rival lord. Thus certain *sergents* who were serfs were called in this manner liegemen; others, who owed homage in its most stringent form, were called by the same name, but for a quite different reason. Both sections shared the name with more or less extensive groups from whom they were distinguished by their functions. These were much too specialised to be carried out by the serfs and vassals as a whole, even the liegemen.

The problem presented by the subject of the administrative classes should perhaps, in truth, be treated as a particular case of a more general problem. German mediaeval law as a whole is characterised by an almost exuberant development of the idea of class, which makes it particularly difficult for French people to understand. Its spirit is eloquently expressed in the theory of the *Heerschild*, which distributes all the holders of fiefs over six or seven 'rungs' of the social ladder. Those who occupy a given level cannot, on pain of social degradation, become the feudal dependants of those belonging to a lower level. No doubt this was a construction by jurists, and as such artificially strict; but its roots were nonetheless firmly planted in fact. There was nothing like this outside Germany. The same tendency is observable in all aspects of legal life. A historical manual of English mediaeval law, in the chapter dealing with the status of persons, can almost leave the nobility out of account. 'Our law', says Maitland, 'hardly knows anything of a noble or of a gentle class; all free men are in the main equal before the law.'[106] A similar book in France will devote considerable space to the nobles, treating them as a more or less unified class. A German work on the other hand will distinguish several groups among the nobility, and they will not all necessarily have the *connubium*. In the same way, the majority of German customs concerning the unfree part of the population, unlike the French ones, distinguish between several quite distinct grades.[107] One cannot be surprised that within this structure of classes one above another one or even several niches should have been reserved over a certain period of time for the seignorial officers, especially for those who were simultaneously serfs and nobles. But this does not resolve the difficulty – it simply pushes it further back and makes it more serious. How can we account for this hierarchical tendency inherent in German law, which makes it so different from all the other legal systems of Eastern and Central Europe? The historian who could supply a satisfactory explanation could preen himself on having searched out the most intimate secrets of past societies. But we have not as yet reached that stage.[108]

NOTES

1. *Revue historique de droit français et étranger*, 1928, pp. 46–91.
2. A German scholar, Ernst Mayer, has attempted to produce a comparative history of German and French institutions:
Deutsche und französische Verfassungsgeschichte, 1899, 2 vols. This work, 'instructive and suggestive as it is' – though also not a little conjectural – cannot be said to give us all we need. No doubt such a vast synthesis must remain a little premature so long as the comparative method has not been methodically applied to particular institutions.
3. *La ministérialité, a-t-elle existé en France?* in *Acad. des Inscriptions. Comptes rendus, 1911.* In 1915, D. Zeglin published, under the title *Der Homo Ligius und die französische Ministerialität (Leipziger Histor. Abn.* 39), an instructive memoir, though too summary and sometimes rather debatable: cf. below p. 122, note 103. The work of Ganzenmüller, *Die Flandrische Ministerialität bis zum ersten Drittel des 12. Jahrhunderts*, has today been superseded by Ganshof's book.
4. *Etude sur les ministériales en Flandre et en Lotharingie*, Bruxelles, 1926.
5. The principal accounts on which Ganshof's book was based have been enumerated by H. Laurent in *Le Moyen-Age*, 1926, pp. xiii – xv. Some of these are of great interest, especially the report by Des Marez, which appeared in *Acad. royale de Belgique, Bulletin de la classe des Lettres*,

ADMINISTRATIVE CLASSES: FRANCE AND GERMANY 109

1924 (M. Ganshof's work had been crowned by the Academy before publication), and printed separately under the title *Note sur la ministérialité en Belgique*; I am in agreement with him on several points. To M. Laurent's list must now be added the very important account by M. Champeaux, which appeared in the *Revue Historique de Droit fr. et étr.*, 1927, pp. 744–756.

6. Along with *ministerialis*, the documents drawn up in Latin use a host of synonyms, some pedantically borrowed from the classical language – *cliens, satelles, famulus* . . . etc., others simply transcriptions of popular terms, *serviens* in particular. In French, *menestrel* appears to have applied above all to the *sergents-artisans*; but in the Jura and in Savoy *mistral* is found in the sense of an administrative officer (p. ex. D. D. Benoît, *Histoire de l'abbaye et de la terre de Saint-Claude*, vol. II, p. 65; J. A. Bonnefoy and A. Perrin, *Le prieuré de Chamonix*, Vol. II, nos. 84 and 96; the same holds good, it seems, of the Provençal *mistrau*.

7. G. Masset, *Cartulaire de Saint-Jean-d'Angély*, Vol. I, no. CCXVI: 'Concedimus etiam ut omnes prepositi corum et vicarii et sutores et pelletani et molendinarii et hortolani et omnes famuli proprii, et qui ballias eorum tenuerint et ministeria eorum habuerint et propria opera corum agerint; quos vel hereditario jure habuerint, vel ipsi de hominibus burgi, qui omnes fere juris eorum sunt, pro voluntate sua, de quolibet gradu elegerint, quieti ac liberi sint ad campestre facere voluerit.' Cf. on this lack of distinctness about the *ministeriales* group Ganshof, p. 279 (Hainaut), note 2 (Utrecht); p. 298, note 2 (Saint-Trond); and 237, note 4.

8. La Mare, *Histoire des ducs de Bourbon*, Vol. III, Pièces suppl., p. 67: 'Item homines usagii ultra quinque non debet dominus recipere in servientes et illos volentes' (Saint-Germain-Laval, Loire, arrondissement Roanne).

9. Guérard, *Cartulaire de Saint-Père de Chartres*, Vol. II, p. 371, no. CXLIX: 'presertim cum plures eorum nobis essent famuli servitutis vinculo obnoxii, quos, si necessitas urgeret, licebat quolibet modo in nostris usibus insumere'.

10. Already in Carolingian times: see particularly *Statuts d'Adalard* (edit. L. Levillain, in *Le Moyen Age*, 1900, II, 1, p. 361; edict of Pitres, 25th June 864, cap., vol. II, no. 273, cl. 31. Cf. for the 12th century Guimann, *Cartulaire de l'abbaye de Saint-Vaast d'Arras*, edit. Van Drival, p. 299 (Dainville); by Lépinois and Merlet, *Cartulaire de Notre-Dame de Chartres*, Vol. I, LI (1139, Jan. 14th).

11. L. Lex, *Eudes comte de Blois*, p. justif., no. XIII (1015–1023): 'De familia autem Sancti Martini, si quis aliquid neglexerit, quoqunque ministeris utatur, tam ingenuus quam colibertus, sive hic qui in ministerialibus servitiis seu forinsecus occupati sunt, quoscumque monachi alunt, vestiunt, nutriuntque nullam vicariam solvant, sed totum quidquid neglexerint ubi et ubi totum in potestate sit abbatis et monachorum ejus perpetualiter.' It will be noticed in what a restricted (and very rare) sense *ministerialibus servitiis* is used – 'household ser-

vices'. Cf. also the charter of privileges granted by Anseau de Garlande to the monks of the priory of Tournan, which was dependent upon Saint-Maur-des-Fossés, for the land at l'Essart (1202, Sept. Arch. Nat., L 460, nos. 11A and 11B); 'Famulus eorum qui major appelatur et omnes *eorum famuli qui de pane ipsorum vivant* ab omni pedagio, theloneo et qualibet alia consuetudine immunes existunt in tota Turnomii potestate, nisi mercatores fuerint'.

12. I have already had occasion to explain the conception of the fief, which will be found outlined below in an address to the 5th International Congress of the Historical Sciences (1923); cf. *Compte rendu*, p. 102ff. I will only recapitulate here the main features necessary for a proper understanding of *ministéralité*. I shall in particular leave completely on one side: (1) the ancient uses of the word fief, in the sense of movable goods, and perhaps in the precise sense of *provende* (before the Capetian epoch); (2) the eccentric development in certain places (the Toulouse region for example, and those governed by Anglo-Norman law), where 'fief' ended by meaning any kind of tenure; I reserve the right to prove that this was a secondary development, the starting point in these regions have been just the same as elsewhere (fief = tenure + service); (3) the use – very instructive everywhere – of the word fief in ecclesiastical language; (4) the rather belated development which often introduced a confusion between the two notions of fief and heredity, which only came about very slowly. In 1142–1143, for example, the Abbot and the Dean of Saint-Avit d'Orléans, when founding the new town of Acquebouille, declared that the steward's office would not be hereditary, and arranged for the steward to hold a fief (*feodum*) composed of a half-ploughland and a fifth of all the fines levied (G. Vignay, *Cartulaire du chapitre de Saint-Avit d'Orléans*, no. 40).

13. This sense is particularly clear in the *Lex Visigothorum (Antiqua)*, XI, 1, 5 and 7 and no doubt 3, 4. Cf. E. Mayer, *Italienische Verfassungsgeschichte*, Vol. I, p. 436).

14. *Cap.* I, no. 32, cl. 50. It will be noticed that all the free grooms have bénéfices; the non-free (fiscalins) are divided between the two systems. The *praebendarii, provendari* are frequently mentioned in the sources from the Frankish period relating to the administration of the large domains, notably in the *Statuts* of Adalard; Mgr. Lesne translates these as '*pourvoyeurs*' (*Mélanges historiques du Moyen Age offerts à M. Ferdinand Lot*, pp. 389ff.), which does not appear to me to give the correct meaning; 'provendier', which was current in the Middle Ages, is better. The co-existence of the two systems of fief and prébende is a common feature in many civilisations; cf. for Assyria, Fossey in the *Revue critique*, Sept. 1st, 1927, p. 321.

15. Cf. for England the interesting remarks of P. Vinogradoff, *English Society in the Eleventh Century*, pp. 76ff.

16. He says in effect (p. 31): 'the fief constitutes at this period (the beginning of the 12th century) a tenure belonging only to knights'.

ADMINISTRATIVE CLASSES: FRANCE AND GERMANY III

17. B. de Broussillon, *Cartulaire de l'Abbaye de Saint-Aubin d'Angers*, Vol. I, no. XLIX: 1082–1106. De Lepinois et Merlet, *Cartul. de Notre-Dame de Chartres*, Vol. II, no. CCXXII (also Guérard, *Cartul. de Saint-Père de Chartres*, Vol. I, p. LVIII, and Fagnicz, *Documents relatifs à l'historire de l'industrie et du commerce en France*, Vol. I, no. 280): n.d.; dated by the editors 'about 1216'. Cf. below p. 511, note 1. In the references that follow, not wishing to make them too long and keeping a fuller critical apparatus for another occasion, I will confine myself here to the most ancient and incontrovertible documents, and for the sake of greater clarity I shall exclude those where the service tenure is called a *beneficium*, although it cannot be disputed that in the language of the notaries this word was synonymous with fief.

18. The documents are fairly numerous, notably: Lacurie, *Histoire de l'abbaye de Millezais*, p. justif, no. LIII (1181, but relying on older) facts). Guerard, *Cartul. de Saint-Père de Chartres*, Vol. II, p. 277, no. XIX (1127). Deloche, *Cartul. de Beaulieu*, no. CI, p. 154 (12th century). E. Laurière, *Texte des contumes de la prévôté et vicomté de Paris*, Vol. III, p. 260: a deed of Richard Cœur de Lion, son of the English king, Count of Poiton; Périgueux, before the siege of Châtillon (consequently 1175 – the text erroneously gives 1277!). *Cartul. du Chapitre de Notre-Dame de Lausanne (Mém. et doc. publiés par la Soc. d'hist. de la Suisse romande*, Vol. VI), pp. 546–547 (1227 Old Style, Feb. 2nd.). In Italy, there is a particularly explicit documentary reference: *Codice diplomatico padovano*, Vol. II, no. 946 (1169, Jan. 3rd).

19. A list of the fiefs of Saint-Maximin de Trèves (about 1200), Beyer, *Urkundenbuch der Mittelrheinischen Territorien*, Vol. II, p. 470.

20. B. de Broussillon, *Cartulaire de l'abbaye de Saint-Aubin d'Angers*, Vol. II, no. CCCVIII (1082–1106); note that there was already a 'bénéfice' belonging to a painter, mentioned in a letter from Einhard, *Ep. karolini aevi*, Vol. III, p. 119, no. 18.

21. L. Delisle, *Instructions addressées par le Comité des Travaux historiques . . . Litérature latine . . .*, p. 61, no. 27 (1228, No., Beauvais).

22. A deed of Megingaud, Archbishop of Trèves (1008–1016), in Beyer, *Urkundenbuch*, Vol. I, no. 287 (the most ancient German document in which the word fief has come to light). J. de Font-Réaulx, *Sancti Stephani Lemovicensis Chartularium (Bull. Soc. histor. du Limousin*, vol. LXIX, no. CXXIX (12th century).

23. Deloche, *Cartul. de Beaulieu*, no. CI, p. 154; Polypt de Prüm (addition du moine Césaire, in 1222), in Beyer, *Urkundenbuch*, Vol. I, p. 161, note 4; H. Bastgen, *Die Geschichte des Trierer Domkapitels im Mittelalter*, p. 298 (13th century, after 1259); H. Pirenne, *Le livre de l'abbé Guillaume de Ryckel*, p. 62 (1261).

24. Beyer, *Urkundenbuch*, Vol. III, no. 289 (1226, Sept. 9th). Cf. *Gesta abbatum Trudonensium*, IX, 12 (edit. C. Borman, p. 152, 1136); there, the *seigneur* was at the same time a locksmith and a glazier; his tenure is not specifically called a fief. It is simply stated that he wished to

transform it (probably from a *sergentine* fief) into a 'free military fief': cf. below p. 95.
25. See J. H. Round, 'The Introduction of Knight Service', in his *Feudal England*.
26. C. Douais, *Cartulaire de l'abbaye de Saint-Sermin de Toulouse*, no. 155 (1139, June 29th): a deed by which the four sons of Pierre Arnaud de Saint-Anatholy (the commune of Lanta, Haute-Garonne, in the arrondisement of Villefranche-de *Lauraguais*) renounced various *convenientie*, in particular this one, 'vel de canonico generis eorum recolligendo, vel de milite generis eorum cum abbate manendo'. Cf. also below, note 61.
27. G. Seeliger, *Die soziale und politische Bedeutung der Grundherrschaft*, says most aptly on p. 46: 'Die Gegenüberstellung der ministerialischen und der freien vasalitischen Lehen als zweier Gruppen militärischer Lehen ist erst das Ergebnis der Entwicklung des 12. und 13. Jahrhunderts.'
28. This has been admirably shown by M. Pierre Petot, *L'hommage servile, Revue historique de droit*, 1927. See in addition to the texts quoted by him, G. Robert, *Les serfs de Saint-Remi de Reims (Travaux de l'Academie de Reims,* vol. CXL), no. XXXI (Jan. 26th 1262): three of the lord's men handed over to Saint-Remi did homage ('hommagium fecerunt') to a monk deputed by the abbot and the convent; the rite is not described. In Italy likewise the word homage denoted a bond between inferior and superior, outside the relationship of vassalage: Santini, *Condizione personali degli abitanti del contade di Firenze nel sec. XIII*, in *Archivio storico ital.*, 4th series, Vol. XVII, 1866, text cited p. 182 (1225): *P. Vaccari, L'affrancazione dei servi della gleba nell' Emilia e nella Toxana*, pp. 61, 124.
29. Galbert de Bruges, *Histoire du meurtre de Charles le Bon*, edit. Pirenne, c. 54, p. 85 ('secundum morem predecessorum suorum comitum'); c. 55, p. 87 (a similar formula); c. 66, p. 107; c. 94, p. 138; c. 102, p. 147; c. 103, p. 149. For Rome, cf. a bull of Anaclet, J.-W., 8390 (Migne, P. L., vol. 179, col. 709, XIX b); for London, Petit-Dutaillis, in Stubbs, *Constitutional History*, Vol. I, p. 859, no. 1.
30. For example: de Ribbe, *La société provençale*, p. 487ff. (a particularly explicit reference); E.-G. Alart, *Privilèges et titres . . . du Roussillon*, pp. 141 and 327; R. Brun, *La ville de Salon au Moyen Age*, p. 204, c. 4; 295 c. 1; 369, c. 12. Cf. Aug. Dumas, *Encore la question 'Fidèles ou vassaux'* in *Rev. hist. du droit*, 1920, p. 218, no. 1 (but the reasons given on pp. 227–228 to explain the disappearance of homage by the common people (*l'hommage des roturiers*') would need to be examined afresh). The *hommage des roturiers* underwent a particular extension in Norman law, which was in many respects anomalous.
31. J. B. Champeval, *Cartulaire des abbayes de Tuile*, no. 176 (July 1216); Ch. Métais, *Cartulaire de Notre-Dame de Josaphat*, Vol. II, no. CCCIV (Nov. 1224). There appear to be analogous examples in Italy (where, as we may note in passing, genuine vassal homage seems to have been much more widespread than Guilhiermoz thought); C. F. V. Rumorr, *Ursprung der Besitzlosigkeit der Colonen im neuren Toskana*, p. 40, no. 4 (1213,

ADMINISTRATIVE CLASSES: FRANCE AND GERMANY 113

May 8, but ind. 2?); P. Vaccari, *L'affrancazione dei servi della gleba*, p. 40, no. 1.

32. Lambert d'Ardres, *Historia Comitum Ghinnesium*, c. 129; E. G. Alart, *Privilèges et titres* . . . *du Roussillon*, pp. 126 and 128; Lodge, *The estates of the archbishop* . . . *of Bordeaux* (Oxford Studies in Social and Legal History, III, p. 25, no. 3); Arch. hist. de la Gironde, Vol. I, nos. XXXIII and XXXIV; J.-A. Bonnefoy and A. Perrin, *Le prieuré de Chamonix*, Vol. II, no. 75, No. 85 (cf. no. 80), no. 90 (the 'hommes liges' in these documents are undoubtedly serfs; cf. below, p. 107); hinojosa, *El regimen señorial en Cataluña*, p. 224. With the exception of the first (12th century), the second and the third and perhaps the fourth (13th century), these documents all belong admittedly to the last two centuries of the Middle Ages; but all the knowledge we have of the development of mediaeval societies would point to survivals rather than to innovations. Except for the first, these testimonies appear to have escaped the notice of M. Petot. Cf. also Pierre Raimon de Toulouse in Mahn, *Werke der Troubadours*, Vol. I, p. 134, I, verse 3. J. Anglade, *Poésies de Pierre Raimon de Toulouse*, Chanson II, verse 3, in *Annales du Midi*, 1919-1920.

33. Marc Bloch, *Les rois thaumaturges*, p. 240, note 2.

34. Ekkehard, *Casus sancti Galli*, c. 21 chevage paid in wax (*chevage en cire*). This due is here perhaps in the nature of an *amende honorable*; cf. besides Petot, loc. cit. p. 82ff., R. His, *Todtschlagsühne und Mannschaft*, in *Festgabe für K. Güterbock*, Berlin, 1910.

35. *Hist. du Languedoc*, Vol. VIII, col. 597 (Aug. 13th 1210).

36. Thillier et Jarry, *Cartulaire de* . . . *Saint-Croix d'Orléans*, no. CCCLXXX.

37. A. Bouthors, *Coutumes locales du baillege d'Amiens*, Vol. I, pp. 317ff, especially §§33 and 124-129 (one of the *monetarii* is at the same time the holder of two mayoralties); the text needs careful re-editing; cf. Massiet du Biest, *Revue du Nord*, 1923, p. 41; E. Morel, *Cartulaire de 'abbaye de Saint-Corneille de Compiègne*, Vol. II, no. DLXXXVI. For Chartres, Bibl. Nat. lat. 10096, fol. 75; cf. the lists of *sergents* in Lépinois et Merlet, *Cartulaire de Notre-Dame de Chartres*, Vol. 11, no. CCCLXXXVI, and Bibl. de la ville de Chartres, MS. 1137, fol. 109; the bishop's enfeoffed porter and carpenter are known from rather later documents: *Cartulaire*, Vol. II, no. CCI and CCXXII.

38. Here is an example taken from a region far removed from the Low Countries: Mathieu and Dreux de Montoire, for the soul's weal of their dead brother, Hugue le Bourguignon, gave to Marmoutier: 'alodun de Charsannia, quod isdem eorum defunctus frater de Hugone, Genetensis castri domino, in foerum tenuerat'; then follows the confirmation of the gift by this Hugo 'de Genetensi castro', who is clearly himself the freeholder (Ch. Métais, *Chartes vendômoises*, no. XLVI – before 1064). Elsewhere, in Rouergue, where the bishop, himself a freeholder, had to a large extent enfeoffed his allod, this word, by a gradual shift in meaning that is easy to understand, ended by taking on the sense of a lordly ownership: it is stated that in such and such a fief the bishop has 'allodium et dominium', has 'l'alo . . . e la senhoria'

(Lempereur, *Les droits seigneuriaux dans les terres de l'ancien évêché dé Rodez, Bullet, histor. et philolog.* 1894). Finally one must reckon with the case where 'Alleu', 'les Alleux' have become settled upon a piece of land – whatever its present legal position might be – as a proper name; cf. a deed of Saint-Serge d'Angers, in the restored version of the Cartulary by Marchegay, Arch. de Maine-et-Loire, H. non coté, fol. 293 (IIII), and the observations of M. Olivier-Martin, *Histoire de la contume de la Prévôté et vicomté de Paris*, Vol. 1, p. 219, no. 2 (dealing with the village Les Alleux-le-Roi).
39. For the serfs, *Revue des Chartes de Cluny*, Vol. IV, no. 3649; Verbiest, *Le servage dans le comté de Hainaut* (*Acad. royale de Belgique, Cl. des Lettres, Mém.*, 2nd series, Vol. VI), p. 106, no. 2; E. Lodge, *The estates of the archbishop . . . of Bordeaux*, p. 56, note 1.
40. Cf. Marc Bloch, *Les transformations du servage*, in Mélange . . . F. Lot, p. 66, note 1. Already among the Roman colonists; C. Th, V, 19, 1.
41. SS., Vol. XXI, p. 622: 'Servus aliquis alodium suum a manu sua nullatenus potent eicere vel feodum facere, nisi assensu domini sui' (July 28th 1200).
42. J. Ahrens, *Die Ministerialität in Köln*, p. 6off; Emil Müller, *Die Ministerialität im Stift St. Gallen*, p. 41; G. Winter, *Die Ministerialität in Brandenburg*, p. 89. Particularly significant is the institution of the *Inwärts-Eigen*, an *alleu* which the *Dienstmann* could freely dispose of in favour of the other *Dienstleute* of his lord, but not for the benefit of other people without seignorial consent; cf. Puntschart, in the *Zeitschr. der Sav. Stiftung*, G., A., Vol. 43 (1922).
43. Guérard, *Cartul. de Saint-Père de Chartres*, Vol. II, p. 301, no. XLVIII. There is need for further study of the rise of the lower *sergents* to the highest positions in the administrative class. I notice, on land belonging to the Chapter of Paris, two *doyens* or sons of *doyens* (the *doyen* was a rural official subordinate to the steward) who acquired stewardships at L'Hay in Feb. 1251, new style, and at Lucy on June 16th 1267 (A ch. Nat., S 315 and 396B).
44. See in Guimann, *Cartul. de Saint-Vaast d'Arras*, p. 346–347, a document that seems to have escaped M. Ganshof's notice, the legal role of the 'servientibus hereditariis coquine'; and for the position of enfeoffed *sergents* at the seignorial court, *Ét. de saint Louis, II, 4* (edit. Viollet, II, p. 338; cf. also *Cartul. de Touraine-Anjou*, c. LXI, *ibid.*, Vol. III, p. 39) – *at the bailiff's court Cont. Touraines-Anjou*, c. CXXII, p. 47. There is an obvious comparison with the *Curia Regis*.
45. *Cap. de villis*, c. 60. As M. Dopsch has noted, *Wirtschaftsentwicklung der Karolingerzeit*, Vol. 12, p. 160, the high position enjoyed by the royal stewards in Carolingian times came from the presence of two of their number alongside the *telonearius* (collector of tolls) of the palace market in the court of justice – quite irregular, admittedly – that was set up in 870 to judge the Bishop of Laon Hincmar; *Hincmari opera*, edit. Sirmond, Vol. II, p. 606.
46. Prou and Vidier, *Recueil des chartes de Saint-Benoît-sur-Loire*, Vol. I, no.

CVI, and Lachaire, *Louis VI, choix de textes inédits*, no. 80: 1109, before Aug. 3rd. This document, which I cannot analyse in detail, is an extremely curious one. There was on the lands of Saint-Benoît at least one other case of subordination of the stewards one to another that was perhaps of a vassal-like character: on Jan. 8th 1254 Girard, mayor of Tigy, who ranked as squire, handed over to the monastery his right of redemption (*rachetum*) of the stewardships of Vienne (en val) and *Tranciacum: Arch. du Loiret*, H. 46. In the same way, at the end of the 13th century, the enfeoffed provost of Santeuil exercised a night of redemption in the stewardships of Montainville and Mongerville (de Lépinois et Merlet, *Cartul. de Notre-Dame de Chartres*, Vol. II, no. CCLXXXVI). It will be seen below (note 54) that there was a provost of Saint-Aubin d'Angers who was the enfeoffed lord of another *sergent*.
47. Guérard, *Cartul. de Saint-Père*, Vol. II, p. 500, no. XLIV. The abuses perpetrated by the officers of the *Seigneur* in the Chartres district are eloquently brought out in the oath which the canons of Chartres, since the episcopate of Geoffroi de Lèves (Jan 24th 1116-1149), had imposed on their mayors: de Lépinois et Merlet, *Cartulaire de Notre-Dame de Chartres*, Vol. I, no. LVIII.
48. Cf. Suger, *De rebus in administratione suis gestis*, edit. Lecoy de la Marche, p. 162; Gutmann, in the *Cartulaire de Saint-Vaast d'Arras*, p. 7.
49. *Perceval*, edit. Potvin, line 970ff; as we shall see in what follows, it is a matter of some consequence to note that this loyal steward had been armed as a knight by his lord (line 1010). K. Bartsch, *Chrestomatie de l'ancien français*, 10th edt., no. 17, line 204ff.
50. Sceau de Dreux, mayor of Saint-Denis à Cormeilles-en-Parisis: Arch. Nat., S. 2336, no. 6 (June 1229). A fortified house, surrounded by a moat, belonging to the mayor of Grand-Puits; he keeps possession of it, holding it in homage from his lord (the abbey of Saint-Denis), after having sold his mayoralty: Arch, Nat. LL 1158, p. 333 (May 1225).
51. As is attested by the deeds for the exchange of serfs in the Paris region, a large number of which concern members of families of this kind who were obliged by their social position to seek a match outside the narrow circle to which they would have been confined by the obligation of *formariage* (prohibiting marriage outside the manor).
52. Arch. Nat. L 848, no. 32 (1234, 24th-30th April or 1235, 1st-8th April). Cf. Cartul. blanc, LL 1157, p. 847 (two deeds of June 1230). Aleaume, not being able to discharge his obligations entirely in money, ceded to the monks his provost-stewardship and some land, which was reckoned at the total sum of 300 livres. For other examples of marriage between mayoral and knightly families, see below, pp. 98, 99.
53. A charter of abbot Herbert and of the convent: Biblioth. de Sainte-Geneviève, MS. 356, pp. 266, 267 (no date), a deed of Louis VIII, Paris, 1225, Nov., in Giard, *Étude sur l'histoire de l'abbaye de Saint-Geneviève* (Mém. de la Soc. de l'hist. de Paris), Vol. XXX, p. 90, note 9.
54. R. Pourpardin, *Recueil des chartes de l'abbaye de Saint-Germain-des-Prés*,

Vol. I, no. CXXXVI (bull of Alexander III, Nov. 26th, 1163 or 1164).
55. Bibl. Nat., lat. 5185d, fol. 1: Louis VII, king of France and Aquitaine (April 1st. 1137–Aug. 1154); Souplainville, Seine-et-Oise, commune of Saclas.
56. Guimann, *Cartul. de Saint-Vaast*, p. 352; 363, 364; 374; 375; 393 (this last example contains 'hôtes', that is to say tenants and *vavasours*). A charter of June 1258 by which Jean, knight, handed over to Saint-Benoît the mayoralty of Sainville, while reserving his enfeoffed men, amongst whom were a knight and a knight's widow: Arch. du Loiret, H. 30[1], p. 260 (according to information provided by MM. Prou and Vidier). An enfranchisement by the monks of Saint-Père de Chartres of William, mayor of Germignonville, who ceded to the abbey, at the same time as his mayoralty, '*duos vavassores qui erant de sua majoria*'; No. 1326, Bibl. de la ville de Chartres, MS. 1136, Vol. III, p. 703, and particularly Guérard, *Cartulaire de Saint-Père de Chartres*, Vol. II, p. 690, no. CXI. In the same way the fief of a provost of Saint-Aubin d'Angers, as revealed to us by a note of 1113 (B. de Broussillon, *Cartul. de l'abbaye de Saint-Aubin d'Angers*, Vol. II, no. CCCCXXX, comprised: 'the tenement of Le Puits Anseau and the fief of Constantin Charbonnel'; this latter person, who thus held his fief from a *sergent* of the abbey, must himself have been a *sergent* of the monks, no doubt of a lower rank; at any rate he appears on several occasions as a witness in the *familia* (i.e. at table); as for the *provost* (*prévôt*) he was a freedman, and consequently not free. In one of the *villae* of Saint-Martial de Limoges, in the 11th century, the 'judge's' fief' included, besides the holding occupied by the *sergent*, ten bordars' holdings worked by his tenants (A. Leroux, *Documents historiques . . . concernant principalement la Marche et le Limonsin*, Vol. II, Premier Cartul. de l'Aumônerie de Saint-Martial, no. 27).
57. Arch. du Loiret, H 30[2], p. 205, the stewardship of Tillay (from information provided by Prou and Vidier).
58. In a deed of 1189 (Arch. Nat. S 2246, no. 7) there is considered a possible case in which the holder of a fraction of the fief of the marshalsea 'equitaverit cum abbate'. In the same way a decree in 1231, quoted in note 61, puts among the functions of the chamberlain the duty of riding with the abbot, or, if the abbot did not desire his company, of providing him with a horse. These obligations are very like the ones attaching to military fiefs. The archives of Saint-Denis provide fairly abundant information about the abbot's administrative officials, which has never yet, unfortunately, been properly utilised; cf. some indications in dom Félibien, *Histoire de l'abbaye royale de Saint-Denys en France*, Vol. V, p. 279, note a. Did the important official who had ceased to fulfil his duties in person have to provide a substitute at his own expense? There are some examples of this in Germany. I don't think I have come across any in French documents.
59. *Gesta abbatum Tradonensium*, IX, 12; cf. Ganshof, loc. cit. p. 173. *Le Livre de Guillaume de Ryckel* (edit. Pirenne) appears no longer to have

ADMINISTRATIVE CLASSES: FRANCE AND GERMANY 117

any cognisance of these hybrid functions; on p. 93 it mentions four 'operarii genestrarum', and notes (p. 94) that a church redeemed the prebend of the fenestrarius (monastic obedientary in charge of windows) *Arnoldus*. Might this be the man in question, under an additional name?
60. Cf. for Saint-Trond, *Le Livre de Guillaume de Ryckel*, p. 93.
61. Arch. Nat., L. 776, no. 36 (witnesses' statements, 1231, June), and no. 35, verdict of the abbot of Saint-Denis, Eude, and Jean de Beaumont, 1231, June 17th).
62. This is what happened in North-West Germany, where the grant to the mayor of the lord's demesne then proceeded to become the type of lease gradually applied to a large part of the ancient tenures (*Meierrecht*): see W. Wittich, *Die Grundherrschaft im Nordwestdeutschland*.
63. In the days of the abbot of Saint-Maur-les-Fossés, Thibaut (1171 at the earliest, 1187 at the latest) the people of Evry (-Petit-Bourg) (Seine-et-Oise, canton of Corbeil) agreed upon a composition of the *taille*. It was from now on fixed at a total of 7 livres, and was levied upon the houses, but four houses were exempt – the one belonging to the steward; Gautier le *Cocherarius* (retailer), bought formerly by him from a certain *Ingerberta*; Ernaud the *caballarius* and finally a house occupied by a certain Robert, which had formerly been part of Ernaud's fief. I think this *caballarius* was a *sergent*; the exemption of a military fief occupied by a knight would not have needed notice; and the knight would have been styled *dominus* (Arch. Nat., LL 46, fol. 108; a deed of the abbot of Isembart, raising the annual sum to 10 livres; 1195).
64. Cap. I, no. 25, c. 4.
65. Landulphi *Historia Mediolanensis*, IV, 2; SS., vol. VIII, pp. 9–10; 'praelio et causis audacissimes assuefacti'. I think that later on 'novis honoratis militibus' should be translated by 'dubbed knights'. This at any rate was the Milanese version of the event of June 3rd. The other sources give different accounts; cf. Meyer von Knonau, *Jahrbücher des deutschen Reiches unter Heinrich IV* . . . Vol. III, p. 475, no. 12. The matter is of small importance here; whatever was in fact the part played by the baker-soldier, the essential point for us is that he bore arms and was considered capable of warlike exploits.
66. Bibl. de la ville d'Orléans, MS. 556, p. 327 (1184); Nemois, commune of Tigy, Loiret.
67. *Inventaire sommaire des Arch. d'Eure-et-Loir*, Vol. VIII, *Introduction*, p. 17 (June 1265) and Layette IV, 5068.
68. *Miracula santi Benedicti*, edit. Certain, VIII, 2 and 3.
69. Deloche, *Cartulaire de l'abbaye de Beaulieu en Limousin* no. L. The document speaks of '*judices servi*'; the fact is that the word 'juge' in the Limousin kept its old sense from Frankish times of official or *sergent*, with particular application to the *ministeriales* entrusted with the administration of a small *seigneurie*; in this sense it was equivalent to 'steward' throughout the greater part of France; numerous documents speak of the manse

L.A.W.I.M.E.—I

or fief, of the juge: 'feodum *al judze*' in J. de Font-Reaulx, *S. Stephani Lemovicensis Cartularium*, no. CXCIV; cf. no. CVII, pp. 126 and 127, no. CXVIII – '*fevum jutzie*' in H. de Montégut, *Cartul. du monastère de Saint-Pierre de Vigeois*, no. CII; cf. no. CCLXVII.

70. Ekkehard, *Casus sancti Galli*, c. 48 (cf. later, still at St. Gall, for the position of the cellarers, who were lower than the steward, SS, Vol. II, p. 161). Also a certain steward's pretensions to 'noblesse'; Polypt. d'Irminon, IV, 36.

71. In Germany likewise a good number of *Dienstleute*, keeping the habits of peasant life, did not pass over into the ranks of knighthood: Weimann, *Die Ministeralität des späteren Mittelalters*, especially p. 7.

72. Information taken from the charters of Hérivaux, Arch. de Seine-et-Oise, H non classé; cf. Bibl. Nat., Duchesne, 77, fol. 17 and 18. It will be observed that Hugo, who had been knighted in 1176, does not bear this title in two deeds of 1183 and 1212 (Duchesne, loc. cit.), a proof that the knightly standing of certain stewards may easily escape our notice. There is the same use of inheritance in the stewards' families of Grant-Puits (Cartulaire blanc de Saint-Denis, Arch. Nat. LL 1158), p. 333; May 8th 1225) et de Souplainville: Bibl. Nat., lat. 5185 D, fol. 2, Louis IX, 1238, July; but in this last case it was contested by the lord. Similarly the application of noble wardship (*la garde noble*) to the stewardships raised certain difficulties; cf. a charter of Saint-Benoît-sur-Loire, Jan. 12th 1270, new style, Bibl. de la ville d'Orléans, MS. 490–491, p. 836 (from information given to me by MM. Prou and Vidier).

73. Compare with the steward's family of Luzarches the one from Tigy (the village – Loiret, canton of Jargeau – belonged to Saint-Benoît-sur-Loire), known to us through two deeds of 1254, new style, Jan. 8th and July 26th, Arch. du Loiret, H. 46; Girard, the steward, squire (*écuyer*); his brothers: Denis, a squire too, and John, a clerk.

74. Above, p. 109, note 11.

75. Above, p. 109, note 9.

76. Guérard, *Cartul. de Notre-Dame de Paris*, Vol. I, p. 383, no. XVI.

77. No one has better shown the variations in sense than Ganshof. (Cf. for *ministerialis*, p. 234, no. 5; for *familia*, p. 233, no. 2). But on other occasions he seems to me to extract from the same words meanings that are hardly justified. Cf. Des Marez, *Note sur la ministérialité;* and for a detailed criticism of Ganshof's thesis on the servile origin of the *minsteriales* as a whole, the review by Champeaux, *Revue hist. du droit, 1927*, p. 751.

78. Cf. P. Petot, *L'hommage servile; Revue hist. du droit*, p. 68, note 1; other examples could be quoted. See also the apposite observations of L. Verriest, *Le servage dans le comté de Hainaut* (*Acad. royale de Belgique, cl. des Lettres*, Mém., 2nd series, Vol. VI, 1900), p. 30.

79. Ganshof constantly uses to designate the status of the serf the word 'demi-libre', which seems to me somewhat unfortunate. The Middle Ages never used it; the serf was considered as completely deprived of

his liberty. This idea of un-freedom is certainly a delicate one to analyse; but we shall gain nothing by substituting another concept, in itself no clearer, and in addition not corresponding in any way to the classifications used by those who were the contemporaries of serfdom. Moreover, does it not smack of an over-subtle legal outlook to term the power of the lord over the half-free men who were his dependants a 'right of property' (pp. 257–258)? It is no good saddling the past with our own theories; we already have our work cut out to explain those elaborated by the jurists of former days.

80. Above p. 97.
81. Above p. 93.
82. De la Boutelière, *Cartulaire de l'abbaye de Talmont* (*Mém. de la Soc. des Antiquaires de l'Ouest*, Vol. XXXVI, 1872), no. LXIII (1078–1081).
83. In February 1243 the stewards of Saint-Mesmin de Micy enfranchised their steward of St. Denis-au-Val 'a jugo servitutis quo nobis *racione majoria* erat astrictus'; it is true that the freedman nevertheless continued to hold the stewardship (Bibl. de la ville d'Orléans, MS. 556, p. 324; cf. MS. 488, fol. 68v) (i.e. v. for *verso*). The care taken by lords that posts of this kind should only be entrusted to their serfs or freedmen stands out prominently in various deeds: for example Halphen, *Le comte d'Anjou*, appendix no. 6; the charter of Louis VI quoted above, on p. 513, note 3; cf. *Les Collibert*, in *Revue Hist.*, Jan.-Feb.-March 1928, and *Mélanges Historiques*.
84. The hereditary nature of vassalage was never anything else but an admitted fact. In law, the tie did not exist, and entailed no legal consequences until homage had been actually performed; and this had to be renewed whenever either of the contracting parties – the lord or the vassal – happened to change.
85. *Miracula Sancti Benedicti*, ed. Certain, VI, 2, p. 219. This 'false knight' was not however a *sergent*; cf. below, note 92.
86. Ed. W. Foerster (*Romanische Studien*, V. line 946ff; trans. P. Meyer, §60; this same expression 'fils de vilain' appears in the passage of the *Couronnement de Louis* quoted below, p. 900. The notion that there is something degrading about agricultural labour is extremely ancient; in the Frankish period it was expressed in the phrase *opera servillia*; cf. Petot, *L'hommage servile*, p. 103, note 2. It crops up in Germany too: between 1154 and 1164 the Count of Ahr dispensed his *ministeriales* from all forced ploughing, as being contrary to 'honour': Lacomblet, *Urkundenbuch*, Vol. IV, no. 624, and P. Sander and H. Spangerberg, *Urkunden zur Geschichte der Territorialverfassung*, Vol. II, no. 97, c. 17. In most places, and notably in France, this idea will be at the root of the notion of 'noble living', the kind of life a nobleman must live if he is to take advantage of his privileges: see in 1235, 1237 and 1238 the statutes of Raimond-Bérenger V of Provence, F. Benoît, *Recueil des actes des comtes de Provence appartenant à la noblesse de Barcelone*, Vol. II, no. 246, C. IVb; 275, c.vb; 227; 228, and cf. V. Bourilly et R. Busquet, *La Provence au Moyen Age*, in *Les Bouches-du-Rhône, Encyclopédie départ-*

mentale, Vol. II, pp. 565 and 715 (off-print pp. 269 and 419). In England the idea was destined to take legal shape in a much stricter form: base services were, from the 13th century onwards, one of the marks of villeinage (a new form of the ancient serfdom).

87. *Rois et serfs*, p. 35.
88. The canons of Chartres, who were excellent administrators, never ceased to demand this.
89. Pérard, *Recueil de plusieurs pièces curieuses servant à l'histoire de Bourgogne*, p. 130: 'cujus nomen praeterimus, ne hereditibus ejus qui militare honore praefulgent grave videatur'.
90. Line, 207. Cf. in Wace, *Roman de Rou*, line 797, the praise of Duke Richard II: 'Ne vot mestier de sa meison – Duner si a gentil home nun', etc.
91. Joinville, c. XX. Jacques de Vitry, *Exempla*, edit. Frenken (*Quellen und Unters. zur lateinischen Philologie des Mittelatters*, V. 1) c. XVII, and the references given by the editor in a note; cf. d'Arbois de Jubainville, *Histoire des ducs et comtes de Champagne*, Vol. II, p. 127. Another example of a fine career in a servile status – a peaceful one this time – but hardly quotable without a question-mark against it: Girard d'Athée, one of the best lieutenants of John Lackland, his seneschal in Touraine, who is named in Magna Carta, which exempts his whole family from feudal dues, was, if Guillaume Le Breton is to be believed (*Phillipide*, VIII, 1. 148), born a serf of the *seigneur* d'Amboise. Is this absolutely reliable information? The reasons given by Lambron de Ligny (*Mém. Soc. archeologique de Touraine*, Vol. VIII, 1855, p. 176) for rejecting the witness of the *Philippide* are not convincing. Nevertheless one cannot but wonder whether Girard was not the victim of a partisan slander: it would have been so tempting to ruin the reputation of a hostile knight by passing him off as a serf's son. For the insubstantial nature of such accusations, and even the slender authority possessed by judicial decisions obtained by methods of proof in which we no longer believe, see Champeaux' perspicacious comments in *Revue hist. du droit*, 1927, p. 751. For the use of this same weapon in ecclesiastical polemics, see Marc Bloch, *Rois et serfs*, p. 26, note 3.
92. Ganshof, pp. 74 and 78, has given a good summary of the date collected before his own work on the serf-knights. We should add to the passages quoted by him or in the works to which he refers, apart from the document relating to Nouaillé, a passage from which will be reproduced at the end of this note, the examples of servile mortmain levied upon knights: Auger, *Les dépendances de l'abbaye de Saint-Germain-des-Prés*, Vol. III, p. 298 (May 1236), and no doubt *Olin*, Vol. II, p. 373, note 8 (1294). All the serf-knights were not necessarily *sergents*; amongst these adventurers of servile status there were some who, having fled from their native country, had made a fortune in distant parts: cf. *Miracula S. Benedicti*, VI, 2, and the deed of enfranchisement of 'foreign' serfs belonging to Saint-Aignan d'Orléans, or, as Hubert testifies in *Antiquités historiques* . . . *de Saint-Aignan*, pr. p. 109, there were among

the beneficiaries some men who 'se milites dicebant' (the fact that this deed concerns some 'foreigners' is made clear by a letter from the Chapter, *Layettes de Trésor de Charles*, Vol. I, no. 819). But one can hardly doubt that the majority of the serfs who reached the ranks of knighthood owed their elevation to the fact that they had exercised administerial functions. And likewise for an adventurer, the best chance of success often lay in getting himself accepted as a *sergent* in some wealthy lord's household. Up till now we have spoken particularly of the serfs who became their masters' officials; but along with them we must also leave room for the serfs who were fugitives and became the serfs of lords at their own choice; these too sometimes managed to thrust their way up to knighthood. Towards the end of the 11th century the monks of Saint-Junien de Nouaillé made the following reproach to Engelaume de Mortemer: 'Servi vero sancti Juniani ad eum venire solebant et ex illis suos servientes in domo sua, vel quoslibet ministros, quosdam autem milites faciebat absque consensu abbatis atque monachorum' (Guérard, *Polypt. d'Irminon*, App. no. XXVI. But does the word *milites* here have the meaning of dubbed knights? Or does it only mean armed men? In a document of this date we may well be doubtful on this point. For the freed knights (culverts chevaliers) and more generally for the freed *sergents*, cf. *Mélanges Historiques, les Colliberti*, pp. 385–451..

93. [Jacques d'Ableiges], *Le Grand Contumier de France*, ed. La Boulaye and Dareste, II, 14, p. 212.
94. The incompatibility of serfdom and knighthood is thrown into clear relief by the developments among English jurists in the second half of the 13th century in proceedings bearing upon serfdom: Bracton, fol. 190b (ed. Twiss, Vol. III, p. 230); Britton, c. XXXII (edit. Nicholis, Vol. I, pp. 207, 208); *Fleta*, II, 51 (Houard, Vol. III, p. 244).
95. Beaumanoir, §§1449–1450. The idea that dubbing in itself set a man free seems to be behind a passage in an unpublished version of the *Chanson d'Aspremont*, if I have rightly understood the passage quoted by L. Gautier in *La Chevalerie*, p. 262, note 2.
96. E.g. J. Thillier et E. Jarry, *Cartulaire de Saint-Croix d'Orléans*, no. CLIII (Feb. 1st. 1210). The case seems a rare one; but wasn't the word 'chevalier' sometimes tacitly passed over in deeds of this kind? Cf. what was said above, p. 118 note 72, about the steward of Luzarches, who was nevertheless a freeman (either by prescription or by origin). One cannot do more than pose the question.
97. G. A. Matile, *Le Miroir de Souabe*: vavassour: c. III (=*Schwabenspiegel*, edit. v. Lassberg, c. 2); c. CII (*Schw.* 104); – *dienstman vavasors*, CXXXVII (*Schw.* 138); – *hautes gens qui ne sunt mie franc*, CLXIII rubric (*Schw.* 158); and more incompletely still, *ome qui n'est frans*, XLVI (*Schw.* 46); – *dienstman, dienstman, dienstman*, LXV (*Schw.* 68); LXVI (*Schw.* 69); CXLIII (*Schw.* 142); CLXIII (*Schw.* 158); rights of fiefs, I, LXXXIIII (*Schw.* 308); rights of fiefs, II, prol. (*Schw. Lehnr.* 1).

98. The lucid account given by Ganshof of the principal German theories will be of the utmost service to French historians, and makes it unnecessary for me to dwell upon the matter here. Unfortunately he did not have the chance to become acquainted with K. Weimann's book, *Die Ministerialität des späteren Mittelalters*, 1924, which, though heavy and obscure in style, is full of useful information. He gives under his bibliography for the administrative classes (p. 38, note 2) the book by Dahlmann-Waitz, *Quellenkunde der deutschen Gechichte*, which is really rather out of date; it would have been better to refer the reader to *Lehrbuch der deutschen Rechtsgeschichte* by R. Schröder, 6th edit., 1919, p. 472, note 8, and p. 1026.

99. For the English administrative classes, see Vinogradoff, *Villainage in England*, pp. 324–325; *Growth of the Manor*, p. 359; and for the *radmen*, analogous to the Frankish Scacarii (escorts and messengers), *English Society in the Eleventh Century*, pp. 69ff. For Italy, see F. Schneider, *Entstehung von Burg und Landgemeinde*, p. 244. Le Frioul, which was very Germanised in its institutions, should be treated as a special case.

100. The *Dienstrecht* of Bamberg, which has been several times published, notably by Altmann and Bernheim, *Ausgewählte Urk.*, 5th edit., no. 77. For Aachen, Lacomblet, *Urkundenbuch für die Geschichte des Niederrheins*, Vol. I, no. 157. Th. Tye's book *L'immunité de l'abbaye de Wissembourg*, which was published since the present memoir took shape, gives (on pp. 72ff.) some very interesting data on the development of the idea of an administrative class. When Henry IV's charter in 1102 simply recognised the abbot's right to 'promovere' any member of the 'familia' 'in beneficiam servientis' and thus to remove him from the notary's power, the spurious charter of Dagobert, drawn up about the middle of the 12th century under the direct inspiration of the authentic imperial charter, expresses the same idea in these words: 'ut in *ordinem* et jus possit promovere ministerialium'.

101. See Ganshof's excellent summary (following Zallinger), pp. 56–57, and also J. Ficker and P. Puntschart, *Vom Reichsfürstenstande*, Vol. II, 1. pp. 209ff.

102. See Weimann, *Die Ministerialität im späteren Mittelalter*; this is the essential conclusion of the book.

103. Loc. cit., especially pp. 70–71. Mlle Zeglin started out from a theory propounded by M. Pirenne – though with some perceptible differences – *Qu'est-ce qu'um homme lige?* in *Acad. royale de Belgique, bulletin de la cl. des Lettres*, 1909.

104. I am not here concerned with its etymology; on this point and on *la ligesse* in general the latest work is that of C. Pöhlmann, *Das ligische Lehensverhältniss*, in *Zeitschrift der sav. Stiftung*, G. A. 1927; it seems to me to contain not a few doubtful views.

105. In *Rois et serfs*, p. 23, note 2 (and *Additions et rectifications*), I have given some information about this use of the term. I could add many other examples. Cf. P. Petot, *L'hommage servile*.

106. Pollock and Maitland, *History of English Law*, Vol. I, p. 408. Cf. more

ADMINISTRATIVE CLASSES: FRANCE AND GERMANY 123

precisely still Maitland, *Constitutional History of England*, p. 171: 'we have never had a *noblesse*'.

107. In France there existed in certain regions, above the level of the serfs, another group of non-free persons, the 'culverts' *(colliberti)*. But from the beginning of the first half of the 12th century they became absorbed into the servile class as a whole.

108. Ganshof has reprinted at the end of his book, with some alterations, two important memoirs which he had previously devoted to the *homines de casa Dei* at Liège and to the *homines de generali placito* at Arras. The problem presented by this latter institution, which is only found at Arras, would need to be taken up again as a whole. It is probable that the obligation to be present in the assize courts (*plaid général*), which was incumbent upon all free men in the Frankish period, gradually became confined to certain tenures. Maitland has revealed an analogous development in the English county courts and hundred courts. The difference is that in England the county courts (not always the hundred courts) escaped being taken under the wing of the Lords, whereas in France the Assize Court became a seignorial institution.

4

TECHNICAL CHANGE AS A PROBLEM OF COLLECTIVE PSYCHOLOGY[1]

Before my address proper, I may perhaps be allowed to say a few words of friendly greeting as well as of gratitude to fellow-scholars.

It seems to me an excellent sign that professional psychologists, to whom we owe this gathering, should have had the idea of inviting to it representatives from very diverse fields of study. I am particularly happy that among the disciplines summoned to take part in these discussions they should have included history. And may I say in parenthesis that I see no reason for ceasing to call it by that time-honoured name, though we are by no means bound to give that term the precise connotation that it had in the days of Hecataeus of Miletus. History may not perhaps at the present time be a branch of knowledge whose boundaries are precisely delimited; but it is certainly a field of study that is very much alive. Assuredly it will be much to the advantage of both historians and psychologists to work in common.

We historians stand in great need of your assistance. Our studies are constantly leading us to consider individual or mass psychology. We are too often content to use rough and ready psychology theories, which are I fear far from being soundly or precisely based. It was this kind of reasoning that led Voltaire not so long ago to deny that the ancient Egyptians could have been so foolish as to worship animals. And today, such reasoning leads certain historians to handle very clumsily a delicate concept like 'sincerity', and to confuse the psychological cause of a social fact with its conscious motivation.

For their part, psychologists feel, I imagine, that they cannot do without the help of historians. For their method of approach to their subject gives them experience which is necessarily limited to the present or the recent past. Should they wish to go back further into the past, they then come up against problems which necessarily require different methods of investigation, which must certainly be called 'historical'. I spoke just now of sincerity, in order to show how the historian cannot on this point dispense with the insights of the psychologist. But the reverse is scarcely less true. The multitude of forged charters at the height of the Middle Ages offers us a genuine example of collective mythomania which no psychologist dealing with truth (or with lies) can, I think, afford to neglect.

It is one of these problems of common interest that I should now like to put before you. Or rather, a whole bundle of related problems, all of them at the very centre of the ordinary concerns of both the historian and the psychologist. Unfortunately I have not been able to put my talk into as exact a shape as I could have wished. I shall therefore not aim at more than setting before you certain debatable points, which will, I hope, call forth from you suggestions more fertile than anything contained in my address.

I

The first problem is a simple one, and may be stated as follows.

Let us suppose that there has been some new technique, either invented within a given society or introduced from outside. It will sometimes be accepted by that society, and sometimes rejected. If it is accepted, this will only take place more or less slowly and sporadically. What causes lie behind these varying reactions?

One idea comes first to mind. The invention will be accepted if it is, or appears to be, useful, and rejected if apparently useless or dangerous. If one pursues this line of thought further, a series of problems arise that have long ago become classic. Some are concerned with technique, others concern economic matters such as the existence of markets, manpower, etc.

No one will deny the importance of these factors. But we are soon led to feel that matters are not quite so simple or so rational. Common speech offers us a word that is pregnant with psychological meaning and which may help us to orient our questions correctly – the word 'routine'. We have a very clear impression that some societies are in themselves more 'routine-minded', and others more 'accustomed to change'; and we feel the need for discovering deeper reasons for attitudes which mere considerations of utility seem insufficient to explain.

Following M. Faucher's example in his very stimulating lecture which you have just heard, I shall choose as an illustration of this problem the case of the peasant's routine.

Now no one will deny that there is in fact a peasant routine; in other words, in any given society the peasant group is generally more attached to its traditions than neighbouring groups. Here then we are confronted by our first 'why?' How are we to explain this particular trait of collective mentality?

I have no intention of attempting to reply in a couple of words to such a large question; I would simply draw attention to a fact of social structure which seems to me to be of great importance. As anyone who knows our countryside has observed on many occasions, it is chiefly the grandparents who more often than not see to the upbringing of children in peasant families. Their work in the fields, among the poultry and in the cowsheds means that neither the father nor the mother has enough leisure to supervise them properly. That is one of the causes, I believe, for the remarkable persistence of tradition in such communities. The youngest generation of adults, being the most active, and consequently the most adaptable, the generation that would perhaps be the first to begin to adapt itself to change, is not the one directly responsible for the education of the rising generation.

But although peasant routine undoubtedly exists, there is nothing hard and fast about it. In a large number of cases we see new techniques being adopted fairly easily by peasant societies, even though under other circumstances these same societies refused innovations which at first sight appear to have been equally attractive. I shall attempt in a few moments to give some examples of this contrast. But I should like first of all to be allowed a digression suggested by what has been put before us by M. Faucher.[2]

M. Faucher has laid before us in the most interesting manner the history of the rotation of crops. He has shown us in particular how the arrival of the Germans in the south of Gaul did not in any way modify the ancient two-course rotation traditionally practised in these parts. There is no doubt about the facts: I only wonder whether we should expect to be surprised by them.

For the invaders in question were the Visigoths, who certainly spoke a language of Germanic type. No one doubts that they originated from Germania, or, more accurately, Scandinavia, but they had not arrived by a direct route. They only reached Gaul by means of a long détour which led them in particular to settle for two centuries or more on the shores of the Black Sea. At the time when they left Germania, was the three-course rotation already known there? Nothing is less certain, for our first evidence on the point is no earlier than the beginning of the Christian era. At all events it was on the shores of the Black Sea that the Visigoth civilisation really took shape. The agricultural customs which they imported with them into our regions were certainly those of the Mediterranean countries, who were traditionally attached to the two-course rotation at a very much earlier date than were the northern countries.

As regards the rest, I am in complete agreement with M. Faucher. The examples quoted by him are extremely instructive. I for my part am going to put before you two other contrasted examples which seem to me to throw light upon the variable attitudes adopted by rural societies when faced with technical improvements.

Here first of all is an example which illustrates attachment to the past.

It is the one that nearly always comes to mind when one mentions 'peasant routine' – namely the agricultural revolution of the 18th century. There is no gainsaying the fact that this great revolution, the essential feature of which was the disappearance of the dead fallow, was the work of elements alien to peasant society in the strict sense of the term; it was the work of nobles, the middle classes, postmasters, and sometimes in addition a few immigrants. The bulk of country people only followed the movement very slowly and with very bad grace. Often at the beginning they deliberately opposed it. There are traces of this resistance even today deep down in agricultural literature. Husbandry today still has a kind of grudge against the peasants for not having rallied round in support of a transformation which undoubtedly had the effect of increasing to a considerable degree the productive capacity of the land.

And now for an opposite example of relatively rapid adaptation to a new technique; for this, surprising though it may seem at first sight, we shall have to go back much further into the past.

There is today one plant, one cereal, that seems pre-eminently characteristic of French agriculture, or rather European agriculture in the past, and this plant is rye. As everyone knows, it disappeared from most of our countryside during the last half of the 19th century. It is a well-known fact, too, that it was very widely cultivated during the Middle Ages, and right on into the middle of the 18th century. In the centre of France, in particular, it was almost the sole cereal. The bread eaten by the majority of our people in those days was not wheaten bread, but rye bread.

Now rye was not really a very old plant; at least in the sense in which the historian uses the word – not perhaps precisely the sense attached to it by the common run of folk. There is every reason to believe that rye, which was unknown to Roman agriculture, scarcely began to spread through Western Europe until the time of the great invasions. It was probably the nomadic civilisations, which left such a deep impress upon the life of the West, who brought it to us from the Steppes. It spread widely in a very short time – apparently in a matter of a few centuries. I have already mentioned what an important position it achieved.

Here then, close at hand, we have a case of an unyielding routine: and much further back in time, an example of adaptability which is no less remarkable. How are we to resolve this apparent contradiction?

On looking into the question more closely, we begin to observe a considerable difference between the two cases.

As M. Faucher so rightly reminded us, the agricultural revolution threatened to ruin the whole social system in which the life of the peasant was enshrined. To the small peasant, the notion of increasing the nation's productive powers made no appeal. He was only within sight – and even then it was a pretty distant prospect – of increasing his own production, or at least that portion of it that was meant for sale. He knew that markets were uncertain, and prices variable, and felt that there was something mysterious and rather dangerous about the whole marketing procedure. He was much more intent upon preserving more or less intact his own traditional standard of life. Almost everywhere he felt that his fate depended upon the preservation of a time-honoured system of communal cultivation which was a burden upon the land. Under this system, the bare fallow was taken for granted. If it were brought to an end, he knew that an attack would inevitably follow upon his rights of common by which, in districts practising a three-course rotation, a third of the cultivated land was thrown open each year to the flocks and herds of the whole community. If robbed of this right, many peasants would no longer have been able to feed their stock. In a word, the majority of peasants were afraid of the great social upheaval which appeared to be the inevitable sequel to the new methods. And they were quite right to be afraid. If they had been better informed about what was taking place at this time on the other side of the Channel, they would have seen their worst fears substantiated. In England, the agricultural revolution took place much more quickly and completely than it did with us, and at the price of crushing out of existence a whole section of the rural population.

On the other hand let us imagine the peasant of the Merovingian period confronted with the choice of growing rye. True, it would be for him a new crop. But the plant itself was probably not altogether unknown to him, for rye seems in the first instance to have come in as a weed among the wheat. In any case it is similar to the other cereals which had long been familiar to the cultivators of Gaul. Above all, the substitution of rye for wheat or barley did not in any way affect the social system. It was simply a means of increasing the value of a particular field, which would continue to be cultivated by the same men as in the past, and according to the same traditional routine.

Thus we are dealing with phenomena of very different significance, and it may be that the contradiction does not need to be explained, for strictly speaking it does not exist. I am willing to admit this. I consider this argument in itself to be perfectly correct. But at the risk of exposing myself deliberately to the reproach of only setting before you a series of possibilities and leaving you to make the choice, I have to admit that I am not at all sure this statement of the case exhausts the realities of the situation. There may be more in it still.

The peasant society that was confronted with the problems of the 18th-century agricultural revolution was a stable and fairly rigidly organised society, a society in which families lived more or less in the same place for generations, and in which there was little mixing between the different social layers.

But look on the other hand at the peasant society that adopted rye. It was during the time of the great invasions; therefore, it was a society in turmoil, which had suffered many different disasters, raids, and forced migrations, and whose ancient framework was being torn asunder. It is surely reasonable to suppose that a society stimulated by such lively and powerful internal movements of this kind will naturally possess greater powers of adaptation. This is simply an hypothesis, to be sure; but we may perhaps find some measure of confirmation in other parallel facts. For rye was not by any means the only innovation that Western society made its own in the course of this disturbed and seemingly infertile period. Think for example of the stirrup. One feels (I would not dare for the moment to express it more strongly) that the conditions of social life at that time, although in other respects terribly tragic, were nevertheless favourable to innovations.

II

The second problem I wish to set before you is more complex, for it involves considering, along with collective psychology, the differential psychology of the individual. It is the problem of invention – and here I only mean to look at it in its collective aspect.

History shows clearly the existence of societies or periods of particular inventiveness. I suggest that we leave aside the question why one man invents rather than another. It remains an observed fact that in the course of social development there are moments when everyone is inventing, and other moments when there are hardly any inventions at all.

Classical antiquity, for example, was certainly a period very poor in inventions. The second part of the 17th century in France confronts us with a still more curious case, the case of a society that wants to invent, but does not succeed in doing so – I mean of course in the technical field.

Let us open a volume of contemporary documents such as Volume I of the *Correspondance des contrôleurs généraux avec les intendants*, published by Boislisle. Let us turn over the pages of the introduction. We shall note that during the reign of Louis XIV a considerable number of patents for inventions were obtained, or, more accurately, privileges were granted to certain monopolists to exploit an invention. These concessions concern the most varied subjects. There was, for example, a method for economical heating, in which Mme de Maintenon invested some money; or, among the new contrivances of secondary importance, a perfectly sprung carriage which could not be tipped over. But there are cases that call for further reflexion: there are references to new methods of driving machinery, which seem to refer to new and hitherto unused forms of motive-power.

Now, one thing is certain: nothing of practical importance came out of all this. Carriages, I have no doubt, continued to bump along. Heating does not appear to have become any more economical. Above all it is certain that no new motive-power came into serious use before the end of the 17th century.

All of which poses a great problem: why did these people who wanted to invent, and who were obviously urged on by the desire to make some money through their inventions, not succeed in their aims?

Here once again we come up against the explanation of economic need. It has already been put forward many times. We read in the *Encyclopédie*, under the article on 'Cordages', as follows:

'Wherever labour is dear, it must be supplemented by machinery: this is the only way to keep abreast of countries where labour is cheaper. The English have been teaching this lesson to Europe for a considerable time.'

In other words, any crisis in the supply of labour should lead to the improved use of machinery.

Simiand took up this idea, linking it with his powerfully argued theory about the alternation of periods of high and low prices. A period of low prices – phase B – is generally marked by progress in inventions. Unfortunately this theory does not apply very well to the 17th century, which – at least in the second half – seems certainly to have coincided with a 'phase B', yet did not produce any inventions.

On the other hand, one might be tempted to look for an explanation in the history of science. It could be maintained that inventors in the 17th century lacked the basic scientific knowledge which they needed to realise their instincts or their desires.

No doubt there is a good deal of truth in all this. But I wonder once again whether these interpretations are not too simple, and whether there are not other reasons too, arising from the social environment, which would explain at one moment the development, and at another the damping down, of the inventive spirit. It will I think be advisable for us, as we did a few moments ago, to look at the internal structure of society and at the mutual interactions of the various groups of which it is composed.

The first question to solve is undoubtedly this: in a given society, which are the groups that produce the inventors? I think we shall come to the conclusion that these have in fact varied according to the period concerned. Certain societies have been particularly productive in artisan inventions. Look for example at the West during the Middle Ages. It was less inventive than has sometimes been stated; it tended rather to borrow the ideas of others. Nevertheless we can place to its credit certain technical discoveries – in particular the spinning-wheel, which was one of the first and finest pieces of machinery invented by man. The spinning-wheel was certainly thought out by artisans, but their names will remain as unknown as the primitive discoverers of fire. Other periods, on the other hand, have seen a multitude of inventions, due almost exclusively to learned men or at any rate engineers.

Let us return to the second half of the 17th century. We can now put the problem in more precise form. We can ask why artisans were no longer inventing, and why learned people had not yet started to invent. A whole series of possibilities at once present themselves. Were there at that time reasons of an economic or social kind which prevented the artisan from aspiring to be an inventor? Was life too hard for him? Was he hampered by the obstinate traditionalism of the guilds? And on the other side, was the learned man's scientific knowledge not sufficiently directed towards practical problems? Was he himself the victim of prejudices which prevented him from putting his knowledge to practical use, judging this to be an unworthy activity? And finally, was it a question of lack of contact between these different groups, a contact which might have enabled both parties to understand each other's needs? I do not propose to put forward an answer to all these questions. My sole purpose has been to point out that if a social analysis were undertaken from this point of view, it would no doubt enable us to understand better than we do today why history offers us the spectacle of two kinds of society – the stable and the inventive.

III

The last problem I shall put before you might be entitled: 'The recognition of the importance of technical facts.' This is a formula that will perhaps strike you at first sight as rather sibylline. A quotation may help to elucidate it.

Let us imagine that we are in the *Chambre des Députés* on July 26th 1838. The government has just proposed to grant a concession for railways to be built in the south-west. The commission is asking for the project to be rejected, and presents in its name a report drawn up to this effect. Amongst other arguments occur the following words: 'We do not admit, when it is a question of examining motives, that two parallel cast-iron rails could bring new life to the *landes* of Gascony: that is our brief.'

To the author of this report, then, it appeared quite insane that anyone should think 'two parallel cast-iron rails' capable of changing the aspect of a region. Now this report was signed 'Arago'; and I cannot decide whether Arago was really a very learned man; but – if you will pardon a crude expression – he was certainly no fool. Nevertheless he spoke the words you have just heard and he could speak them without calling down ridicule upon himself. Such a thesis appeared quite natural, it seems, in 1838; whilst our difficulty today is just the opposite – to understand how anyone could fail to realise the fact that in a new country – Morocco for example – two rails running across the ground possess full power to make a radical transformation both in the territory's economy and in its social structure.

Nor is this an isolated case. More than one similar declaration can be found in the documents of this period. The omissions, moreover, are no less significant. Take the correspondence of Thiers, for example. In the public part of it, I defy anyone to discover the slightest allusion to the tremendous industrial transformation which he nonetheless witnessed, and – what is more – from which he made considerable private profit.

Now not all societies have uniformly adopted this attitude. Our society of today, as we are well aware, is positively haunted by the technical world. But its importance was equally well understood or divined in very much more remote periods, and in quite different environments. In the Greek *Anthology* you will find an epigram dating from about the beginning of the Christian era which explains most pertinently, in mythological form, how the invention of the water-mill, by doing away with the hand-operated millstone, will liberate slaves from one of the hardest of their former tasks.

We are thus confronted with another 'why'. Why are there periods in which this realisation is so clearly evident, and why are there others, quite near to our own day, from which it seems to be completely absent? Where are we to look for an explanation? Does it lie in certain mental habits, certain systems of education, which at times direct the minds of cultivated men exclusively towards theoretical science, or towards literature? Or are we to look for the explanation also in those facts of social structure that we have so often come up against in our search? When classes become closed to one another; when the richer and more powerful classes cease to communicate with those ranged beneath them on the economic ladder, it can happen that the governing elements, by this very circumstance, come to consider everything that has to do with the material aspects of work unworthy of their attention. I am not making a categorical statement on this point, any more than I did a little while ago. But you will see that this is a problem of very great interest both in itself – for the reaction of a society to phenomena controlling its existence will differ according to the way it sees (or fails to see) their importance – and also from the point of view of general psychological research.

Well, gentlemen, you will see that I have hardly done more than formulate certain questions, and even those very superficially. Not, I fear, a very good specimen of the contribution historians can make to the study of psychology; but it may at any rate serve as an example of the things that puzzle them.

NOTES

1. *The Journal of Normal and Pathological Psychology*, Jan.–March 1948, pp. 104–115.
2. M. Bloch is referring to information given by M. Daniel Faucher in the course of the *Journée de Psychologie et d'Histoire du travail et des Techniques* of June 23rd 1941. Cf. *Le Travail et les Techniques*, a special number of the *Journal de Psychologie*, 1948.

5

THE ADVENT AND TRIUMPH OF THE WATERMILL[1]

I

When the first water-wheels began to turn in the rivers the art of grinding cereals, in Europe and in the civilised lands of the Mediterranean, was already more than a thousand years old. In the beginning, the procedure must have been rudimentary in the extreme, the grain being simply crushed with rough stones. But in prehistoric times – we are not here concerned with the exact moment or place – the invention of real tools brought a decisive advance. Then came the pestle and mortar, or a stone roller moving to and fro on a long flat surface, as depicted in Egyptian statuettes, worked by women, usually in a kneeling position. Next came the revolving millstone. Invented in the Mediterranean basin – perhaps in Italy – in the course of the two or three centuries before the Christian era, it had found its way into Gaul shortly before the Roman Conquest.[2] It too could be worked by manpower, and often was in fact. Although if Samson, whom the Bible depicts as grinding corn for his masters the Philistines, certainly never turned a millstone because it was still unknown in Palestine at the period when the story of this worthy Strong Man was written, there were later on in the Roman world innumerable slaves – and even some free men, such as Plautus in his penniless youth – who braced their muscles to this monotonous task. But the new invention made it possible for the first time to substitute animal for human effort in the grinding of corn – usually the horse or the ass. When Caligula on one occasion requisitioned all the horses in Rome, bread became scarce because there was no means of turning corn into flour.[3] But the same invention made possible another and much greater advance. The simplicity and regularity of rotary motion compared with the complicated movements required by the older method opened up the way for the use of a force which, although more blind than any animal-power, naturally moves in one constant direction – namely the power of running water. Without the *mola versatilis* there would never have been a watermill.

These two stages did in fact follow in fairly quick succession. There was a watermill about the year 18 B.C. at Cabira in Pontus among the outlying buildings of the palace formerly built by Mithradates, and no doubt contemporary with the buildings as a whole. In that case this would be the earliest specimen of precise date – from 120 to 63 B.C. A Greek epigram generally attributed to the Augustan Age features some nymphs who are grinding corn, and the expressions used in it make it quite clear that the water goddesses have only recently been obliged to submit to this enslavement. About the same period, the Latin author Vitruvius describes the apparatus in detail; a little later Pliny notes mill-wheels in the rivers of Italy.[4] Although, as usual, these texts do not throw any light on the actual moment of birth of the invention, it cannot be mere chance that they are massed together in such a short space of time. All the indications point to a narrowly restricted period – the last century before the Christian era – and in all probability to the Eastern Mediterranean as the place of origin. It is significant that Vitruvius should only know the new machine by its Greek name, *hydroletes*: and from Greece it must rapidly have spread to Italy.

These conclusions are supported by what we know of its history in the rest of Europe. On the rivers of Gaul, the first mills to which our documents vouchsafe a reference are the ones turned by a small tributary of the Moselle in the 3rd century.[5] In southern Germany, these contrivances spread sufficiently quickly and widely after the invasions to claim the attention of the Alaman and Bavarian laws from the first half of the 8th century onwards. In the north, in regions less open to Gallic and Roman influence, they spread more slowly. Our documents clearly show the broad lines that they followed. There were slaves, like the Bavarian who was taken captive by the Thuringians about the year 770 and built his master a mill; there were colonists, like those Frankish warriors whose village, founded in 775 on the Unstrut, was given the evocative name of Mühlhausen; there were monks and nuns, like the inmates of Tauberbishofsheim, who settled in the great Odenwald forest about the year 732. The construction of water-wheels went ahead as fast as immigrants came in with the technical skills of their own countries.[6] In Great Britain, there is no known example before 838. In Ireland, the legal collection of Senchus Mor mentions watermills in the 9th and 10th centuries. According to a legend which was probably not far from the truth, the oldest of these was said to be the work of a foreigner summoned for that express purpose 'from beyond the seas'.[7] Among the Slavs of Bohemia and on the shores of the Baltic, this invention, though familiar for more than a thousand years to the waterside populations of the Mediterranean, does not seem to have penetrated before the 12th century. There, too, it had made its way from west to east, following the immigration routes. We have evidence of this in an incident reported in a chronicle by a priest of Holstein. Some Saxon peasants had settled during the 10th century in Schleswig and Wagria. Their settlements were later destroyed in a Slav offensive. When almost two hundred years later another group of Germans arrived and re-settled in the country, they came upon traces of the previous occupation, amongst which were the embankments that had been raised to form ponds for working watermills. From this point onwards, then, these were among the most characteristic material signs of Western civilisation in any territory that came to be colonised.[8] And lastly as regards Scandinavia, watermills were introduced into Denmark in the second half of the 12th century, and into Iceland round about 1200; but they hardly became general in Nordic societies until the 14th century.[9] There must of course be a good deal of uncertainty about this information. We would never dare to assert that in such and such a year among this particular people the mill-wheel began for the first time to be turned by water-power. But the few landmarks upon which we are forced to rely do nevertheless provide us with a sufficiently lively image of events. They provide an almost regular series of isochromes which radiate without the slightest doubt from the Mediterranean world.[10] Moreover linguistics come to the aid of history at this point. In the

Germanic and Celtic languages, and even in certain Slav languages, the word for watermill was directly or indirectly borrowed from the Latin.

There is, of course, good reason to be astonished at first sight by the undoubted Mediterranean origin of this great technical improvement. For the uneven flow usually characteristic of rivers in this kind of climate would not seem to make them suitable for the production of motive power. On the other hand it is equally true that they did not suffer from the disadvantages of frosts and ice which often interrupted the supply of flour under more northerly skies, once the watermill had come into almost general use. Nevertheless the apparent anomaly still remains. But it may perhaps be possible to resolve it. Nothing is more certain than that the revolving millstone was the creation of Mediterranean civilisations. Now this first invention – for which no one will be tempted to find an explanation in geographical determinism – did, as we have seen, condition the second. But there is more to it still. A water-wheel driven by a current is adaptable to many other uses besides the turning of a millstone. More particularly, if fitted with scoops attached to its rim, it can actually pick up water and deliver it into any given basin or irrigation channel. This is still the practice, as it was at the beginning of our era, among the Mediterranean peoples. Nay, it goes back to a very remote past. Strabo, to whom we owe the mention of the oldest known watermill at Cabira, was the first writer to make express reference to these water-lifting wheels. He saw them at work in Egypt, where, although unknown in the time of the Pharaohs, they seem in fact to have spread widely under Roman rule. A little before this date, however, in a passage that is unfortunately obscure, Lucretius appears to allude to them.[11] Let us however go back to Vitruvius. He classifies the mill among the machines for drawing up water – rather a peculiar method of classification, which one is tempted to explain in terms of some historical reminiscence. In more precise terms, he describes it as follows: a wheel with scoops attached to the rim, simply worked by a man's foot; then a wheel with scoops attached, but also having water-vanes, so that it can be turned by the water-power of the river; and finally the evolution into a watermill. This order might well represent the relationship between the three contrivances. In other words we should probably see in the watermill the further development after a short period of an invention which had been contrived in early times to facilitate irrigation, and which was naturally at home in regions where agriculture was always one long struggle against the drought of summer. It must be freely admitted that this is no more than a hypothesis of a most conjectural kind; but it will serve at any rate to give at least a provisionally satisfactory answer to one of those 'why's' that are both the torment and the delight of the historian's craft.

The first and most obvious effect on the social order of this technical advance was a new step forward in the specialisation of skills among artisans. The tool created the trade. In the days when a Greek poet described the villages wakening at dawn to the sound of grain being crushed by the pestle, and later on when the revolving millstone had been introduced, the preparation of flour in the countryside was the domestic task of the slave or the housewife; in the large towns, it was one of the tasks of the baker. *Pistor* – 'the grinder': this remained to the very end the Roman baker's name. The millstone, worked by hand or by horse, figured among his familiar attributes on monuments, and in his shop, along with the oven, as one of the instruments of his trade.[12] For watermills on the other hand millers were needed. Their guild, clearly differentiated from all others, appears at Rome for the first time on an inscription in 448.[13] It is not part of our present purpose to trace the history of this profession, whose nature varied moreover to a large degree according to the time and the place concerned. At first, as at Rome, the miller was a member of a guild; then generally he became a *sergent* or seignorial farmer; finally he became a self-employed craftsman who was his own master, for the miller in ancient Europe enjoyed great variety of status. He provoked a good deal of hostility too, often expressed in the small talk of an idle moment. 'An art or a science? Is the miller's an honest calling?' – this was the question that occupied the first pages of Hans Hering's *Traité singulier des moulins*, which the 'philosopher of Oldenburg' wrote in 1663. The

THE ADVENT AND TRIUMPH OF THE WATERMILL 141

German proverb was no more in doubt about the matter than Chaucer: 'Why do storks never nest on a mill? Because they are afraid the miller will steal their eggs.'[14] But let us turn aside from the echoes of these ancient village spites, however instructive they may be in their dogged persistence, their overtones still continuing to sound in the *cahiers* of 1789. In any analysis of former rural societies, as of the middle classes who had so often risen from the ranks of the small craftsmen peasant, the miller is always seen to have his allotted place alongside the innkeeper or the cattle-dealer. And all this, thanks to the ingenious mind which first entrusted the millstone to the 'water-sprites'.

But it is more especially in the history of technology that the initiative taken by this nameless pioneer constitutes a date of real importance.

The generations immediately before ours, as well as our own, have witnessed a tremendous revolution in transport, animal traction giving place to purely mechanical forms of energy. Not very different was the revolution that took place in another sphere with the coming of the watermill. But in the course of all this progress towards relieving the animate world of physical effort, the history of which more or less summarises the essentials of technical evolution – iron replacing wood, coal supplanting charcoal, chemical dyes taking the place of cochineal and indigo – in the course of this increasingly direct control exercised by man over elemental natural forces, without recourse to the power of animals, the advances made shortly before the birth of Christ were, in one sense, the most decisive of all. For the force thereby harnessed was one of the most familiar and most easily used, as well as one of the most powerful; it is the self-same force that our turbines aim at harnessing today. Its importance lay moreover in the fact that the creature who stood to gain by saving his muscle-power was man just as much as the animal. Finally, it was important because it was the first such step, and was in effect to be the only one up to the time when the steam engine was invented. For a wheel fitted with vanes could with only slight modifications transmit its motion to a great many other contrivances as well as millstones. Olive-presses and tanning-mills were no more than simple applications of the process of crushing and grinding by stones. But it was only a short while before the invention spread widely. The hydraulic saw dates from at least the 3rd century. By the 11th century the first fulling-mills recorded in our texts were already echoing with their heavy and urgent throb through some of the alpine valleys where the last survivors of the race were still at work in the 20th century.[15] The bellows and the smithy's trip-hammer do not seem to have been much later in their appearance by the riverside. Then other multifarious and novel uses were devised, so much so that the earliest manufactories of the 17th and 18th centuries, whose machines used a system of interconnected wheels roughly similar to what Vitruvius describes, and were driven by water-power, were really nothing more than descendants of the ancient watermill; and in England they long continued to be called 'mills'.

But that is not the end of the story. For the internal mechanism of the watermill also represented a step forward in the equipment of humanity whose significance far surpassed the fairly modest history of milling. This was not, of course, true of all watermills. Up to quite recent times one could see working, in various regions where mechanisation was still fairly primitive, mills with horizontal mill-wheels, fixed at water level, and connected by means of a simple rigid beam to the moving millstone placed immediately above it. The existence of this singularly rudimentary type raises some vexing problems. Scattered as it appears to be from one end of our world to the other, in regions as remote from one another as Syria, Roumania, Norway and the Shetlands, it is hardly possible to ascribe its invention to any specific civilisation.[16] Moreover it is totally different from the apparatus described in the clearest of the ancient texts like Vitruvius. Hence we are led to wonder whether this is not a genuine example of a technical regression such as might well have occurred among peoples accustomed to a very crude level of material existence. It may well have seemed easier to them to imitate the action of a force like that of water, well known to everyone, rather than reproduce mechanical contrivances that had already reached some degree of complexity. Whatever the truth may be about this hypothesis, the question is clearly still an open one, and would be worth going into more fully. But there is no doubt at all that the Greco-Roman mill contained a vertical wheel. It seems originally to have been quite often driven from underneath, 'by the river as it flowed on its course', as Pliny puts it. This is also how Vitruvius describes it. But quite early on – for this is the picture we already get in the epigram in the *Anthology* – a system of simple canalisation made it possible, when required, to let the water flow on to the vanes 'towards the top'. Now in one way or another this arrangement confronted the constructors with a mechanical difficulty, the original magnitude of which tends to be concealed from us today by the common spectacle of an all-too-cunningly mechanised world. The difficulty was that the movement, in passing from the vertical millwheel to the necessarily horizontal millstone, had to change its plane. An arrangement of cogwheels made this possible, thus introducing a principle with an immense future ahead of it, of which the mill was one of the very first examples.

About the beginning of the Christian era, the Greco-Roman civilisation, whose consumption of flour was enormous, had therefore at its disposal for the production of this essential foodstuff a piece of machinery that had already been brought to a remarkable degree of perfection. It was in fact the first machine whose use seemed capable of ameliorating the lives of countless numbers of human beings. The astonishing thing is that, having it at their disposal, they were so slow at bringing it into general use.

II

For – let us make no mistake about it – although the invention of the watermill took place in ancient times, its real expansion did not come about until the Middle Ages. It is possible to collect significant evidence of this fact relating to Gaul: one reference in the 3rd century; another round about the year 500, showing the machine to be still exceptional; five to my knowledge in the 6th century (one of which is contained in the Salic Law, which suggests the existence of a great number of mills);[17] and finally a great many references during the rest of the Frankish period. The disproportion between the amount of documentary material – quotations included – of the Roman period and of Merovingian age is not so great as to be considered merely fortuitous. But the most telling example is provided by Rome itself. Under Caligula, as we have seen, flour was supplied to the city by horse-driven millstones. In order to find references to watermills, we must – despite the relative abundance of texts – pursue the matter as far as the middle of the 4th century. At that point there is a reference to mills at the Janiculum, fed by a stream from Trajan's aqueduct, which continued to appear in documents of all kinds right up to the 7th century. From then on they were considered indispensable to the life of the population: witness the care with which emperors and Gothic kings vied with each other in ensuring that no water from the mill-races should be channelled off for other uses; witness above all the predicament in which Belisarius found himself during the siege of Rome by Totila through the destruction of the water conduits. The only defensive measure he could take was to set up improvised millwheels in boats floating on the river Tiber.[18]

Now this failure to develop to the full the possibilities of technical devices that lay ready to hand was not an isolated instance in the ancient world. 'Rome', writes Gautier, 'did not exercise over the forces of nature any dominion comparable with the development of her political organisation.'[19] I fully agree; but one may be allowed to wonder whether Rome did in fact really desire any such dominion. And if we should reach the conclusion that she was not particularly keen to exercise such a dominion, it may not be altogether impossible to understand the reason why.

Suetonius relates that when Vespasian was rebuilding the Capitol which had been burnt down during the last of the civil wars, an artisan put before him proposals for a machine that would have allowed the columns to be cheaply transported to the top of the slope. The prince rewarded the inventor but declined the invention. 'Let me still be allowed,' he said, 'to give the people a livelihood.'[20] This anecdote is instructive on more than one count. Greco-Roman civilisations were well enough endowed with quick eyes and ready minds, and it is

THE ADVENT AND TRIUMPH OF THE WATERMILL 145

unlikely that they lacked the quality of technical inventiveness; consider for example the ingenuity displayed in their siege-engines or their methods of house-warming. Nor were the generations contemporary with the first millwheels stupid enough not to realise that all progress in mechanisation would economise in human muscle-power. 'Spare your hands, which have been long familiar with the millstone, you maidens who used to crush the grain. Henceforth you shall sleep long, oblivious of the crowing cocks who greet the dawn. For what was once your task, Demeter has now handed on to the Nymphs.' This epigram from the *Anthology*, which we have already invoked as a witness, might well deserve to be selected as the motto of a society in a position to make machinery a source of joy and dignity for mankind. There is the same note of rejoicing, though expressed in less poetic terms, in the work of an agronomist like Palladius.[21] Much later on, and under very different skies, Irish legend traced the origin of the first watermill to a king's love for a beautiful captive, telling how he would fain spare his mistress the fatigue of turning the millstone when she was great with child.[22] But the ancient world hardly seemed to feel the need to spare human effort because, in relation to its agricultural capacity, it was at the beginning of the Christian era very thickly populated. Moreover, although these rough tasks could have been accomplished by an impersonal natural force, it was the custom to hand them over to a body of labour that was among the cheapest and the commonest of any of the resources of that age. For it must of course be realised that the case of building works for the Capitol was exceptional. Rome, hypertrophied in its economic functions, saw its streets seething with a hungry proletariat whom the governing classes were only too glad to help find a living by employing them in public works. People like this would not have been willing to push the millstone, which was no doubt why the majority of the City's mills were worked by horses. Elsewhere, on the great estates, the millstones were not usually turned by paid workers nor by horses or asses, nor – as Pliny tells us in a reminiscence about even more primitive methods – did people pound the grain in antiquated mortars.[23] This hard labour belonged to the slaves, sometimes men, more often women, the sisters of those menials to whom the poet in the *Anthology* so mercifully promised repose. The lords of the great *latifundia*, who were much less sympathetic to the burdens of humble people, had no reason to instal expensive machinery when their markets and their very houses were overflowing with human cattle. As for more modest households and for bakers, who would in any case have been unable to afford such heavy expenditure, many of them were quite well enough off to have their own domestic slaves; or else they did their own work themselves. In the large towns like Rome, no doubt, watermills would have been of the greatest service. But as is common knowledge, an invention rarely spreads until it is strongly felt to be a social necessity, if only for the reason that its construction then becomes a matter of routine.

Now this necessity was just becoming apparent towards the end of the Empire. In general the population was declining, there were in particular difficulties in the supply of slave labour; there was a tendency for the great gangs of slaves formerly fed directly by the master to be broken up and their members dispersed among holdings that were separated from the domain – though this is not the place to enquire into the reasons for these phenomena. It is enough for us to accept them as we find them – solid facts, among the most incontrovertible of all those that have dominated the evolution of European societies in the period between Antiquity and the Middle Ages. The proof that men were then beginning to run short of man-power for the millstones lies in the fact that they thought of supplementing the supply of slaves by using condemned criminals. Up till then, the latter had only been put to work in the mines. Constantine was the first to add another alternative to this ancient penalty, that of forced labour in the public mills.[24] As a palliative it was obviously of limited use, and, even in its own field, clearly insufficient. It was better to turn to a machine that had long ago been thought out, but had only been very incompletely exploited. We know what was in fact done. Perhaps the invention owed its birth to some individual flash of genius. But effective progress lay in transforming the idea into practical reality and this only took place under the pressure of social forces. Just because these two stages seem to have been so sharply marked off from one another, the history of the watermill, being part of the general history of technology, has the peculiar merit of being a spontaneous event; and it illustrates features of development which are more or less universal.

III

However, we must beware of imagining that this was a victory achieved at one stroke. Before the ancient processes of grinding by animal or human power finally retreated in face of the watermill, and later on the windmill, and even in face of steam flour-milling – for in some places the struggle continued as late as this – they were to have a further lengthy span of life, marked by bitter social conflicts. Unfortunately this story, which we shall attempt to sketch, is veiled in considerable obscurity.

Handmills, grain crushed by the hands of men – these terms which frequently occur in our texts are ambiguous. Leaving on one side the stone roller, which does not seem to have had a very long period of use in the West, we are left with the mortar and the revolving millstone. How are we to tell which of these two methods, one still very rudimentary and the other already much more sophisticated, is being referred to on each occasion in the texts? To set and maintain a heavy stone in motion is such hard work that one might be tempted to rule it out in cases where a woman is shown grinding corn. But nothing of the sort: for there are various accounts of an exceptionally clear nature which describe slaves or housewives 'pushing' or 'turning' the millstone.[25] Moreover the *molae trusatiles* of early Roman times, which could only be heavy because they were at first confined to the homes of the rich, where they were worked by slaves or horses, were soon replaced even in classical times. As rotary millstones made their way into the humblest dwellings, so the *molae trusatiles* were replaced by smaller, less powerful and lighter models for domestic use.[26] Taken in their strict sense, expressions like *manumolae* suggest the idea of a millstone rather than a mortar. But how can we have much confidence in the precision of a vocabulary which we know on other counts to have been so hazy? One can hardly say more than that the language of the texts, reports by certain travellers at periods not far removed from our own day, and the testimony of some rare objects that have unfortunately never been inventoried, give the impression that the millstone gradually supplanted the old prehistoric device which had held the field so long. It is better frankly to admit our ignorance of the early periods. It is an ignorance that furnishes a good example of the difficulties lurking in the path of the historian of science as soon as he attempts to come to grips with the facts. Moreover, the old types of mill handed down from classical times to the Middle Ages can surely not have remained without improvement in the course of so many centuries. And this holds good whatever the motive-power may have been. By a strange piece of application of the most recent to the most ancient device, handmills or horse-mills seem sometimes to have been provided with a system of cogwheels.[27] But here, too, our sources nearly always leave us in the dark. We shall therefore be forced in what follows to adopt a necessary though inconvenient schematisation, and simply compare and contrast the different types of apparatus according to the nature of their motive-power.[28]

There was one important and elementary reason which for a long time slowed down the victory of the watermill. Throughout the world there are regions which lack rivers and streams. As transport difficulties made it impossible to rely upon a supply of flour from mills situated at any distance, people lacking water power had no alternative but to content themselves with the ancient methods, at any rate until the day when their problems were solved by an even newer invention – the windmill. It was probably borrowed from the Arab world, coming into the West about the end of the 12th century, and thereafter making rapid progress, at least in Northern France, during the next ten or twelve decades.[29] When we find that a land-register at Orsonville in 1360, in the dry district of the Beauce, notes windmills and horse-driven mills side by side, it does not need a very bold imagination to conjecture that the latter had preceded the former. We must add to this the fact that not all water-courses were equally suitable for turning water-wheels; moreover even the best of them could not escape being frozen over, or flooded, or even becoming dried out. The Abbot of Saint-Alban was a wise man when he repaired the monastic watermills in the 13th century, and replaced one of them, whose feed-channel had dried up, by 'a very fine horse-driven mill'. Even in 1741, although the suburbs of Paris had an abundance of watermills on their rivers, and windmills on their hills, the Controller General, remembering both the great frosts of the previous winter and the floods of the year before, invited the city to equip itself also with handmills.[30]

But it was doubtless not only the vagaries of nature that prompted these ministerial recommendations. Traditionally it was considered prudent to guard against siege. There was not a single fortress in the Middle Ages that did not have its handmills. Philip Augustus was careful to see that the castles on which he lavished so much attention were provided with them. The inhabitants of Nîmes, when they were putting their defences in order in the year of the battle of Poitiers, placed 'ten or twelve' of these contrivances within the walled city. And it was not a question of guarding against an imaginary danger: the inhabitants of Parma, when besieged for months on end by the Emperor Frederick II, had all their water-courses and canals cut off, and would have succumbed to famine if they had not had hand- and horse-driven mills at their disposal. Thus it came about that warfare, upsetting as usual all normal economic conditions, constantly forced men back upon ancient and rudimentary techniques.[31]

Finally the need for mobility seemed for a long time to make portable machines advisable. It was only natural that mills – evidently hand-worked – should have been loaded on to the Carolingian army waggons at a period when enormous tracts of territory – particularly in Germany – existed in ignorance of the watermill. It is stranger to see the Norman merchants as late as the 13th century providing themselves with this kind of equipment in their peregrinations. No doubt this was due to other than strictly technical considerations. One of these was of an economic nature: in many places, bread and flour were only supplied one day at a time, and the traveller often had no other course open to him but to buy and even to import unground corn. The other reason is connected with a social institution whose importance will become clear later on: the privately owned mill enabled people to avoid the dues for grinding as they went on their travels. These seignorial rights (*banalités*) could be very burdensome.[32]

But apart from these admittedly exceptional cases, the fact remains that even where water was plentiful, and even where there was no risk of warfare, the old contrivances continued to do duty for a long period. We must no doubt take into account during the first centuries of the Middle Ages the slowness with which any innovation was likely to spread, the continued existence of considerable bands of slaves in the service of important people, and finally the habits brought with them from their original homes by the barbarian conquerors. The slave who ground the corn was looked down on with peculiar contempt, and was always less effectively protected in her life and in her honour than her sisters employed in household duties; and she remained for a long time a familiar figure in the home of the German chieftain – witness the Northern sagas and the ancient laws of Frisia and of Kent.[33] In the royal *villa* of Marlenheim in Alsace, quite close to the clear-flowing waters of the Mossig, handmills were still in use at the end of the 6th century, worked by female servants.[34] But fairly rapidly, at least in ancient *Romania* and the adjacent districts of Germania, wherever natural conditions were not unfavourable to the change, hand- and horse-operated mills disappeared from the great domains. It was an accomplished fact in Gaul at the time of the Carolingian *Polyptyques* and the *Capitulare de villis*, and in England at the time of Domesday Book, all of which, for those who have ears to hear, are loud with the music of the millwheel. But there was one out-of-the-way place left where the old-fashioned methods were still carried on – namely the homes of the peasants.

Let us imagine the various conditions that would be required for the establishment of a water-driven mill. Not only did it require the legal right to draw on the water; but the costs of construction and repair prevented its being profitable unless there was a sufficiently large quantity of grain to grind. It is a striking fact that among the earliest-mentioned mills in our documents, many of them – from the 4th century onwards in

Rome, from the 6th at Dijon and Geneva – were intended for supplying urban populations.[35] The Roman ones were managed by a corporation under very strict State control: the later Empire had no intention of entrusting the capital's food-supply to private initiative. We do not know the status of those at Dijon and Geneva. But there is clear proof that there was no difficulty in making them a paying concern. In the country, there may well have been collective bodies administered by the village communities. This system may perhaps have existed in Ireland, where the ancient tribal structure of society was favourable to group effort. In the barbarian kingdoms, on the other hand, there is no documentary evidence of any such system. If Bavarian law held mills to be public places, this was not on the grounds that they were common property. Even if this latter description could have applied to some of them, there were certainly others to which it was not applicable, at any rate those constructed by the monasteries. Now the law lumped them all together indiscriminately under the same label; they were deemed 'public', and therefore enjoyed a special 'peace', granted by whatever master they may have been dependent on, because they embodied a common effort by a number of men for a purpose that was worthy of protection, in the same way as a market, for example.[36] Even where – as in Frisia – the community was exceptional in managing to avoid being stifled by seigniorial authority, the peasants only took advantage of their liberty to remain obstinately faithful to their own individual mills.[37] They were not prepared to come to a friendly agreement with one another and adapt technical progress to their own requirements.

All the mills whose history we can more or less follow were in fact seigniorial in origin. Many of them were dependent upon monasteries, which were already fairly numerous. In addition they were obliged to feed an equal and often larger number of servants, domestic vassals and passing travellers. Hence their consumption of flour was considerable – about 2,000 *muids* a year (more than 9 tons at Corbie in the 9th century, according to Abbé Alard's estimate, which left out of account the provision of food for guests).[38] We can be quite certain that no possible economy in manpower would have escaped their attention, even though under the strict Rule the monks were themselves in duty bound to carry out the heaviest tasks. Ascetics like Germain d'Auxerre and Radegonde might well take upon themselves as a mortification the heavy and menial work of grinding corn; but the wise abbot of Loches preferred a watermill, which 'allowed a single brother to do the work of several', thus setting free a whole group of pious souls, probably for the work of prayer. About this same time, Cassiodorus boasted, among the advantages of the site he had chosen for his model foundation of a *Vivarium*, the fact that it had a river suitable for watermills.[39] There can be no doubt that these monastic constructions – as the story of the Saint of Loches bears witness – often served as an example to lay lords. They, too, maintained on their estates imposing numbers of armed retainers and agricultural servants. In order to be able to feed such large numbers, all manors, whether they were ecclesiastically owned or not, possessed some demesne land, cultivated directly by the lord, as well as dues paid by the tenants, largely in the form of agricultural produce. Once it was harvest-time there would be growing piles of corn, ready for the mill. It is probable moreover that from this point onwards an appreciable part of the revenue of the seignorial mill came from the dues levied on the peasants of the surrounding district, whether or not they were tenants, who found it convenient to have their own corn ground at the central mill.[40] Perhaps local despots were already trying to transform this permission into an obligation. But as yet custom did not support their efforts. This would be the explanation, for example, of the tenants of the Saint-Bertin monks in the 9th century, the serfs of Saint-Denis at Concevreux in the 10th century, and no doubt many others like them, whose humble story is not mentioned in any document, continuing to grind their corn at home, more often than not with their own hands.[41]

From the 10th century onwards, however, a profound change took place in the economic and legal framework of rural life. Using their power of command – which was called the '*ban*' – and fortified by their right to deal out justice, a right whose growth was at that time facilitated by the absence of any adequate machinery of justice in the State, the lords – or at

THE ADVENT AND TRIUMPH OF THE WATERMILL 153

least a large number of them – succeeded in setting up certain monopolies very much to their own advantage, monopolies concerning the use of the baking-oven, the wine-press, the breeding-boar or bull, the sale of wine or beer, at any rate during certain months; monopolies in the supply of horses for treading out corn, when this custom prevailed; and lastly – probably the most ancient and certainly the most widespread of all – a monopoly over the mill. Now society at this period was on principle inclined to confuse the ideas of what was just with what was customary. Novel claims were soon converted into custom, and the *banalités* soon became an integral part of seignorial right, and remained so as long as the seignory survived. (In Canada, where the French social system had been imported under the Bourbons, they lasted as late as 1854.)[42] From this point onwards the lord's mill was the only one where tenants of land on which it was erected were allowed to grind their corn, subject, of course, to a respectable payment to the lord of the mill and the millstream. Sometimes – since rights regularly overlapped – this obligation would even extend to villagers living in neighbouring lordships whose lords were too feeble or too unskilful to succeed in winning this privilege on their own account. For French legal theory in the 13th century with its tendency to schematize was inclined to regard this as one of the highest judicial rights (*haute justice*) – a right that belonged to none but these. Thus it came about that when from the 11th and 12th centuries onwards the great demesnes began to crumble away, and a little later on when money payments gradually began to replace the payment of dues in kind, the seignorial mills, which under the old free system would have risked standing idle, were certain of a long and useful life since they were guaranteed a steady supply of customers bound by hard custom to bring them their corn.

As may be guessed, such compulsory rights did not prevail without a struggle. It was no very difficult matter to prevent the construction of other watermills, windmills or even horse-driven mills on the lord's land. A little vigilant policing and timely agreements were quite enough to prevent the peasants from taking their corn to any local competitors. But a serious obstacle of another kind arose from the multiplicity of domestic mills, which had gone on steadily working down the centuries in almost every cottage. The lords decided to declare war upon them.

It will unfortunately never be possible to give a detailed account of this long dispute as far as the greater part of France, and perhaps also Germany, is concerned. This is at any rate true as far as I have been able to ascertain from a somewhat incomplete enquiry made more incomplete by one of the most unfortunate gaps in the technical equipment of historians in France. I refer to the regrettable – let us bluntly call it the ridiculous – habit which allows editors of charters to deprive their readers of any subject index. As if these collections only existed to provide the genealogists with tables of proper names with which to do their gymnastics! The absence of testimony in any quantity seems however quite certain. Moreover for France in particular the silence of the documents is easily explicable. This country revelled in seignorial rights (*banalités*). They not only extended over a greater number of activities than elsewhere, but they scored their greatest successes at a remarkably early date. Now by reason of this very precocity the period of their establishment, covering roughly the 10th and 11th centuries, happens to coincide with a time when documents are more scarce than at any other period of the Middle Ages. When source-material once more became abundant, the decisive stage of the struggle was already over. A very great piece of luck enables us to see the monks of Jumièges, in an agreement dated 1207, breaking up any handmills that might still exist on the lands of Viville. The reason is no doubt that this little fief, carved out of a monastic estate for the benefit of some high-ranking *sergent* of the abbot, had in fact escaped for a long period the payment of seignorial dues.[43] The scenes that took place in this corner of the Norman countryside under Philip Augustus must have had many precedents in the days of the last Carolingians or the first Capetians. But they escape the meshes of the historian's net.

The victory was not however complete by the end of the Middle Ages, for many old hand-operated mills still existed here and there, in more or less intermittent use. If they had not still been a familiar object in the 14th century, we should surely not have seen the Ecorcheurs (brigands) stationed by the Dauphin in Alsace, forcing their prisoners, as the slave-master had forced his charges in former times, to turn the millstone.[44] In the towns, people whose rank put them outside seignorial jurisdiction did not disdain on occasions to go in for a little hand-milling at home. An example of this was a canon of Montpezat in Quercy, in the years before 1380.[45] But the most important reason of all is that in the countryside seignorial authority, harassing though it was, was very poorly served. It was therefore often incapable of acting with that continuity which alone would have made it possible to reduce the peasants, past masters in the art of passive resistance, to complete submission. At least in certain regions it was left with a great deal to do when, during later centuries, new forces came into play, destroying the routine of country life.

In Germany, the Sovereigns of the territorial states had gained possession of a considerable number of seignorial rights which had always been less split up there than in France, and had, perhaps from the very start, been recognised as royal privileges. They threw all their energies into the business of supervision, as did the Prussian State for example in the 18th and at the beginning of the 19th century, in Westphalia, Pomerania and Eastern Prussia. But in this last province hand-mills were such an inseparable part of the equipment traditionally dear to the heart of the Slav population that it was sometimes only possible to forbid their use to German settlers, and for the rest of the inhabitants simply to limit their number.[46]

In France, the struggle was taken up again with more powerful weapons during the period of feudal reaction in the 17th and 18th centuries. An effective ally was found in the great judicial bodies that were such citadels of privilege. One after the other the *Parlements* of Dijon and Rouen pursued the handmills. The struggle was specially bitter in Brittany, where country life remained for a long while – and even down to our own times – very little mechanised and still peculiarly primitive. Attachment to the ancient methods of grinding seems moreover to have been much less widespread in western Brittany, entirely Celtic in language, than in the eastern cantons, largely Gallic, and at that period probably the most impoverished. The villagers would seem by their own accounts to have fallen back upon these practices only in times of drought or when the common mill was not working properly, or for milling buckwheat, which it appears that millers were often in the habit of refusing to grind. There can however really be no doubt that the competition of so many 'hand-mills' hidden away in the cottages must have made serious inroads on the profits from the legal monopoly. For that matter, the lords did not so much claim to suppress them as to make the use of them subject to the payment of a due. The very multiplicity of the successive decrees passed by the *Parlement* of Rennes shows how dogged the resistance must have been. Among the various forms of 'feudal tyranny', this particular one still roused some of the most lively of all the registered protests in the Breton *cahiers* of 1789.[47]

But it is in England especially that the war of wind and water against human muscle is seen in its clearest light.

Manorial rights were not an institution native to England. The Norman conquerors had imported them from the continent as one of the principal elements in the 'manorial' system which after the almost total dispossession of Saxon aristocracy they methodically established, by superimposing it on what remained of a much looser form of dependence. It is true that in England the system of seignorial monopolies always remained less complete than on the other shore of the Channel. But manorial rights over the mill were generally introduced, though not without resistance. Opposition was all the more passionate in this country because by reason of its remoteness from Mediterranean influences, and the strong impress of German and Scandinavian civilisation, the watermill, though familiar from the end of the 11th century on the great estates, only won its way very slowly among the middle classes. It is characteristic that among the privileges granted to English burgesses there should frequently figure this clause, totally unknown in French and German urban charters, allowing the use of the handmill, or more rarely the horse-driven mill. This was the state of affairs at Newcastle, Cardiff and Tewkesbury during the 12th century, and in London even in the middle of the

14th century.[48] But the pressure of rich and powerful communities was needed to overcome this tolerance. 'The men shall not be allowed to possess any handmills' – such was the clause inserted by the canons of Embsay in Yorkshire between 1120 and 1151, in a charter in which a noble lady made over to them a certain watermill. It expressed their own attitude and that of all lords of rivers and manors.[49] There were occasions when milling stones were seized by the lord's officials in the very houses of the owners and broken in pieces; there were insurrections on the part of housewives; there were law-suits which grimly pursued their endless and fruitless course, leaving the tenants always the losers. The chronicles and monastic cartularies of the 13th and 14th centuries are full of the noise of these quarrels.[50] At St Albans they assumed the scale of a veritable milling epic.

In this small Hertfordshire town, to which the monks who were lords of the place obstinately refused to give any privileges, the example of neighbouring citizens stirred up – in the words of the monastic chronicler – a particularly 'indomitable tenantry'. They were a collection of artisans rather than peasants, and it was not only the dues for milling grain or malt and the miller's exactions that they sought to avoid by milling at home. The drapers among them also claimed, in defiance of the lord's fulling-mill, the right to set up their own fulling stocks for the pressing of material, at least for the coarser kinds of cloth, for it was generally considered at this period that fine materials must be fulled under foot. The first quarrel broke out in 1274, accompanied by the usual incidents. Millstones and lengths of cloth were confiscated; there was mutual violence perpetrated by the lord's officials and by tenants; a league was formed among the inhabitants, who clubbed together to establish a common purse to maintain their cause at law, whilst monks, barefoot before the High Altar, were chanting penitential psalms; attempts were made by the women to win the queen over to their side, but the abbot had taken the precaution of having her smuggled into the monastery by a secret entrance. Finally there were lengthy proceedings before the royal court, ending inevitably in the defeat of the recalcitrant party, who sought to appease their offended lord by the gift of five fine barrels of wine. Another incident took place in 1314. Then in 1326 the citizens demanded a charter which should contain among other clauses the right to domestic milling. This led to an open insurrection, in which the monastery was twice besieged. Final agreement was only reached under pressure from the king, but it left the problem of the lord's monopolies unresolved. Taking advantage of this uncertainty, the inhabitants soon had anything up to eighty handmills working in their homes. But in 1331 a new abbot – Richard II, the terrible leprous abbot – entered the lists. He won the day by going to law. From all over the town the millstones were brought in to the monastery, and the monks paved their parlours with them, like so many trophies. But when in 1381 the great insurrection of the common people broke out in England and Wat Tyler and John Ball emerged as leaders, the people of St. Albans were infected by the same fever and attacked the abbey. They destroyed the notorious paved floor, the monument to their former humiliation, and as the stones were doubtless no longer any use for grinding, they broke them up and each took fragments of them as a sign of victory and solidarity, 'as the faithful do on Sundays with the holy bread'. The deed of liberation which they extorted from the monks recognised their freedom to maintain 'hand-mills' in every home. The insurrection however proved to be like a blaze of straw that soon burns itself out. When it had collapsed all over England, the charter of St Albans and all the other extorted privileges were annulled by royal statute. But was this the end of a struggle that had lasted more than a century? Far from it. The chronicler, as he draws to the close of his story, has to admit that for malting at any rate the detestable handmills have come into action again and have been again forbidden.[51]

They were destined to give humble service throughout the length and breadth of England for a long time to come. It is true that the narratives we possess hardly make any further mention of them. But here and there a manorial 'record' allows us to lift the veil for a moment. The Tudors had long ago succeeded the Plantagenets when in 1547 the people of the royal manor of Kingsthorpe obtained recognition for their right to grind at least a certain quantity of their grain at home.

At Bury in Lancashire, it was not until the restoration of the Stuarts that the lord of the manor succeeded in suppressing competition with his own mill; and even so the obstinacy of those representing the parish made the suit drag on till 1713. This was only seventy-three years before the first large-scale flour-mill was opened in London.[52]

In short, when the iron and coal age opened, the ancient prehistoric tools had nowhere yielded altogether to the 'engines' which for so many centuries had also relied upon the inanimate forces of wind and water. There is therefore nothing surprising about the survival in working order of handmills in Ireland, Scotland, the Shetlands, Norway, East Prussia, and nearly everywhere in Slav territory, right up to the end of the 19th century; and even perhaps in our own day they have not altogether ceased to function. For these regions, situated as they are on the fringe of the West, had in all respects long been faithfully wedded to a fairly rudimentary degree of mechanisation. Prussian villagers were still grinding grain in 1896 according to the elementary methods of their ancestors, and felt obliged, like them, to hide from strangers as they did so – as though the lord's monopolies were still in existence. In these actions we can recognise, not only the dim potency of tradition, but also the fact that in the North winter frosts were not very favourable to the use of running water-power; moreover, in the Shetlands, Norway, Scotland, and even Ireland, there was no seignorial authority comparable to that prevailing in France. But even in the heart of our own civilisation, a more searching enquiry would no doubt reveal more than one scattered example of a similar survival. The Breton handmills, whose history might well tempt a scholar more familiar with the province than I am, were surely given something of a new lease of life by the suppression of the seignorial regime. In the second half of the 19th century Lamprecht observed near the tributaries of the Moselle, whose waters had turned some of the earliest millwheels in Gaul, material traces of the relatively recent practice by which, with the aid of human power, corn was crushed between two revolving stones.[53]

These anomalies should not however be allowed to lead us astray. When the steam engine arrived to put the finishing touches to the defeat of the handmill and mortar, by far the greater part of the flour consumed in the countryside and in the towns of the West had for centuries been milled by wind- or water-power. No doubt the peasants, if left to their own devices, would have clung still longer to the old ancestral ways. And by imposing heavy milling dues seignorial lords, owners of the manorial mills, may sometimes have encouraged unintentionally a fidelity to the past; but in the end they destroyed it through the use of force. In more than one respect these seignorial undertakings were not unlike some of our great present-day commercial enterprises. First of all they saw them- selves constrained by the shortage of manpower to bring about this great improvement in human equipment; then they harshly imposed the system on all around them. Thus technical progress resulted from two constraining forces; and this, we may be quite sure, is not the only example.

NOTES

1. *Annales*, no. 36, Nov. 1935, Vol. VII, pp. 538–563. For the Biblio- graphy, see the bibliographical note at the end of this article. In the course of what I have to say I shall limit myself to simple documentary references. Works whose full titles are given in the bibliographical note will be referred to in these notes in abbreviated form where this is practicable.
2. J. Déchelette, *Manuel d'archéologie*, Vol. II, 3rd part, pp. 1386ff.
3. Suetonius, *Caligula*, 39.
4. Strabo, XII, 556; *Antholog. Palat.*, IX, 418. The epigram is generally attributed to Antipatros of Thessalonica. The latest editor, H. Stadtmüller (*Anthologia Graeca*, Vol. II, 1, 1906), gives its author as Antiphilus of Byzantium, who was more or less contemporary moreover with Antipatros; Vitruvius X, 257; Pliny XVIII, 23.
5. Ausonius, *Mosella*, line 362.
6. *Lex Alamannorum*, LXXX; *Lex Baiwariorum*, IX, 2; *S.S. rer.˙merov.*, Vol. IV, p. 513; *Diplomata Karolina*, Vol. I, no. 104; *S.S.*, Vol. XV, 1, p. 127. The quotation of 837 which W. Arnold, *Ansiedlungen und Wanderungen der deutschen Stämme* (p. 592), has borrowed from Dronke, *Codex diplomaticus Fuldensis*, no. 504, is not decisive, since the word *farinariis* only appears in the stereotyped formula of the *'appartenances'*. The case of Mühlhausen shows how valuable for the history of the spread of the mill would be a systematic study of toponomy.

THE ADVENT AND TRIUMPH OF THE WATERMILL 161

7. Kemble, *Codex Diplomaticus*, Vol. I, p. 317, no. CCXXXIX; W. de Gray Birch, *Cartularium Saxonicum*, Vol. I, no. 418. There is a further reference, shortly before the Norman Conquest, in the *Gerefa*, c. 9 (Liebermann, *Gesetze*, p. 454); *Ancient Laws of Ireland*, Vol. I, pp. 125 and 141; J. Vendryes, in *Revue archéologique*, 1921, H. p. 370.
8. L. Niederle, *Manuel de l'antiquite slave*, Vol. II, pp. 198, 199; Helmold, *Chronica Slavorum*, I, c. 12 (edit. Lappenberg-Schmeidler, p. 24).
9. Axel Olbik, *Danmarks Heldedigining*, Vol. I (Copenhagen, 1903), p. 2⁻.
10. Perhaps these concentric lines should be extended towards the east. According to the Byzantine historian Cedrenas, in a passage probably inspired by a lost account from Ammianus Marcellinus (cf. Pauly-Wissowa, *Realenclyclopädie*, under the word *Metrodorus*), the hellenised Persian Metrodorus, during a journey to India in the days of Constantine, is said to have constructed watermills there 'which had up till then been unknown to the Brahmans' (*Historiarum Compendium*, 516, in Migne, P.G., Vol. CXXI, col. 562). I hand this problem over to the specialists. According to Feldhaus, *Die Tecknik* (p. 70), a Jesuit is said to have published in 1612 a book in Chinese on the hydraulic machines of the West; but (p. 65) the existence of watermills in China had been attested since 1609. There are further questionable points which would be well worth the attention of competent authorities.
11. Strabo, XVII, 807. For Egypt, cf. E. H. Winlock and W. E. Cram, *The Monastery of Ephiphanius at Thebes*, Vol. I, New York, 1926, p. 65 (*The Metropolitan Museum of Art, Egyptian Expedition*); Lucretius, V. line 517.
12. Pherecrates in the *Athénéé*; VI, 263; *C.I.L.*, Vol. VI, 1002; a photograph of a bakery in Pompeii, *Dictionnaire d'archéologie chrétienne* (art. *Moulin*).
13. *C.I.L.*, Vol. VI, 1711.
14. *Tractatus singularis de molendinis eorumque jure*, Lugduni, 1663. *Quaestio prima*: 'An ars sive scientia molitoria sit honesta, nec ne?'; *Zeitschrift für deutsches Altertum*, Vol. III, 1843, p. 32, c. 44.
15. Ausonius, *Mosella*, line 393 (dealing with a saw for cutting marble); *Cartulaires de l'église cathédrale de Grenoble*, edit. J. Marion (*Doc. inéd.*), p. 119, no. XLVI; an undated document from about the year 1050. A. Dopsch, *Die Wirtschaftsentwicklung der Karolingerzeit* (Vol. II, 2nd ed., p. 150), is wrong in thinking that there is a reference to a fulling-mill in the *Formulae Sangallenses Miscellaneae* (c. 11). The *Pilae* here mentioned are similar to those drawn by the author of the famous plan of Saint-Gall – a crushing-instrument which the plan certainly does not represent as water-driven, and was doubtless not so driven in the case referred to in the *Formulae*. There was a fulling-mill still at work in 1910 in the Herens valley for making a coarse local cloth called 'guide's cloth'.
16. This type has been studied at length by Bennett and Elton, *History of Corn Milling*. It seems moreover that by interpreting certain textual references in a rather rash manner they have exaggerated its wide-

162 THE ADVENT AND TRIUMPH OF THE WATERMILL

spread use. They are for example wrong in representing it as clearly attested on the Garonne by Paul Hentzner in his *Itinerarium*, 1619 edit., p. 56.

17. Ausonius, *Mosella*, line 362; Gregory of Tours, *Vitae Patrum*, XVIII, 2 (the episode is placed in the reign of the Visigoth Alaric II; 484–507); *Historia Francorum*, III, 19; Fortunat, *Carmina*, III, 12, lines 39ff; Marius d'Avenches, *Chronica*, a. 563; *Lex Salica*, XXII, 2; *Vita S. Romani* in *S.S. rev. merov.*, Vol. III, p. 142, c. 18 (I adopt as the date of this text the one defended by Mgr Duchesne and R. Pourpardin). Cf. also the *Lex Visigothurum*, VII, 2, 12 and VIII, 4, 30 (*Antiqua*, that is to say referring to conditions before the death of King Léovigild in 586). For lack of easy access to the documents, I have had at this point to leave completely on one side all that refers to the history of the watermill in Spain, and from the Middle Ages onwards, in Italy.

18. For the Janiculum mills see the *Description des 14 regions de Rome* in O. Richter, *Topographie der Stadt Rom* (Iwan Müller, *Handbuch*), p. 374, *Regio XIII*; *Cod. Theod.* XIV, 5, 4; Prudence, *Contra Symmachum*, II, line 950; Cassiodorus, *Variae III*, 31 (cf. XI, 39); *C.I.L.*, Vol. VI, no. 1711; Procopius, *De bello Gothico* I, 19; *Liber Pontificalis*, edit. Duchesne, Vol. I, p. 324 (cf. p. 327, no. 20): Honorius I. Naturally, at the time of the siege of Rome the difficulty was increased by the lack of forage, which prevented them from falling back upon horse-driven mills.

19. *Genseric*, p. 32.
20. *Vespasian*, c. 18.
21. *Opus agriculturae*, I, 41.
22. J. Vendryes, in *Revue archéologique*, 1921, II, p. 369.
23. XVIII, 23.
24. *Codex The. d.*, IX, 40, 3, 5, 6, 9 and XIV, 17. 6.
25. Gregory of Tours, *Historia Francorum* IX, 38; Flodgard *Historia Rememsis ecclesiae*, I, 24; *Miracula S. Bertini*, in Mabillon, *A.A.*, *S.S. ord. S. Benedicti*, III, 1, p. 112, c. 13.
26. Déchelette, *Manuel*, Vol. II, 3rd part, pp. 1386ff.; Lindet, in *Rev. archéol.*, 1900, I, p. 30ff.
27. A. P. Usher, *A History of mechanical inventions*, pp. 126ff.
28. A passage in the Strasbourg chronicler Jakob de Königshofen would seem at first sight to attest the co-existence of both types of instrument up to the 14th century. During the siege of 1392, he tells us, when the besiegers had diverted the course of the Ill and when moreover the summer drought had almost dried up the Bruche, the poor people, 'if they had no friends', were compelled 'to crush their corn in mortars', whilst divers persons set up in their own homes handmills or windmills and so came to the rescue of other poor people. (*Die Chroniken der deutschen Städte*, Vol. IX, p. 694). But the handmills were obviously improvised, and the mortars which were pressed into service in this emergency for crushing corn were no doubt used in normal times for other purposes. This passage, in sum, simply bears witness to the ingenuity of the population.

THE ADVENT AND TRIUMPH OF THE WATERMILL 163

29. The history of the windmill has been vitiated for a long time by false examples wrongly attributed to the 11th and even the 9th century. Cf. L. Delisle, *Études sur la condition de la classe agricole* . . . *en Normandie*, p. 514, where the earliest French documentary reference so far discovered is quoted – about the year 1180. The first testimony in England is clearly of about the same date, since it refers to abbot Samson, of Bury St. Edmunds, who was elected in 1182. It has been preserved for us by the chronicle of Jocelin de Brakelonde, which was put together about the year 1202; *Memorials of St Edmund's Abbey*, edit. Thomas Arnold (*Rolls Series*), Vol. I, p. 263, c. 45.

30. Terrier of Saint-Martin-des-Champs (Arch. Nat. LL, 1879), folio 1; Thomas Walsingham, *Gesta S. Albani* (Rolls Series), Vol. I, p. 323. Cf. the supporting passages in L. Delisle, op. cit., p. 518, note 37; M. Malouin, *Descriptions et détails des arts du meunier*, p. 55; Leon Cahen, in *Cahiers de la Révolution française*, Vol. I, 1934, p. 56.

These prudent precautions explain how in the celebrated plan of the monastery offered to Abbé Gozbert de Saint-Gall (816–836), mills, of the hand or horse variety, are shown in one of the out-buildings (F. Keller, *Bauriss des Klosters S. Gallen*, Zürich, 1844; reproduced on a smaller scale in C. Enlast, *Manuel*, 2nd. edit., 2nd part, Vol. III, p. 10). They were for use in an emergency. The watermills possessed by all the large religious establishments of the period could not be shown on a typical plan, as their position was bound to vary according to local conditions, and because they were not generally located within the precincts of the monastery. Cf. also for Augsburg (1442), *Chroniken der deutschen Städte*, Vol. IV, p. 324.

31. F. Lot and R. Fawtier, *Le premier budget de la monarchie française* (a reproduction of the account published by Brussel, *Nouvel examen de l'usage général des fiefs*, Vol. II, pp. clvi and clxxv); L. Delisle, *Études sur la condition de la classe agricole*, p. 518, note 38; Ménard, *Histoire de la ville de Nîmes*, Vol. II, 1702, p. 181, col. 2. In this text, as in Vol. I, p. 10, col. 1, in a passage occurring in a catalogue of the bishops of Nîmes, relating to Bishop Jean de Blanzac (1348–1361), the handmill is called *molendinum sanguinis*; this expression has puzzled the wits of many, and I confess myself unable to produce a satisfactory explanation of it. In any case its character as something local and rather late in origin seems to be averred; *Annales Parmenses maiores*, in *S.S.*, Vol. XVIII, p. 674. For other examples of handmills in fortresses: J. A. Brutails, *Étude sur la condition des populations rurales en Roussilon au Moyen Age*, p. 23; V. Mortet et P. Deschamps, *Recueil de textes relatifs à l'histoire de l'architecture*, Vol. II, nos. CXXIV (p. 264) and CLVII (p. 330). Cf. also for the siege of Strasbourg in 1392 above, note 28.

32. *Capitularia*, Vol. I, no. 77, c. 10. The existence of handmills which merchants took with them appears to be attested by this passage in an agreement concluded in 1207 between Thomas de Viville and the monks of Jumièges: 'Moltam de tota terra Thome abbas habebit. Si homo de terra Thome ad aliud molendinum ierit, molendinarius

abbatis per servientem Thome ea[m]dem justitiam faciet quam faceret in terra abbatis et tantum ... Si mole ad manum in terra Thome ad aliud molendinum ierit molendinarius abbatis per servientem Thome ea[m]dem justitiam faciet quam faceret in terra abbatis et tantum ... Si mole ad manum in terra Thome reperte fuerint, omnes frangentur, preter unam propter egros. Si mercator de terra Thome undecumque venerit cum blado vel frumento et in domo sua comedere voluerit vel quippiam aliud facere et statim recedere, licebit ei. Si nocte una morabitur, vel redam suam sub solario vel super limen domus sue deposuerit, moltam debebit' (*Arch. de la Seine-Inférieure*, Grand Cartulaire de Jumièges, no. 218). A fragment of this charter has been quoted by L. Delisle, *Études sur la classe agricole* (p. 518, note 39); I owe this copy to the kindness of the archivist, M. Cacheux. Although the handmills had to be broken up, the merchant on his side was allowed to grind his corn elsewhere than at the lord's mill; and so it seems that he had what I have ventured to call a travelling mill.

33. *Lex Frisionum* (9th century), c. 13. Cf. also, at the beginning of the 13th century, the *Ueberküre*, c. 7, in Richthofen *Friesische Rechtsquellen*, pp. 100–101; Lois d'Aethelbert (597–617), c. 11. Cf. below, note 48, for a similar arrangement in a Gallic law; and see J. Grimm, *Deutsche Rechtsaltertümer*, 4th edit., Vol. I, p. 485.
34. Gregory of Tours; *Historia Francorum*, IX, 38.
35. *Ibid.* III, 19; Marius d'Avenches, *Chronica*, a. 563.
36. *Lex Baiwariorum*, IX, 2. For the 'peace' of the mill and the long survival of this notion in Germanic law, cf. M. Krammer, in *Neues Archiv*, Vol. XXX, 1904, p. 278. 'The mill', says the Mirror of Swabia in the 13th century, 'enjoys a more secure legal position than other houses' (edit. Lassberg, Ldr, c. 249). For the legal position of mills, see C. Koehne, *Das Recht der Mühlen bis zum Ende der Karolingerzeit*, pp. 22ff.; for the 'peace', ibid., pp. 33ff.
37. Cf. in the 13th century the *Ueberküre*, referred to above, note 33.
38. I take these figures from the *Statutes* of Abbé Alard, published by L. Levillain, in *Le Moyen Age*, 1900; it is impossible here to go into a critical examination of the text. It is not surprising that at Corbie the watermills should stand out as particularly important.
39. *S.S. rer. merov.*, Vol. VII, p. 252, c. 3; II, pp. 369–370, c. 16 and I, p. 734 (Gregory of Tours, *Vitae Patrum*, XVIII (2); Cassiodorus, *De Institutione*, c. 29. Cf., although much less precise, the Rule of Saint Benedict, c. 66. At Bobbio, a mill was part of the first installations of Saint Columba (*Vita auctore Iona*, II, 2, in *S.S. rer. merov.*, Vol. IV, p. 115).
40. This seems to emerge in particular from the study of the revenue that the monks of Corbie were wont to draw from their mills.
41. As Guérard saw clearly in *Polyptyque d'Irminon*, Proleg. Vol. 1, 2, p. 633, the existence of domestic corn-grinding on the lands of Saint-Bertin arose from the numerous flour-dues exacted from the tenants. Moreover there is precise evidence on this point in an account –

THE ADVENT AND TRIUMPH OF THE WATERMILL

unfortunately of uncertain date – inserted in a collection of the miracles performed by the monastery's saint: cf. above, note 25. (The compilation, dating from the 13th century, has incorporated some older elements; cf. the notice by Holder-Egger, *S.S.*, Vol. XV, 1, p. 508). For Concevreux, see Flodoard, *Historia Remensis ecclesiae*, I, 24.

42. W. B. Munro, *The seignorial system in Canada*, New York, 1907 (Harvard Historical Studies, 13), pp. 245ff.
43. The text is quoted above, note 32. Why was permission given to retain a handmill 'for the sick'? No doubt because by avoiding the delays frequently occurring at the lord's mill it would be possible to supply them promptly with the required flour.
44. The continuator of Königshofen in F. I. Mone, *Quellensammlung der Vadischen Landesgeschichte*, Vol. III, p. 530.
45. R. Latouche, *La vie en Bas-Quercy*, supporting document no. v., p. 472 (posthumously indexed): 'unum molendinum brachiorum pro molendo blada'. Handmills are mentioned, about 1150, in the treatise *De Ustensilibus* by Adam du Petit-Pont (Mortet et Deschamps, *Recueil de textes*, Vol. II, p. 85). But this account, with its wealth of classical reminiscence, inspires a certain distrust.
46. Ad. Dorinder, *Die Entwicklung des Mühlenwesens in der ehemaligen Grafschaft Mark* (Diss. Munster, 1909), p. 38; A. Treichel, in *Zeitschrift für Ethnologie*, Vol. XXVI, 1894, pp. 415ff.; Koehne, in *Zeitschrift der Sav. Stiftung*, G.A. 1907, p. 68. In Prussia the war by the State against handmills, which had increased in number as a result of the abolition of the lord's manorial rights in 1808, was resumed in 1810 when Hardenberg had imposed a heavy 'excise duty' on milling, the collection of which would have been made impossible by milling at home; but this extremely unpopular tax was abolished in 1811. See G. Cavaignac, *La formation de la Prusse contemporaine*, Vol. II, pp. 55 and 60 (with references). On handmills, there is a very informative chapter in A. Maurizio's *Histoire de l'alimentation végétale*, pp. 377ff.; they had for a long time been used to crush grain for porridge for human consumption and for animal foods, even after they had fallen out of use for bread flour.
47. Decree of Dijon, 1653, July 29th, quoted by Bouhier, *Les coutumes du duché de Bourgogne*, Vol. II, 1846, p. 367; decree of Rouen in 1743, March 9th, quoted by Guyot and Merlin, *Répertoire*, 1830 edit., Vol. XI, p. 327, according to a commentator from Basnage; Mainsard, *Les banalités en Bretagne*, 1912, pp. 142ff. and 177; M. Sauvageon, *Coutumes de Bretagne*, 1747, on art. 387 (1629, July 16th and 1684, April 13th); Poullain du Parc, *Journal des audiences et arrêts du Parlement de Bretagne*, Vol. II, 1775, pp. 321ff. (1751-1752-1755); H. Sée and A. Lesort, *Cahiers et doléances de la Sénéchaussée de Rennes* (with a reference in the Table of Contents under 'Meules à bras'). On the other hand the *Cahiers de doléances des Sénéchaussées de Quimper et de Concarneau* (edit. J. Savina and D. Bernard) do not mention handmills at all; this is all

the more striking because they protest violently against the lord's monopolies. The cahier for Pouldrezic (p. 54, c. 1) even puts forward a clear case for the abolition of the lord's monopoly, arguing that it would not result in any falling off in the patronage of the mill, whether water- or wind-driven.

48. Ballard, *British Borough Charters*, 1916. To the list of towns quoted above should be added Bristol, although the text of its charter is less precise. For London cf. *Liber Albus*, edit. Riley, p. 74. In Wales, about the 12th century, corn was still commonly hand-ground by women of servile status (*Ancient Laws of Wales*, Vol. II, p. 7, c. 17).

49. Bennett and Elton, Vol. I, p. 211, and a fascimile as frontispiece to the volume (for the date, cf. *Victoria County Histories*, Yorkshire, Vol. III, p. 195). See also, in Edward III's reign, the regulation of the Chester mills (Bennett, Vol. I, p. 212).

50. *Chronicum Petroburgense*, edit. Stapleton (Camden Society, 1849), p. 67 (1284); E. A. Fuller, *Circencester: the manor and the town* in Trans. Arch. Soc. *Bristol & Glos*, Vol. IX, 1884–85, pp. 311ff (1306–1307); Glos, *Registra quorumdam abbatum monasterii S. Albani*, editl Riley (*Rolls Series*), Vol. I, pp. 109ff. (1499: a rising by the women provoked by the prohibition of horse-mills); in 1381, the people of Watford, like those of St. Albans, had extorted from the abbey a charter recognising their right to use handmills; see Th. Walsingham, *Gesta S. Albani*, Vol. III, p. 325.

51. Thomas Walsingham, *Gesta S. Albani*, edit. Riley (*Rolls Series*), Vol. I, pp. 410ff; Vol. II, p. 149, 158, 287ff.; Vol. III, pp. 286ff.; 360–361, 367–371. Cf. the *Historia Anglicana* by the same author, edit. Riley (*Rolls Series*), p. 475. For the events of 1381, see C. Oman, *The Great Revolt of 1381*, pp. 91ff.

52. Bennett and Elton, Vol. I, p. 224; P. Mantoux, *La Révolution industrielle*, 1905, p. 341.

53. Bennett and Elton, Vol. I, p. 167; *Revue archéologique*, 1900, I, p. 35;. *Zeitschrift für Ethnologie*, Vol. XXII, 1890, p. 607, and Vol. XXVIII, 1896, p. 372; Lamprecht, *Deutsche Wirtschaftsgeschichte*, Vol. I, p. 585. Research in provincial areas would undoubtedly shed much new light on the life-span of hand-milling. It is in this way that A. Demont (*Le blé dans les traditions artésiennes*, in *Revue de folklore français*, 1935, p. 49) discovered that a handmill was found in 1856 'right in the middle of the belfry of the church at Hermaville. The millstones showed signs of long use. The oak framework was a timber construction in 18th-century style.' Cf. also *Bull. Soc. Archeol. Limousin*, Vol. CXXXV, p. 47 and LXXV, p. 58.

Bibiliographical Note

For the history of technical development in general, the best guide is Abbott Payson Usher's *A History of mechanical inventions*, New York, 1929 (with bibliography); cf. *Annales*, Vol. II, 1931, p. 278. The work by Franz M. Feldhaus, *Die Technik der Antike und des Mittelalters*,

Potsdam (1931) (*Museum der Weltgeschichte*), will prove less useful, apart from its excellent illustrations (cf. *Annales*, Vol. IV, 1932, p. 482). The work by A. Vierendeel, *Esquisse d'une histoire de la technique*, 2 vols, Louvain, 1921, only gives very brief, and not always very reliable, information on the Ancient World and the Middle Ages.

For the mill, the fundamental work remains R. Bennett and J. Elton, *History of Corn Milling*, 4 vols., London, 1898–1904. Unfortunately it is virtually unobtainable in the libraries of France.

More recently, a useful general conspectus has been produced by Carl Koehne, *Die Mühle in Rechten der Völker*, in *Beiträge zur Geschichte der Technik*, 1913; (in spite of its title, the memoir deals as much with the history of technical development as with that of the law). The same author earlier made a study of strictly juridical problems in a series of works. Certain of his themes (the origin of the *banalités*, in particular) are debatable, but the documentary value of the work is considerable: *Das Recht der Mühlen bis zum Eude der Karolingerzeit*, Breslau, 1904 (Untersuchungen zur deutschen Staats – und Rechtsgeschichte H. 71); *Studien über die Enstehung der Zwangs – und Bannrechte*, in *Zeitschrift der Savigny Stiftung*, G.A. 1904; *Mühlenbann und Burgbau*, ibid., 1904.*

The articles under *Mola* in Daremberg and Saglio's *Dictionnaire des Antiquités grecques et rojmaines* – by A. Baudrillart, $M\acute{v}\lambda\eta$ in Pauly-Wissowa's *Realenencyclopädie der classischen Altertumswissenschaft* – by W. Ruge, *Moulin* in Cabrol and Leclerq's *Dictionnaire d'archéologie Chrétienne* – by Don Leclercq – provide much useful information. The articles under *Mühle* in Max Ebert's *Reallexikon der Vorgeschichte* and J. Hoop's *Reallexikon der germanischen Altertumskunde*, the article under *Mahlen* and *Mühle* in O. Schrader's *Reallexikon der indogermanischen Altertumskunde* (2nd edit. 1923) are simply straightforward recapitulations.†

There are some indications as to the origins and the various technical types in L. Lindet, *Les origines du moulin à grains*, in *Revue archéologique*, 1899, Vol. II, and 1900, Vol. I.

The principal linguistic works are: R. Meringer, *Die Werkzenge der* pinsere – *Reihe and ihre Namen; Zu den Werkzengen der* pinsere – *Reihe; Zu den Werkzengen der* molere – *Reihe*, in *Wörter und Sachen*, Vol. I, 1909, pp. 1, 164–165; A Meillet, *Le nom indoeuropéen de la meule* in *Mélanges publiés en l'honneur de M. Paul Boyer*, Paris, 1925 (Travaux publiés par l'Institut d'Etudes slaves, Vol. II). Cf. also the article

---

* The work by William Coles Finch, *Watermills and Windmills, a historical survey of their rise, decline and fall as portrayed by those of Kent*, London, 1933, is of the picturesque and anecdotal type, and not of much significance for the historian of the mill. I have not been able to see M. Ringelmann's *Essai sur l'histoire du génie rural*, Paris, 1907(?).

† The explanations given by d'A. Maurizio in *L'Histoire de l'alimentation végétale* (trans. F. Gidon, 1932, pp. 377–422) are of interest for hand-milling, about which much useful information is given, rather than for watermills.

by J. Vendryes, referred to below, on the subject of Celtic civilisations.*
For the civilisations of Western Asia: B. Landsberger, *Zur Mehlberei-tung im Altertum*, in *Orientalische Literaturzeitung*, Vol. XXV, 1922 (almost exclusively linguistic).

Classical antiquity: H. Blümner, *Technologie und Terminologie der Gewerbe und Künste der Griechen und Römer*, Vol. II, Berlin, 1879, p. 83; Th. Mommsen and J. Marquardt, *Manuel des antiquités romaines*, Vol. XV (J. Marquardt, *La vie privée*, Vol. II), p. 45.

Celtic civilisations: J. Vendryes, *Les moulins en Irelande et l'aventure de Ciarnot*, in *Revue archéologique*, 1921, II.

On the technical details of the mill before the steam-engine: M. Malvin, *Description des arts du meunier, du vermicellier and du boulanger*, Paris, 1767.

It goes without saying that a complete inventory of the sources relating to the history of the mill is out of the question, for the material is extremely scattered. A fairly lengthy enquiry has enabled me to offer some new evidence. There is no doubt that there is much more material waiting for the research-worker who is patient and skilful enough to find his way through editions where the lack of any index often forces the student to grope his way. I will not do more here than call special attention to the conspicuous merits of one particular category of documents.

Some of the information above has been taken from the legal literature of the Ancien Régime. Commentaries on customary law, collections on jurisprudence, systematic treatises on seignorial or feudal law – all these dusty folios and quartos are a mine of astonishing richness. Unfortunately, in the present state of our scientific equipment, the task of mastering their contents bristles with difficulty, primarily because there is no satisfactory inventory of them. The one that was attempted some time ago in Vol. II of the *Profession d'Avocat* by Camus and Dupin (5th edit. 1832), though still useful today, is not sufficient for all requirements. Above all, in the only library which contains an extensive collection of this kind of work – I mean the Bibliothèque Nationale – the working rules are about as unfavourable as possible to researches which involve the handling of many volumes in a very short space of time. When the historians of France's past find all these old law-books collected in one room, and ready to hand, then it will become an easy matter to throw light on many of the dark areas of our history. Our colleagues in the Natural Sciences justly complain of the state of their laboratories: what would they think of the material conditions under which most of our enquiries have to be conducted?

* The excellent articles by P. Aebischer, *Les dénominations du 'moulin' dans les chartes italiennes du Moyen Age* (*Bulletin du Cange, 1932*), and *Les termes servant à désigner le 'moulin' dans quelques anciennes chartes relatives à la Belgique* (*Bulletin du dictionnaire Wallon*, Vol. XVII, 1932), are of purely linguistic interest.

6

MEDIAEVAL 'INVENTIONS'[1]

I

During the Middle Ages, 'apart from the invention of gunpowder, technical progress . . . was to a large extent non-existent'.[2] This sentence was written less than fifteen years ago, and was immediately judged by a few specialists to be an outrageous statement. But the fact that today all historians, and no doubt many other knowledgeable people, consider it to be so is chiefly due to the discoveries and the vigorous writing of M. Lefebvre des Noëttes, to whom all honour is due.[3] We now know beyond all doubt that at the time when European societies were embarking on the conquest of the great oceanic routes they had at their disposal a technical equipment infinitely superior to what was possessed by the Roman Empire in its declining years. But we are still very much in the dark about the exact dates when these various advances were made, and their causes. In another article I put forward some facts and conjectures with regard to the history of one of these advances. To establish the argument beyond all reasonable doubt would require whole teams of research-workers. But in the hope of forwarding their labours I should like to bring together here a variety of observations, though many of them will not be much more than queries.

II

At first sight nothing could be more disconcerting in the historical literature commonly set before the public than the almost complete absence of information about changes in technical equipment between prehistoric times and the 18th century. For several years now people have expressed their astonishment at this fact, in lively fashion and with very good reason. There have been histories of the countryside whose heroes, as Lucien Febvre puts it, seem to do their ploughing with charters; administrative histories full of the grand doings of a 'central power' which rules the provinces, seemingly regardless of such mundane realities as the condition of roads, the availability of animals for transport, the supply of fodder for horses, and travelling time. These are just a few typical examples taken from two books, among a thousand, that are grotesquely out of touch with their real subject-matter. Their errors are inexcusable. Ever since *Annales* has been in existence, its editors have never ceased to demand that learning shall be kept in touch with reality. But having recalled their notable campaign, have I also the right to plead mitigating circumstances on behalf of poor groping researchers?

It will be as well at the outset to remind ourselves that we are not after all without some useful works on the technical equipment of societies in the past.[4] To be sure, there are not enough of them, and they are too widely disposed over the whole field of enquiry. They are often the work of several groups of researchers who are frequently ignorant of one another's existence – archaeologists, ethnographers, linguists, historians almost exclusively accustomed to dealing with texts. And most of all, they have never been systematically catalogued, so that even those who are most skilful at finding their way among libraries risk missing the best of them altogether. Above all, these works of research lie on the frontiers of the territory traditionally marked out for our studies and are, so to speak, towed along in the wake of 'history in the grand manner'. Yet the results which are being elaborated at the cost of infinitely laborious work do not deserve to be left in the shadow just because explorers are sometimes inclined to let discoveries go to their head.

But this is not all, or even the most serious of the difficulties. However close the historian may stick to the realities of life, he will always remain the slave of certain other realities, which are nonetheless concrete and compelling even though his readers (through his own fault) are unaware of them – I refer to the meagreness of the available information. There is general agreement that the history of technical progress is in a very backward state; but it is only fair to ask whether this backwardness is not due, at least in part, to the extreme difficulty of writing it. However, the obstacles are not, I think, insurmountable, provided that we see them clearly for what they are.

There seem to be three large groups of documents which appear in themselves to be capable of shedding some light on mediaeval technical equipment – namely texts, iconography, and material objects. Unfortunately, the information that comes to us from all these three sources is extremely fragmentary and uncertain.

The labours of artisans lack glamour, and have very seldom attracted the notice of chronicles. An episode picked out by chance in the annals of an English monastery gives an accurate idea of what may be hoped for from this kind of source, and more particularly reveals the extent of our ignorance. In 1295, the Dunstable annalist relates, Brother John de Charpentier constructed a horse-driven mill of a new type, which he was quite certain could be worked by a single horse. But when the contrivance was finished it became apparent that it could scarcely be operated by four of the stoutest animals, and there was nothing else to do but abandon it.[5] This adventure finds a place in the annals because its hero was a monk, and perhaps also because it shows up a fellow-monk in a slightly ridiculous situation. But its interest for today lies in the taste for experiment that it reveals. How many similar groping efforts, sometimes doomed to failure, sometimes crowned with greater success, must have gone to the making of technical progress! But Brother John was alone, or almost alone, in finding a historian. Here and there, no doubt, a chronicle or a charter makes a more or less obscure reference to some new instrument or procedure; but what proof is there that this indicates the date of the invention rather than simply the date of its adoption? The very words are lacking in precision: technical vocabulary has always shown itself conservative in devising new expressions, and the motorist who talks at the present time about his *voiture* is not the first man to stick an ancient label on a brand-new object.

Because they are visible objects and were intended to be looked at, miniatures, bas-reliefs and seals might at first sight appear to be rather more reliable in their testimony. But they were often very clumsy in design, and for a long time fidelity to the truth was the last thing their designers took into consideration; human portraiture was not the only province of mediaeval art in which realism was a late growth. Above all, the artists or craftsmen were only too ready to go on reproducing traditional and conventional patterns, in the same way that the clergy whose business it was to seal the decrees of the German boy-king Louis went on using an ancient jewel which depicted the prince – who died at the age of nineteen – with a growth of beard as luxuriant as that of the Emperor Hadrian.[6] In the same way, as M. Lefebvre des Noëttes informs us, many illuminated manuscripts continued obstinately to depict obsolete kinds of harness when no one for generations had harnessed their oxen or horses in that manner.

As for the material objects, the majority of them have perished. Even if there are by chance a few survivors, there is no inscription or guiding mark as a rule to enable us to determine even within broad limits the date when they were made. By way of contrast, consider an exceptionally favourable case – the Gothic arch. Although the origin of this admirable creation is veiled in obscurity, and although its true significance – practical or purely ornamental – is hotly debated at the present time,[7] we can at any rate more or less follow its development. This is because the building of churches seemed sufficiently important events for writers to take the trouble to record them. More particularly, it is because a large number of ancient churches are still standing, and the experts engaged in classifying them as national monuments are provided with valuable cross-checks both in their style of building and in their decoration. A millwheel, a plough, a horse-shoe, a rustic spinning-wheel on the other hand have no style. Moreover the long and peaceful use to which these instruments have usually been put is an additional obstacle to fixing their precise date of origin. Our civilisation is mortal, but it is not yet dead: the archaeologist has a perfect right to say that it has at present no ruins. No doubt a skilful research-worker, by scrutinising a piece of equipment, or the remains of it, can reconstitute some extremely useful chronological series, as students of prehistory have so brilliantly demonstrated. But here the very limitations of his knowledge work to the scholar's advantage. As soon as he has succeeded in establishing the order in which the various techniques have succeeded one another, he can happily rest content with very rough guesses as to the length of time a particular process was used and the intervals that elapsed between the adoption of each process. For as he has at his disposal, in the nature of the case, only one single kind of document, he has no need to concern himself with synchronising his findings with other chains of evidence. In short, for the student of prehistory, it is permissible to say – with a touch of exaggeration – that a civilisation is willy-nilly nothing but a workshop. For the historian properly so-called, it is this (though some are apt to forget the fact), but it is at the same time something much more than this. Hence it comes about that we feel much more obliged than our colleagues to date things 'to a nicety', as the old saying was; for without this there could be no possible comparison between the various categories of events, and so no possible research into causes.

The candid picture I have set before you may perhaps make the historians of mediaeval techniques hope that they will be judged with some indulgence. But I should be extremely sorry if any research-worker were to take this as a counsel of despair. Hard as the task may be, not all the possible fields of exploration are equally unfavourable. It has sometimes chanced that inventions have led to legal battles, as in the case of the watermill, but not for instance in the case of harness. The word 'lawsuit' or even 'quarrel' at once conjures up a vision of much paper – in other words, of documents. If the men of the Middle Ages had not been so fond of lawsuits, what would the mediaevalists have to work upon? Moreover, when one kind of testimony taken by itself is unable to provide us with information, it often happens that several series put side by side do produce extremely fruitful results. We must once again stress the point that it is only through the various disciplines working in alliance that we can hope for a little more light upon the fact – an alliance, let me reiterate, deliberately planned and provided with adequate material equipment in the way of catalogues and indexes. We shall never know all we should like to know. But we could know a great deal more than at present. And what we need to know touches the very depths of our social life; it concerns not only the most obviously influential factors but others exerting a more subtle influence. If the historian is to provide a history of science, he will have to exercise a little of the patience and ingenuity that the great scholars of former generations brought to the unravelling of royal genealogies.

III

Mediaeval 'inventions', we often call them. It is quite certain, however, that this is an over-simplification covering, in fact, a range of singularly diverse phenomena. Without in the least claiming to exhaust a very lengthy list which is full of uncertainties, we can perhaps give a few examples that will show how necessary it is to have some classification.

Sometimes the Middle Ages did not do more than spread, under the influence of new social conditions, a piece of equipment or a method that had long been known in Europe. The watermill is an example. So is the three-course rotation of crops, the first evidence of which comes from the Treviri at the beginning of our era when it was used as a purely temporary expedient.[8] It is moreover common knowledge that a large part of Europe always refused to adopt the system. These two examples are significant inasmuch as each of them represents the heritage of different civilisations which have come down to the Middle Ages and to ourselves. The watermill came from the Mediterranean: but the three-course rotation of crops came from the agricultural communities of the North. The intellectual sphere is not the only one which can benefit from a blend of traditions.

Elsewhere, there was more borrowing, but this time from foreign civilisations. The stirrup, as far as we can see, was a gift from the horsemen of the Eurasian steppes, the Alans, and the Sarmatians. Several groups of these people settled as military colonies in the Roman Empire; there was a long period when the Goths lived alongside them, on the Black Sea; finally both groups fled before the Huns and came into close contact with the Western world towards the beginning of the Middle Ages. At almost the same moment China – and through her Japan – seems to have had the same gift conferred on them. These roving bands of raiders who one after another threatened the settled peoples of the East and the West were forging a kind of link between these distant societies.[9] A good deal later on, the windmill must have come to us from the Islamic East. These actions and reactions open the mind to large problems, which likewise deserve further study. It is fashionable nowadays, even in the text-books, to set side by side in carefully arranged parallel columns the history of Asia and the history of Europe. But this procedure does not do much to solve the problems of mutual influence, which are of paramount importance. It may well be that they hold some surprises in store for us. For instance, M. Georges Bratiana recently showed us how the hennin worn by Christian ladies in the 15th century, giving them a silhouette 'like horns and branches', had been passed down through the courts of the Levant, and was an imitation – almost a copy – of a headdress much favoured by elegant Chinese ladies in the reign of Hang.[10]

Other improvements, even inventions in the full sense of the word, certainly seem to have taken place during the Middle Ages and on our soil. This is true of the 'modern' methods of harnessing whose appearance in illuminated manuscripts, dating from shortly after the year 900, has been described by M. Lefebvre des Noëttes; this is probably also true of the mysterious spinning-wheel, the first known mention of which occurs at the end of the 13th century;[11] perhaps likewise for the compass, if, as its most recent historian seems to have proved, we must consign to the realm of fable the tradition of its Chinese or Arabic origin.[12] Here, the problem confronting us is no longer to trace on the map the routes along which influences may have travelled; it is above all to search for causes, about which we shall have something to say in a moment.

Let there be no mistake, however. Borrowings and inventions, when looked at closely, all bear witness to one thing: the remarkable dexterity of hand and mind and eye. In this faculty for renewal, widespread even at the artisan level, we must surely recognise one of the sources of European greatness which can be seen rising with such astonishing vigour in the most troubled times. In other words *homo europaeus* was essentially *homo faber*, not only because he knew how to create, but also – at least up to the 19th century – because he knew how to imitate or adapt; and with this mixture of ability he succeeded in building up a technical civilisation.

IV

The title of M. Lefebvre des Noëttes's book, which has been considerably modified in its second edition, and has now become famous, is as follows: *L'attelage et le cheval de selle à travers les âges*; and the sub-title is: *Contribution à l'histoire de l'esclavage*. In other words, it is concerned both with the purely technical world and with its relationship to the structure of society.

I will not here hark back in detail to the first group of problems, although they open up enormous fields of thought, as is shown by the article of M. Jules Sion on this work.[13] It is questionable, for instance, whether those wishing to compare the tractive effort of draught-animals nowadays and in former times have sufficiently realised that they are following a fallacious line of argument. For the motive power itself has changed, thanks to the patient selective breeding carried out by stockmen, thanks above all to the agricultural revolution, and in particular to the coming of artificial food-stuffs. What help could the country ploughs expect from those oxen or cows described in a curiously unanimous fashion in folklore from Norway to Maine, who were so weak after the famine conditions of winter that they had to be helped on to their feet by their tails?[14] The strength of animal muscle has not proved a more stable factor in history than human muscle – perhaps even less so. Moreover, among all M. Lefebvre des Noëttes's equine and archaeological science his most significant discovery was obviously that which concerns the methods of harnessing animals, for the saddle-horse never played anything like as important a role in human destiny as the waggon or the plough. But this fundamental progress was itself the result of several improvements taking place at the same time, namely the replacement of the throat-collar – which threatened to strangle the animal as soon as it made the slightest effort – by the shoulder-collar, the invention of which allowed it to exert the maximum pull; the shoeing of oxen and horses; and harnessing in line. The history of the harnessing in line and even the history of the horseshoe – not perhaps a native invention of the West – still leaves us with more than one obscure point to clear up.[15] On the subject of harnessing, I am not aware that the author's conclusions have ever been seriously contested. The most one can hope for by carrying out a fresh search through the illuminated manuscripts is to arrive at a few more accurate dates.[16] For – to state it another way – that would be the next great discovery. I think I was one of the first historians to put this in so many words. And I stand by what I have said. For let us once more admit that the first requirement for anyone aspiring to write history is a good pair of eyes – not to be used only for poring and straining over charters.

M. Lefebvre des Noëttes, however, attributes an enormously far-reaching effect to this technical revolution that he has so effectively brought to light – nothing less than the abolition of slavery by rendering it useless. When animals had become capable of ten times their former tractive effort, he argues that they set men free. But this is certainly not true. To posit a cause is to establish an order of precedence; but the decline of slavery did not follow the transformation of harnessing methods – it took place before it.[17]

The purest type of slave in antiquity has been a veritable domestic animal – a comparison often used by the texts themselves. We must remember that his whole working potential was at the disposal of his master, without restriction as to the kind of work he did or the length of time he was employed; consequently it was from his master that he received board and lodging, seeing that he himself was incapable of earning anything or cultivating land on his own account. From the end of the Roman Empire onwards, however, this system, which had figured prominently in the economy of the preceding centuries, began to show signs of decadence. It is possible that the invasions, by throwing a large number of prisoners of war on to the market, revived it for a time. But under the early Carolingians, its fate was sealed. No doubt there were still slaves in existence, in the legal sense of the term. But they were relatively few. Some of them were attached to seignorial houses or enterprises, and certainly went on in the ancient traditional ways of servile labour. But most of them were now settled on lands which they worked themselves and for which they paid dues. They had ceased to live at their master's expense, or to work continuously for him. To be sure, the slaves who had been 'housed' ('*chasés*'*) were still obliged to render very onerous services, as well as pay a variety of taxes; and these services were often enough, in theory, quite unlimited. Nevertheless in practice the lord was not allowed to command more than a share of their time, for it was necessary to leave them leisure to cultivate their own fields. From these they drew both the living that they were no longer supplied with direct and the necessary income for paying their dues, in money or in kind. Indeed, it was only the hope of such revenues that had induced the proprietor to break off so many fragments of land from his estate. Now a slave who is responsible for his own subsistence, who pays rent and has control over a good deal of his time, would hardly seem, either by his way of life or by his role as producer, to be still a slave. And so the relaxation of economic subjection rapidly brought about the weakening of the bonds of slavery in general. From the 11th century onwards, it was freely admitted that whereas in former times the tenant of servile birth had been under no law but the arbitrary caprice of his master, his obligations henceforward, like those of 'free' dependants, were regulated by the custom of the group. By the time that modern harnessing had appeared on the scene – about the 10th century, as M. Lefebvre des Noëttes reckons – the great social revolution, whose first fruits we have just considered, had taken place. It did not altogether follow the lines which had seemed likely when the ancient world was crumbling to pieces. For new circumstances had arisen since

* For a discussion of this development see Marc Bloch's *Feudal Society*, Vol. 1, p. 163, trans. L. A. Manyon, pub. Routledge, Kegan Paul (paper), 1965. (Trans.)

the invasions, multiplying the ties of personal dependence among all ranks of society from the top to the bottom. Among contemporaries of the first Capetians, there were an infinitely larger number of people whose status was deemed servile than in Charlemagne's days. But these 'serfs' who had inherited the former name for slaves (*servi*), were not in most cases their descendants, nor did they live in a state of submission like that of the one-time slaves. What had changed in the meantime was the very notion of freedom or absence of freedom. From now onwards a man would be considered free if he could escape from all hereditary subjection; on the other hand, it became more and more usual for a man to be deemed unfree if he had been bound to a lord from birth, and was unable to sever the bonds for the whole of his life-time, and if his lord was unwilling to release him. This did not mean however that their persons or their labour belonged to him in an unlimited fashion. Settled as he was on land whose whole produce – apart from the dues – belonged to him, and liable only to charges defined by custom, and subject, moreover, to constantly diminishing labour services, the serf was not in any respect mere 'motive-power' at the disposal of his master.

This is not to say that slavery properly so called had completely disappeared from the face of Europe. On German estates the conditions of life imposed on some of the lord's dependants, who owed him almost daily services, were closely reminiscent of ancient slavery. More particularly in the various regions on the fringe of the Catholic world, or in those which had close trade relations with exotic civilisations, such as Eastern and South-Eastern Germany, Spain, Provence and Italy, the fortunes of war or the slave-trade continued to provide the propertied classes with a supply of human cattle. As many of these poor creatures came from the Slav countries, it became customary to use their very general ethnic label as a name for their status, and this is the origin of the word 'slave'. The very appearance of this term – though it cannot as yet be accurately dated – is enough to show how far the old word *servus* had strayed in common parlance from its primitive significance. This was a very ancient wine which really needed a new bottle. The progress of trade from the 12th century onwards had the effect of making human merchandise much more plentiful in the Mediterranean basin than it had been in previous centuries. Except in certain parts of Spain, however, these Greek, Slavonic, Negro and Moorish slaves were hardly ever employed at anything but household or artisan work. Their economic role remained therefore a good deal inferior to that of their equals in the Roman world; but this is not to say that it was negligible. Thus it was that when modern methods of harnessing first appeared and found slavery moribund, they were not even capable of completing its downfall.

It would be extremely rash to attempt at this point to analyse in a few words the causes leading to its long and rather irregular decline. But a few very simple remarks will at least allow me to point out one of the paths which it looks as though research should follow. Servile labour – as the Ancient World perfectly well knew – nearly always produces an extremely feeble output. Many hands are needed to accomplish relatively little work. It was thus a form of capital that only brought in a very mediocre return, especially as the slave's subsistence had to be reckoned as a cost, reducing the value of his work. Moreover slavery was a fragile form of capital, and frequent replenishments were necessary. Now the birthrate among personnel on the estate was practically never high enough to furnish the necessary supply. Experience proves that human livestock are one of the most difficult of all to rear. In order therefore to prove profitable, large-scale slavery needed – almost on its doorstep – an abundant supply of new and cheap human flesh. What other ways were there of procuring it except through war and raiding? For the slave has always been first and foremost a captive. In other words, a society could hardly found its economy on human slavery unless it had within easy reach other more decadent societies whom it could fight and plunder. Thus from the 16th to the 19th centuries colonial Europe confronted black Africa; today it is Abyssinia (or was until very recently), surrounded by primitive and poorly armed tribes; in former times it was the Roman Empire. The military decay of Rome beneath the repeated onslaughts of the Persians and the barbarians was one of the most powerful causes of the decline of slavery in the twilight days of the classical civilisations. As for the West during the Middle Ages, it certainly indulged in plenty of fighting. But its wars were mostly internal struggles. And by this time a religious idea was beginning to have some influence over affairs. The Church did not condemn slavery in itself; but having imposed upon the ancient notion of the city the words *societas christiana*, it held all Christians – or, more accurately, all Catholics – to be fellow-countrymen. It would not therefore permit them to make slaves by warfare among themselves. Thus the servile masses of former times dwindled in number as slaves were transformed into tenants without any new entrants being recruited to make up this constant drain. This essentially explains why the ancient word *servus* came to describe a very different set of dependent relationships; and why slavery on the ancient model only survived or reappeared under a new name in places where infidel territories lay close at hand or were within easy reach by means of trade.

Even if they had not done more than remind us of the great contrast between civilisations with, and without, slave labour M. Lefebvre des Noettes's researches would have justified themselves. For this is one of the problems which the historian of the Middle Ages has for too long passed over in silence. But there is more to it than that. It seems that the idea of function ought to be retained in the bold causal connection that our author proposes between two apparently very remote phenomena – the invention of a new harnessing collar, and the disappearance of the cruellest form of human subjection; but it ought to be widened, and the order of its terms should be reversed.

It would certainly be puerile to claim that all improvements in the technical equipment of the Middle Ages were inspired by one ruling idea. Nevertheless one can hardly fail to observe that several of them – and not the least important – are linked by a common factor. Mills driven by water or by wind; mills for corn-grinding, for tanning, for fulling; hydraulic saw-mills, blacksmith's drop-hammers; shoulder-collars, the shoeing of draught-animals, harnessing in line; even the invention of the spinning-wheel: all these represent progressive steps towards a more effective use of natural forces, animate or inanimate, and hence led to economies in human labour, or – what comes to much the same thing – a more productive return. Why was this? Perhaps because there were fewer men available; but most of all because the master had fewer slaves. Consider the history of the mill, which provides such a perfect test case. The spread of this admirable contrivance was certainly not, as M. Lefebvre des Noëttes would appear to believe, a result of the improvement in methods of harnessing. The evidence of the dates is plainly against any such supposition. On the contrary, the more effective use of animal motive-power and the harnessing of water-power were developments that took place simultaneously, for the very good reason that they originated in the same need. Was the decline of slavery then a result of this? By no means: it was much more probably a cause, leading on to a technical revolution, which was destined in its turn – we need hardly say – to have powerful repercussions on the structure of society. This at any rate is a working hypothesis and for the moment, this is all that can be claimed for it; but if in the course of closer investigation it were to lose much of its first simplicity, it is to be hoped that it will have proved sufficiently fertile to justify putting it forward.[18]

NOTES

1. *Annales d'histoire économique et sociale*, no. 36, Nov. 1935, pp. 634–644.
2. A. Vierendeel, *Esquisse d'une histoire de la technique*, Louvain, 1921, Vol. I, p. 44.
3. M. Lefebvre des Noëttes has given a general list of technical inventions and improvements which he considers to be mediaeval in origin in the *Mercure de France*, Vol. CCXXXV, 1932: *La 'nuit' du Moyen Age et son inventaire*. His original study came out first in 1924, when its title was *La force animale à travers les âges* (cf. a résumé of its essential themes of the author himself in *La Nature*, 1927, Vol. I. The book was re-edited in 1931, with considerable additions and under a new title: *L'attelage et le cheval de selle à travers les âges. Contribution à l'histoire de l'esclavage*, Paris, 1931; 1 vol. of text and one of plates (cf. my review in *Annales*, Vol. IV, 1932, p. 483). It contains more especially some very novel views on the Roman roads already advanced in an article in the *Revue archéologique*, 1925, Vol. II, p. 105. Nowhere has M. Lefebvre des Noëttes better expressed his healthy scepticism towards conven-

tional history than in this brief study of roads. And it has breathed new life into our historical studies. At the same time he came to grips with the problem of the rudder in *Le gouvernail: contribution à l'histoire de l'esclavage*, published in *Mémoires de la Société des Antiquaires de France*, Vol. LXXVIII, 1932; *Autour du vaisseau de Boro-Boudour: l'invention du gouvernail (Contribution à l'histoire de l'esclavage)*, in *Nature*, 1936, I; *De la marine antique à la marine moderne*, Paris, 1935. A mere landsman like myself must observe a discreet silence when it comes to delicate questions of naval archeology. A whole literature of reviews and criticisms has grown up round what I shall venture to call the 'Lefebvre des Noëttes problem'. I confine myself to citing one article by M. Roger Grand, *La force motive animale à travers les âges et son influence sur l'évolution sociale*, in *Bulletin de la Société Internationale de Science Sociale*, 1926; and because I shall later take up some of the ideas expressed in them – my two comments in the *Revue de synthèse historique: Technique et évolution sociale*, Vol. XLI, 1926, and *La force motive animale et le rôle des inventions techniques*, Vol. XLIII, 1927 (with a letter from M. Lefebvre des Noëttes). On the other hand it does not seem as though M. Lefebvre des Noëttes's studies have generally met with the attention abroad that they certainly deserve.

4. For general histories of technical improvements, see above pp. 166 ff. the 'Bibliographical Note', added as an appendix to M. Bloch's article on the watermill.
5. *Annales monastici*, edit. Luard, *Rolls Series*, Vol. III, p. 402.
6. Percy E. Schramm, *Die deutschen Kaiser und Könige in Bildern ihrer Zeit*, Vol. I, 1928, p. 5.
7. Cf. the notice by M. Louis Lacrocq, *Annales d'Hist. Ec. et. Soc.*, no. 37, Vol. VII, pp. 644–646.
8. Cf. *Annales*, Vol. VI, 1934, p. 479.
9. On the stirrup (apart from M. Lefebvre des Noëttes's book) see E. H. Minns, *Scythians and Greeks*, 1913, pp. 250 and 277. (cf. p. 75), and especially M. Rostovtzeff, *Iranians and Greeks in South Russia*, 1922, pp. 121 and 130. The Scythians, who were the predecessors of the Sarmatians, had no knowledge of the stirrup. Cf. also the fruitful suggestions made by E. Gautier, *Genséric, roi des Vandales*, p. 80. For Spain, see the useful information in Cl. Sanchez-Albornoz, *Estampas de la vide en León hace mit años*, 2nd edit., 1934, p. 134, no. 18.
10. *Anciennes modes orientales à la fin du Moyen Age*, in *Seminarium Kondakovianum*, Prague, Vol. III, 1935, pp. 165–168. This short article is full of ingenious and suggestive lines of thought.
11. At Spires, to be precise, in 1298 (*Zeitschrift für die Geschichte des Oberrheins*, Vol. XV, 1863, p. 281).
12. See O. von Lippmann, *Geschichte der Magnetnadel*, 1922, in *Quellen und Studien zur Geschichte der Naturwissenschaften*, Vol. III, 1. The argument appears to be convincing. On the other hand the author does not seem to have produced any proof for the Scandinavian origin which he attributes to this invention. At the beginning of the 14th century Hank

Erlendsson, reproducing the ancient stories of the capture of Iceland by the Norwegians (*Landnámabók*), observed that at this period 'the seamen of the North did not as yet possess the magnetic compass-needle' (cf. E. M. Carus Wilson, *The Iceland Trade*, in E. Power and M. M. Postan, *Studies in English trade in the fifteenth century*, 1933, p. 160). On this subject I would like to point out that in all studies bearing on the technical equipment of ships and the possibilities that lay within their reach adequate attention should be paid to the ocean exploits of the Vikings. 'We have recently become aware that large-scale voyages dates from the 13th century,' wrote M. Paul Valéry in *L'idée fixe* (p. 38). Fortunately this is not so; if we accepted this statement we should be making a great mistake.

13. *Annales d'Histoire économique et Sociale*, No. 1935, Vol. VII, pp. 628–633. Cf. also, by the same author, *Notes sur les répercussions sociales d'une technique*, in *Annales sociologiques*, Series E, section 1, 1934, pp. 117–123.

14. R. Musset, *Le Bas-Maine*, p. 307, and Magnus Olsen, *Farms and fanes of ancient Norway*, p. 10.

15. Cf. G. Méautis, *Les Romains connaissaient-ils le fer à cheval?* in *Revue des études anciennes*, 1934, p. 88. On this subject, great importance should be attached to the *Tactica* of the Emperor Leo. Contrary to what I suggested in the *Annales* (Vol. V, 1932, p. 484), recent work agreed with the dating of this treatise adopted by M. Lefebvre des Noëttes, who attributes it to Leo VI; cf. *Byzantinische Zeitschrift*, Vol. XXX, 1929–1930, p. 396. On the other hand the MS. no. 764 from Saint-Omer is certainly of the 10th, and not of the 9th, century.

16. At present nothing is more uncertain than this chronology. As M. Roger Grand rightly observes in the article quoted above, note 3, the shoulder and collar had probably been in use a good while before the artists, who liked always to reproduce traditional forms, decided to introduce it into their pictures. It would be safest to say that the new-style harness was illustrated for the first time (as far as we can tell) in the 10th century, and not that it was *invented* at that time. It would seem that M. Lefebvre des Noëttes has sometimes allowed himself to slip inadvertently from the first statement into the second.

17. A Belgian scholar, M. Ch. Verlinden, is at present engaged in important research on mediaeval slavery, the results of which will no doubt open up the subject afresh. Moreover the history of slavery proper is closely linked up with that of ties of dependence in general as conceived by the societies of the West. There, too, our knowledge is in a state of flux and growth. The outline put before the reader here aims only at presenting in a deliberately schematic form the most important facts that are more or less generally agreed. More especially I have had to give up any attempt to do full justice to regional shades of difference. For the bibliography of slavery, I refer the reader – while awaiting M. Verlinden's results – to my two notes in the *Revue de synthèse historique* quoted above in note 3, and the various reviews in *Annales* (notably Vol. I, 1929, p. 98, and Vol. IV, 1932, p. 597). On

ties of dependence and their connection with the idea of liberty, see especially my article entitled *Liberté et servitude personnelles au Moyen Age*, in *Annario de historia del derecho español*, 1933, and *Mélanges historiques*, Vol. 1, pp. 286–355. See also M. Ch. Edmond-Perrin's review in *Annales*, Vol. VI, 1934, p. 274.

18 As M. Sion has rightly observed, an exact relationship between the invention of a new system of harnessing and conditions of human labour will only be clearly proved if it can be demonstrated that before the spread of the new-style harness, men generally carried loads on their backs. When I was correcting the proofs of this article I happened to read about some of these mediaeval coolies. Part of the forced labour that the monks of Saint-Vanne exacted from their *homines de potestate* domiciled at Laumesfeld in Lorraine was 'the obligation to carry grain a distance of six miles *cum collo*' (quoted by Ch. Edmond Perrin, *Recherches sur la seigneurie rurale en Lorraine*, 1935, p. 666, note 4). On the other hand the polyptique of Saint-Germain-des-Prés mentions several times, along with carts, certain services designated as *portaturæ*; and here too the distances mentioned are far from negligible (cf. B. Guérard, *Polyptyque de l'abbé Irminon*, Vol. I, 2, p. 773). I do not think any requirement of this kind can be found later than the 12th century. The disappearance of the *portaturae*, however, is of no interest to the historian of slavery proper. Although most – but not indeed all – of the dependants of Saint-Germain on whom this obligation fell are characterised as *Servi*, it must not be forgotten that in spite of their personal status, these tenants enjoyed a kind of life vastly different from that of the ancient slave. As for the *homo de potestate* of the 11th century, it goes without saying that there was nothing of the slave about him. It seems then that there is a real relationship between the progress of animal traction and forced labour in the broadest sense of the term, though it would be difficult to state precisely the nature of the connection – whether for instance technical improvements reduced the previously heavy demands, or whether, on the other hand, the difficulty of getting people to perform such hard labour drove men to find a more efficient method of using draught-animals. In any case our available documentation is still rather slight. Enquiring research-workers, please take note!

7

THE PROBLEM OF GOLD IN THE MIDDLE AGES[1]

Of all the barometers capable of revealing to the historian the deeper movements of an economy, monetary phenomena are without doubt the most sensitive. But to look upon them as a symptom only is to do them less than justice: they have been, and they are, in their turn, effective causes. One might think of them as a seismograph that not only registers earth tremors, but sometimes brings them about. This amounts to saying that when we really know the history of gold – or, more accurately, the history of gold as a medium of exchange – during the Middle Ages, a flood of light will be shed upon many hidden trends and connections which at present elude our understanding. Unfortunately the facts are far from clear; they have moreover been inadequately studied, and often from a point of view different from that of today. The study of numismatics has had difficulty in emerging from the world of museum displays and curiosity shops. For the present, I do not propose to do more than state the big problems and suggest some solutions, which, though admittedly provisional and conjectural, will nevertheless serve as a working hypothesis.[2]

*   *   *

Mediaeval Europe inherited its money system from the Roman Empire. It could not well have been otherwise, since the Germans – in this respect more backward than the Gauls – did not with some exceptions possess any monetary system of their own before the time of the Conquest. In more precise terms, Europe inherited a system that had been reorganised by the Constantinian monarchy after the troubles of the 3rd century. The fundamental unit was a piece of 'solid gold', the *aureus solidus*, the *sou*, which in principle contained 4 qr. 48 of fine metal, equivalent in gold content to a little less than 76 French francs of today.* There were also gold coins of lower denominations in circulation, worth half a *sou* and a third of a *sou* respectively. Alongside these gold coins, silver and copper ones were also minted. The rate of exchange as between these various coins was regulated by the State. The barbarian monarchies at once took over this regime as far as they were able. But in the event (except in the North of England, where precious metals were no doubt rather rare), a copper coinage soon had to be abandoned; it was a true money of account whose value bore no relationship to its metal content. Neither the State – which had become too feeble – nor the private moneyers had the necessary authority to validate the circulation of a purely token coinage. Gold and silver, on the other hand, continued to be worked at the mints; the Visigoths, the Lombards, the Franks and the Anglo-Saxons all struck *sous*, and more particularly coins representing a third of a *sou*. But this did not continue for very long.

From the beginning of the Carolingian period, in fact, a monetary schism, which was a symptom of deeper divisions within the economic order, came into being and split Europe. The Byzantine world remained faithful to gold. Under the new names of νόμισμα and then ὑπέρπυρον, the Constantine *sou* never ceased to be minted. Its metallic content was no doubt far from stable, and it underwent various fluctuations, now rising and now falling in value. Above all it seems that a series of slow convergent movements combined to whittle down its value. A variety of reasons appear to have been relentlessly at work leading to this inevitable conclusion; the principal among these seems to have been the necessity to put new coins into circulation at the value of the old, which were constantly becoming worn. In spite of all these hazards, however, the *aureus* survived triumphantly down the ages. About 1200 the *hyperperon* was still worth, in fine metal weight, some three-quarters or thereabouts of its Roman ancestor. The Arab monarchies, for their part, found in the two sets of traditions upon which their administrative system was based – that of the Sassanidae of Persia and that of the Basileis of new Rome – the tradition of a monetary system based on gold; and to this

* Presumably of January 31st, 1933, the date of this article. (Trans.)

system they remained faithful. Let us not forget, moreover, that neither Byzantium nor Islam was during the Middle Ages synonymous with the East. Gold pieces bearing the names of the masters of each country continued to form the basis of the coinage not only in the Balkans, the Levant and the Magrab, but even in southern Italy, which was first Byzantine and then partially Arab, in Sicily – Byzantine at first and then Arab – and finally over the greater part of Spain. To this list we must add, far away in the east and for a short while only, Russia under the Varangians.[3] Thus we have before us a map of the official minting of gold from the middle of the 9th to the middle of the 13th century.

The West on the other hand, whether in the Latin or the Germanic tradition, had followed quite a different path. In the Frankish State – which by the end of the 8th century had absorbed northern · and central Italy – Charlemagne and Louis the Pious were still issuing some gold pieces; but the latter at any rate only from a very few mints and for quite exceptional needs. None of their successors repeated the experiment. With the Anglo-Saxons, the minting of gold, – imitations apart – (we shall return to this matter later on), had by this time long ceased to be of any importance, though one can still discern sporadic activity down to the time of Ethelred II (998–1016). From then onwards the mints working in ancient *Romania* – which soon became innumerable – together with the new mints that gradually grew up in the countries formerly without any national coinage (Germany to the east of the Rhine, Bohemia, Poland, the Scandinavian States), seemed only to produce silver coins, and nearly always of one single denomination – the *denier*.[4] The *denier* first saw the light in Frankish Gaul – or more accurately, in the form in which it spread across Europe – in Carolingian Gaul. It was gradually adopted by the whole of the West, England for her part abandoning her *sceatta*, which were far too light. The *denier* itself however still weighed very little: in Charlemagne's time it would have been the equivalent of about ·30 pre-war francs; in the France of Philip Augustus – taking the *denier* '*tournois*' as a basis of comparison – about ·08 francs. The *sou* existed simply as an accounting unit: reckoning was still done in *sous*, but whenever payment was made in coin and in native coin, it was made in *deniers*, the equivalence being generally fixed – though not in all countries – at twelve *deniers* to a *sou*. It was in this sense that people spoke of silver *sous* – meaning *sous* represented by a payment in silver pieces; similarly when it was a matter of a payment in kind they spoke of '*sous de grains*'.[5] Over long centuries, the word 'money' in the West meant almost exclusively silver; an equivalence of meaning which has left clear traces in the French language.

There came a moment however when it ceased to be based upon actuality. True, it is wrong to invoke the effects of events occurring in countries snatched from Islam or Byzantium by the Catholic princes, as has sometimes been done. When Alphonso VIII began to strike the first Castilian gold coins at Toledo in 1175, he was only following the example of the Khalifs or emirs who had preceded him, on whom moreover he modelled himself. If he made the decision at this particular moment, the reason doubtless was that the Musulman mint at Marcia, which was largely responsible for supplying Léon and Castile, had just ceased operations.[6] Moreover, this continuity was such a perceptible feature that in France during the 13th century it was current practice to call the Christian *anfous* by the same name that was customarily given to the Almoravid *dinars*, namely *marabotins*.[7] In the same way, the Norman conquerors of southern Italy and Sicily, with their famous *taris*, simply replaced the former masters of the land. Nothing in the monetary map of Europe had changed. Nor was there any change when Frederick II created the *augustales*, issued at Messina and Brindisi. The real revolution came when the countries which until that moment in the High Middle Ages had minted nothing officially, except silver, returned to gold.

The merchant cities of the Mediterranean lost the initiative. In 1227 Marseilles, which had been provisionally made into an autonomous commune, induced the Imperial Vicar to grant her the right to strike gold coins, though she was certainly not able to take advantage of it.[8]

The step was not taken till 1252, at Genoa and Florence simultaneously. Then the movement reached Perugia (1258),

Lucca (shortly before 1273), Milan towards the end of the century at an uncertain date, and finally Venice, which began in 1284 to issue its famous ducats. Minting at Florence in particular underwent a great expansion in the early years. By 1265 at the latest, its florins, stamped with the emblem of the fleur-de-lys, were being negotiated in the fairs of Champagne. A rise in the rate of exchange occurred that year at the fair of Saint-Ayoul of Provins through the purchase of florins by Charles of Anjou for the purposes of his Sicilian expedition.[9] These coins served as a model for most of the transalpine minting houses, for the example of Italy was soon followed beyond the Alps. Naturally, the first effort in this direction came from the two chief monarchies of the West – from England in 1257, and from France at about the same time, under Saint-Louis. In neither country was the issue more than moderately successful. It was only in the reign of Philip the Fair that the French coins became really important. In England, where the Florentine Pegolotti noted about 1340 that there were no gold coins on the London market,[10] the attempt was not resumed till nearly a century later, in 1344. Meanwhile, however, the rich principalities of the Low Countries – Flanders between 1300 and 1312, Brabant between 1300 and 1315, Hainault, Luxembourg, the bishopric of Liège in the first half of the century – had undertaken the minting of their own 'florins'.[11] In the same way Hungary issued them between 1308 and 1342, taking advantage of her own deposits of precious metal. Then in 1325 it was the King of Bohemia's turn, quickly followed by various German princes, such as the Archbishop of Cologne, the Emperor Louis of Bavaria, the Comte de Görz, the Duke of Austria, and in 1340 by the greatest banking centre of the north – Lübeck.[12] The Roman Curia, which was then at Avignon, had joined the movement in 1322. But this tale of conquest must end here. In the present state of research and with the limited tools available, the story has to be left incomplete. If we knew more of the detail it would doubtless reveal many periods when the trend was reversed (to these we shall later return) and many hesitations. Poland, on the extreme fringe of the Catholic world, only decided to take the plunge in 1528.

The minting of silver had of course not ceased meanwhile so that the new monetary regime may conveniently be called bimetallic, so long as we do not press the analogy with classical bimetallism, as it was to be defined in the 19th century. There was no free right to mint coin – no more than under the Roman Empire. Moreover, as we shall see later, the roles of the two metals in the economy were so different that one cannot call them really interchangeable.

It looks as though the double problem posed by these events can be put fairly simply: why did the greater part of Europe give up the official minting of gold in or about the 9th century, and why did it resume the practice in the 13th? Let us see whether it is possible to find a solution which fits the data outlined above relating to the issue of coins. We can then put it alongside some much more complicated phenomena, which up till now we have had to disregard – namely the state of the circulation, and the existence of a counterfeit coinage.

* * *

One great fact must dominate all attempts at explanation: Western and Central Europe produced very little gold and could not produce more.

This was not the case with silver. The mines at Melle in Poitou helped to provide metal for the Merovingian coinage. Those in the Massif Central not only contributed silver to the French mints during the whole of the Middle Ages; their produce was also exported to England and as far as 'the lands of the Saracens'.[13] The silver-mines in Sardinia largely account for the attraction which this island exerted upon the great conquering republics of Italy – Genoa and Pisa. The opening up of the veins in the Harz Mountains, in the heyday of the Saxon dynasty, gave a solid financial basis to the power of this race of monarchs, and metal from these mines was sold on the English market, too.[14] These are only a few examples picked out from among many. No doubt the mint was often held up by lack of silver; also the right to mint coins was so extremely split up between the various authorities that there were often many mints in the hands of princes who possessed no mines. As late as 1455, the Duke of Bavaria apologised for his inferior coinage on the grounds that he was obliged to buy the raw material from outside sources.[15] It is none the less true that Western and Central Europe as a whole were self-sufficient for their own needs.

On the other hand the shortage of gold was a nuisance worse during the High Middle Ages than previously or subsequently. Since the prehistoric period and since Roman days many of the veins had been exhausted or only yielded minimal quantities of gold; the mines in Ireland, for example, which had produced so abundantly in the Bronze Age, and these in the western Pyrenees, which had been worked in the early days of the Empire. There is nothing peculiar about these facts: 'a vein of gold, *a fortiori* a strip of alluvium,' writes M. de Launay, 'is not like a field that produces a new crop every year; it is like a bag from which one takes the contents until it is empty'.[16] The methods of working, which were extremely elementary, accelerated the exhaustion of the deposits. Moreover the still untapped mines of the eastern Alps and Silesia were apparently not yet known; they do not seem to have been worked before about the year 1200.[17] True, there remained the native gold patiently collected from running water, from the torrents of the Cevennes and the Pyrenees, for example. The Ariège placers* continued to make a contribution to the coinage of Toulouse up to the beginning of the 19th century; and there were also the waters coming down from the Alps to the plains of the River Po and to the terraces of Bavaria.[18] The 'Rheingold' was no myth; it was collected from the 'golden sands' which the poets of Louis the Pious's time, in competition with one another, celebrated in Frankish and Latin verse as one of the greatest gifts of the river. Three centuries later, the monk Theophilus was still describing the work of the searchers for grains of gold-dust along the river sides; and the Alsatian monasteries set such store by the possession of washing-places that they did not scruple to make use of forgeries in order to secure them.[19] But all these sparkling grains, when put together, would certainly not have amounted to much in weight – very little at all events compared with the output of the Urals, the Caucasus, the Altaï and Hindustan, or the rivers of tropical

* An English term, meaning a place where gold is washed. (Trans.)

Africa. There is something strange in the spectacle of countries who were destined, from the end of the Middle Ages to the present day, to be the most lively centres of the world's economic activity, being deprived by nature of the material which an old tradition – stronger now than ever – requires us to consider as the sign and embodiment of all wealth. Perhaps this is only an apparent paradox. Europeans have been condemned to acquire this 'fabulous' metal either by exchange or by conquest; and their original lack of it was no doubt one of the reasons that made them dominate or exploit the world.

But in the High Middle Ages things had not yet reached this point. It is obvious that the minting of gold would only have been possible if one or other of two conditions had been fulfilled. Either it would have been necessary to maintain a pre-existing stock in sufficient quantity; or to establish an exchange rate which would have attracted westwards the gold of the producing countries, or of those who possessed abundant stocks. Let us see what the facts tell us of this matter.

* * *

There is no doubt that in the western part of ancient *Romania*, gold grew steadily more and more scarce from the end of the empire. Symmachus, writing about 384 or 385, notes this phenomenon.[20] The natural result was a rise in the value of gold coins as compared with silver. Whereas in 397 five *sous* equalled the value of a pound of silver, in 422 only four were needed.[21] It was inevitable that the coinage itself should be adversely affected. Such was the case first of all beyond the Alps. The Emperor Majorian, in 458, noted the poor quality of the Gallic *sous*. More than a century later, Pope Gregory the Great noted, in his turn, that they were not accepted as current coin in Italy. This time the remark applied, at least in part, to the coins struck by the barbarian kings established in Gaul. The Burgundian *sous* of Geneva or Valence and those of the Visigoth king Alaric I had a particularly bad reputation.[22] In general there was a marked deterioration in all the barbarian coinages. The *sou*, which was over-heavy, ceased almost completely to be minted. As for the *tiers de sou* (third of a *sou*,) a comparison of its gold-content at the beginning and at the end of the decline is most significant. Under Constantine it weighed 1 gr. 51 of fine gold; under Charlemagne, the total weight was 0 gr. 972 only, of which rather less than 0 gr. 39 was gold – a large proportion of the coin being in fact made of silver.[23] There is no doubt that this was due to the dearth of the prime material, and not merely – as one might be tempted to think – to a weakness in the monetary system. We can tell this from the evidence of the goldsmith's art. To be sure, jewels of gold were still being worn, but the metal in them (as the specialists testify) was being used with the 'strictest economy'.[24] It is clear that when the Carolingians ceased to issue any more gold coins, this was the final stage of a long process of decline.

And it was not only specifically economic facts that were responsible: religion played its part as well. Pagan custom, often continuing after conversion, required that a German chief should be buried with his finery; how many splendid jewels were hidden from human eyes by being shut up in the tomb! Again, political events caused numerous treasures to be buried for safety, and they were not always recovered after the emergency. The gold coins among the treasure found at Beaugisière, in Vendée, were reckoned to number more than three thousand.[25] But it was above all the tribute paid to the invaders that had so cruelly impoverished the imperial stocks of gold. Governments had been disturbed by the fact, but could find no remedy. 'It is not only forbidden to furnish the barbarians with gold' (runs an edict of Valentinian, Valens and Gratian about the year 374), 'skilful efforts must be made to get back from them the gold they already possess.'[26]

Part, no doubt, of the riches thus drained away came back subsequently to *Romania* when it was reconquered. But large quantities – quite independently of the reasons for loss already noted – disappeared for good and all, to find their way into the coffers of the Scandinavian world, for there was a considerable to-and-fro traffic between it and the Empire, some of it being the price of subjection, some of it plunder. Later on, in the days of the sea-kings, the North added to this first influx the booty from raids and the money paid by Frankish or Anglo-Saxon sovereigns by way of ransom, together with other coins or bar metal more honestly come by, such as the wages paid to the merceneries employed by the Greek emperors, or the price of the merchandise brought down the long Russian rivers to the Baltic, en route for the markets of the East. If anyone had ever wanted to see great masses of gold in 9th- and 10th-century Europe, anywhere outside Byzantium, he could probably only have done so in Scandinavia. 'Piracy', so Adam of Bremen informs us, had caused precious metal to be heaped up in the island of Zealand; it glistened from the prows of Cnut the Great's vessels, as it still gleams nowadays in the museum showcases of Stockholm and Copenhagen, whose treasures recall the heroic age.[27] But it was precisely these countries who were at that period ignorant of the art of minting. Gold was used for ornament; and if it was sometimes used for exchange or for the payment of wages, it was only in the form of gold bracelets which the chiefs 'broke' and then distributed to their followers. Towards the end of the 10th century, when the kings began to mint coins, they naturally imitated the coinage of neighbouring States, which was in silver. Soon, moreover, profound changes in the conditions of life – the end of sea raids, and the decay of trade with the East and of Scandinavian trade in general – put an end to the former abundance.

These various considerations, however, are not enough to account for the dearth of gold in the West. The Byzantine East had been equally affected by most of the factors set out above. A victim, like *Romania* in the West, to invasions, she had certainly been exhausted perhaps, even more than her sister, by tribute; she had furnished most of the gold *sous* dated between 395 and 565 which constituted the finds in Scandinavia. In the 6th century Byzantium, too, had experienced a very serious crisis, which was notably a crisis of gold.[28] But it made a remarkably successful recovery, whilst the West continued to struggle in its grip. What was the reason for this contrast? The usual explanation concerns the balance of trade insofar as the complete absence of any statistics allows us to use such terms. In order to discuss this hypothesis, it will be as well to formulate it first of all as clearly as possible. But I must warn you straight away that it does not seem to me to be an acceptable hypothesis without a good deal of qualification, the necessity for which will be evident at a later stage. None of the facts invoked in its support is wrong; but the picture is not altogether complete.

It is probable that from the end of the Empire onwards, the West received from the East more than she sent to it. There is no doubt about this fact from the Frankish period onwards. Trade in both directions was considerably slowed down. It had begun to experience this decline before the Arab invasions, but these – as M. Pirenne has rightly stressed – hastened the process. From that time onwards hardly anything was exchanged by way of trade except objects that were small in volume but high in value, such as precious stuffs, ivories, luxury weapons, and particularly spices. All these came from the East, and the West in exchange sent back nothing similar. It was therefore obliged to pay for its imports in coins or in ingots. And this metal, whether in the form of coins or not, which was thus gradually withdrawn from circulation at home, was first and foremost gold – the only medium of exchange possessing a truly international value. When we hear, for example, of a great lord's will mentioning an 'Indian sword' and 'Saracen tablets' (whatever these may be), we can be certain that these objects were responsible for the loss of yet another small amount of gold.[29] There are moreover many historical analogies to support this explanation. If we find Vladimir of Kiev minting gold coins at the end of the 10th century, it is because Russia, with her great rivers, maintained at that period with Byzantium and Asia an active trade whose balance was by no means unfavourable to her; for had she not slaves to sell, and furs, and honey and beeswax from the forests and the steppes? As early as the 1st century, moreover, ancient writers were calling attention to the threatened effects of the trade with the Far East (with India in particular) upon the monetary stocks of Europe, more especially the stock of gold. If Byzantium contrived subsequently to avoid the exhaustion of its supplies, a substantial part of its success was no doubt due to the introduction into the Mediterranean Levant, from the 6th century onwards, of various luxury industries, in particular the manufacture of silk. The same shortage of money denounced by Pliny and Dion Chrysostom, and arising from precisely similar causes, was to be a source of anxiety in modern England before the export of cotton goods.[30]

From the 12th century onwards, however, the trade balance of Western Europe began to improve. She now began to export to all parts of the Eastern Mediterranean, and to the south as well, weapons, wood, corn and cloth, especially those precious materials, coming mostly from Flanders and Brabant, which began from the early years of this century to be piled in bales on the quay-sides of Genoa – and a little later on – Italian cloth too, which was discovered by a Florentine traveller of the 15th century in the markets of Timbuctoo.[31] At the same time gold started to flow into the ports and spread from there to the rest of the country. It was not long before the minting of gold, coins began.

*   *   *

This reconstruction of events would appear at first sight to be solidly based on reliable evidence. But it suffers from one serious defect – it takes no account of an important fact that I have so far left on one side, just as it has been so often neglected by historians. From the 9th to the 13th centuries, without a shadow of doubt, the minting of gold coins – at any rate of the native pattern – ceased in Western and Central Europe; but gold in general, and even gold coins, never ceased to circulate, in relatively small, and yet quite significant, amounts.

We do not need to be reminded of the existence of gold ornaments in ecclesiastical and seignorial treasuries. True, they would appear to have been perceptibly less numerous than silver ornaments, as far as one can judge in the absence of any corpus of inventories. Yet they were by no means lacking. This did not mean, however, that the metal thus hoarded was removed from circulation. To believe this would be to fail to recognise the economic role played by the goldsmith's craft, a source of much hidden wealth among mediaeval barons. Jewels and church ornaments were the great stand-by against a rainy day – and these times of need occurred frequently. These treasures would then be handed over as security to the money-lenders – often without hope of redemption – for was there any dynasty in existence that did not several times pledge its crown? Or they might meet an even sadder end: they might be handed over to the foundry, as happened to the golden crucifix given by Archbishop Willigis to Mainz Cathedral. The donor's successor surrendered one foot to pay the Pope for his *pallium*; another successor surrendered a second leg to pay for his war against a neighbouring baron.[32]

Gold also was constantly circulating in the form of ingots, dust, or even rings. In England, where gold seems to have been particularly widespread in the 10th and 11th centuries, Domesday Book frequently contains stipulations that rents must be paid in weighed gold.[33] Throughout Europe payments of this kind are mentioned here and there in charters. How often do they occur? It would no doubt be possible to make a great collection of available documents and statistics – which would of course have to take account of the different kinds of stipulation and the different classes of debtors; but in France, at any rate, no one has even attempted the study of payments – which is the key to the history of the exchanges.[34] Mere lists of examples picked here and there are useless. I will confine myself to two which, apart from their value as typical examples, have a certain individual and intrinsic interest. In 1060, the abbot of Saint-Laurent, in the diocese of Narbonne, enfeoffed an estate in return for an annual payment of 33 deniers and a lump sum of an ounce of gold. Clearly, gold by reason of its relative scarcity was more suitable for an exceptional payment than as a recurring obligation. Between 1009 and 1012 two ladies each received an ounce of gold in gratitude for their consent to a donation to Saint-Pierre-de-Bourgueil. One of them received into the bargain a thousand dried fish, which goes to show that the use of goods in kind as part of a price could perfectly well be associated with the use of media of exchange of a less strictly household character.[35]

Lastly, and perhaps most important of all, gold circulated in the form of foreign coins. The author of the *Chanson de Roland* was well aware of this when he spoke to his audience of '*besanz*' – les *besants* '*esmerez*', that is to say gleaming *bezants* and of '*mangons*' (*mancusi*). Everyone knew what these words meant, familiar as they were in the charters as well as the

THE PROBLEM OF GOLD IN THE MIDDLE AGES 199

epics. The *'bezant'* was the Byzantine *hyperperon*, called after its place of origin. As for the *'mangon'*, it was the *mancusus* of the Latin texts, a word of uncertain origin. Christians were wont to give this name to the golden *dinars* struck by the Arab khalifs, and then by the emirs, in Syria, in the Magrab, or in Spain. Towards the end of the 11th century it disappeared from written documents, to be replaced by the term *'marobotin'*, which applied especially to the Almoravid coins. In documents relating to the Jews of Catalonia, issued by Miret y Sans and Schwab, the *mancus* is mentioned for the last time in 1070, and the *marabotin* makes its appearance in 1120.[36] From time to time a certain amount of confusion crept into the nomenclature: people talked, for example, of *'besants Sarrasinois'*;[37] but the money-changers, you may be sure, made no mistakes.[38]

The *mancus* appears to have been the commonest of these various coins. Gold *sous* had not entirely ceased to be minted when the Arab *dinar* was already beginning to spread throughout the West. It is found in Italy as early as the year 778. About the year 800, Istria paid its taxes to the Carolingian treasure in *mancusi* and it was in *mancusi* too that the king of distant Mercia, the Anglo-Saxon Offa, promised in 786 to pay the annual tribute due to Saint Peter. A *dinar* has come to light at Maysan, in Brabant, among Carolingians *deniers* or half-*deniers*, all of them prior to 877; another, dated between 724 and 743, has been found at Eastbourne, on the south coast of England. Others, together with Byzantine and Beneventine gold pieces, formed the treasure of an unfortunate traveller – no doubt a merchant – who was drowned in the Reno near Bologna not long after the year 820.[39] Italy, Catalonia and – strange as it may seem at first sight, England – were to continue for centuries as the favourite homes of this foreign coinage. Anglo-Saxon wills mention it on almost every page. It was so familiar to the English that they made it the standard unit of weight for gold metal. But it was known too in Gaul, in Lotharingia and in Germany. It was by the present of a gold piece 'engraved with Arabic words and characters' that a litigant tried in 798 to corrupt the *missus* Theodulphus. The context shows clearly enough that for Theodulphus, who related the story himself, any golden coin conjured up the idea of Arabic letters, whilst a silver coin suggested letters in Latin. In 870, when the Bishop of Metz drew up an inventory of the treasure at Saint-Trond, the only coins contained in it were five *mancusi*.[40] These infidel *mancusi* were in fact so widely known in Latin Christendom that an almost constant rate of exchange with the native coinage had been established. It was currently valued at 30 *deniers*, which had long been the customary rate in various countries (and notably Bavaria) for the oriental *aurei* and the older, and therefore heavier, of the Frankish *sous*.

Gold coins from Byzantium were for a long while much scarcer. But they appeared in Bavaria not later than 1024 – 1031, having doubtless made their entry because of the very active trade existing at that time with Eastern Europe, not so much along the Danube as by way of the caravan routes that ended in the markets of the Kiev district of Russia.[41] It was coins from this source that were placed on the altar by great Italian ladies in 1065 when Peter Damien was celebrating Mass.[42] In 1071, the abbot of the Lotharingian monastery of Saint-Hubert was able, in return for the promise of an 'allod', to lend 500 of them to the Countess of Hainault.[43] About the year 1100, they are mentioned in Normandy.[44] Then, in the 12th century, the evidence of them becomes more and more frequent. In England, they figured among receipts in the royal budget from Henry II's reign onwards. In 1146, when Louis VII of France was preparing to leave for the Holy Land, he invited the abbot of Saint-Benoît-sur-Loire to pay him 500 *besants*. The abbot protested; but the astonishing thing is that it was possible to carry out the request. About 1178, 80 *besants* were bequeathed to a monastery in the diocese of Auxerre, along with 18 marks of silver, by a noble lady of the district.[45] From Louis VI's time at the latest, four of these coins were paid annually on behalf of the King of France to Saint-Denis, as a token of religious obedience.[46] In Philip Augustus's circle, these Hellenic coins had become so plentiful that he used their metal for making himself gold rings. Soon, as was to happen to all specie that became at all plentiful during the Middle Ages, it was destined to pass into the hands of certain groups of artisans in Paris, who used it as a measure of weight. In 1254, it still formed – along with the augustales – the greater part by far of the gold coin in the king of England's treasury.[47]

Truth to tell, the interpretation of this testimony has to be undertaken cautiously. It often happened in the Middle Ages that the standard of value mentioned in a price was distinct from the method of payment. Silver *deniers* might be stipulated but one paid in merchandise that had been duly 'priced'. In the same way when payment in gold was stipulated, it often happened that it was made in silver. Nothing is more characteristic than the payments imposed by the Papacy on the monasteries under her jurisdiction. Rome preferred to receive gold, and usually fixed the sum in *besants*, *mancus* or *marabotins*; but in practice she often had to be content with payment in silver coins or ingots, according to a rate of exchange which tended in each case to become traditional.[48] In 10th-century Italy, it was common to speak of 'silver' *mancus*, in exactly the same way that one spoke of silver *sous*; the *mancus* or *sou* served as an accounting unit, but the debt was settled in coins of a different metal. In the same way at Genoa and Marseilles, two or three centuries later, the expression on '*besants de millares*' was used, the *millares* being a small silver coin. Much the same applies to the mention of gold not in the form of coin: it, too, was often not actually paid over. Towards the end of the 11th century, a certain lady renounced, in favour of the Priory of Saint-Martin-des-Champs, all claim to a country church, and fixed the price of this concession at two ounces of gold; but the monks made her accept instead 60 *deniers* of Provins.[49] Unfortunately many of the contracts were content to specify the standard chosen, without bothering even to mention the material in which the final payment was made. And so when a text contains the words *besants*, *mancus* or *marabotins*, it would be rash to conclude, without some cross-checking, that these were in fact the medium of payment. There are in addition certain documents of a more precise nature which allow us to track down operations that really were effected by a transfer of gold; but quite apart from these, the custom of using accounting units borrowed from Arabic *dinars* or Byzantine *hyperperons* is an assurance that these coins were universally recognised.

It will be convenient to deal separately with the facts relating to the 12th century. At a time when the balance of trade in the West was, without the slightest doubt, being redressed, it was quite natural that there should be an influx of gold from abroad. At Genoa during this whole century a large number of commercial contracts stipulate payment in gold, in coin or other forms. The Commune of Genoa in 1160 paid the inhabitants of Placenta 2·815 pounds of *besants* (here reckoned by weight); and in 1162 the Count of Provence paid over to the Imperial Court 15,000 *marabotins*.[50] Far from the Mediterranean, even a French abbot in 1146 could command the sum of 500 *besants*; and some German canons, thirty years later, imposed a fine of 20 *marabotins* on those of their colleagues who improperly alienated the community's possessions.[51] But all these examples are after all but the natural signs of a resumption of the minting of gold. To these must be added – as far as the upper classes are concerned – the profits from conquests in the Latin East, and the results of social obligations incurred during the crusades. Shortly before 1167, a seigneur from Avallon had married a lady from Beirut. The couple sold their lands near Acre to the Hospitallers and settled in Burgundy, enriched by the sum of 200 *marabotins*.[52]

But these observations are valid only for a very short period. During the whole period of official silver monometallism, *dinars*, *hyperperons* and ounces of gold did in fact serve for current payments. A little episode from monastic history will give a more accurate idea of the part played at this period of the two metals. At the very beginning of the 12th century – that is, at a time when southern Germany had not yet been affected by the new monetary trends, spreading out from the Mediterranean – the monks of Hirsau in Swabia were condemned by the king to pay a fine of five and a half marks of gold. As they were unable to pay they fell back upon the good offices of a friendly lord. But he, too, had none of the required metal, and was obliged to buy the necessary amount at the price of 44 silver marks. Thus it was possible even for the coffers of the rich to be lacking in gold; but it was not difficult to procure some on the market, and that at a very moderate rate of exchange. The relationship between the two metals implied in this account – namely 1 to 8 – bears witness to a much less marked appreciation of gold than is signified in the law of year XI, which fixed the proportion at 1 to 15·5.[53] Everything leads us to the same conclusion: gold undoubtedly was relatively scarce; but it was neither completely absent nor economically useless.

* * *

The first revision made necessary by observations concerns European trade. It remains highly probable that the West imported more in value than it exported. But the total balance did not show as large a deficit as was at one time supposed. Trade with Byzantium, it is true, seems constantly to have showed an unfavourable balance up to the end of the 11th century, for how else should we interpret the scarcity of *besants*? Clearly, the most profitable exports went to the Islamic countries over a long period, whence there was an ample flow of *mancus* in return – particularly into Spain, for the 'rupture' brought about by the Musulman invasions had never been complete. What merchandise had Latin Christendom to offer these Saracens? To obtain an accurate answer, we should have to comb the Arabic documents – in the hope that they are rather less desperately uncommunicative than our own.[54] There is no doubt that large quantities of slaves were exported thither; even when native slavery had disappeared from Gaul, Germany and Italy, the slave-raids into Slav territory continued to feed the trade, and caravans convoyed these captives to the far side of the Pyrenees. As for England, the trade in slaves – Celts for the most part, but also prisoners taken in the course of internal wars and even children sold by their parents – seems to have been very active over a long period. This is apparently the explanation for the remarkable abundance of Arabic coins in the internal monetary circulation of the island. Perhaps – though this is no more than a hypothesis – Great Britain also sold its tin in the markets of Spain. As for Italy, especially the eastern parts, it may be conjectured that a good number of the *mancus* came from

Syria, for the Adriatic was never closed, and Venice was not above indulging in the trade in human livestock.

But the most troublesome enigma concerns the history of money. It is absolutely clear, in the light of these new facts, that the state of trade is by itself incapable of explaining why gold should have ceased to be minted. However rare the metal had become, the dearth of it was not so complete as to make minting seem impossible; for it was easy to melt down foreign coins, and, in view of the profits accruing to the mints, this procedure, it seems, would have had some advantages. Between 1076 and 1080, Adelaide de Forcalquier brought the Comte d'Urgel 5,000 *mancusi* from Valence as a dowry.[55] Why did not his father, the Marquis of Provence, think of turning all this gold into new coin? And there is another point to add: in the 11th century the gold-washers along most of the Lombardy rivers were obliged to take all the gold-dust they recovered to the royal 'chamber' at Pavia;[56] and however moderate the amounts may have been, there would no doubt have been enough to strike a few coins. Why did the mint at Pavia, in the very centre of a country where a foreign gold coinage was circulating freely, never strike anything but silver *deniers* in the king's name?

*　　　*　　　*

A fact that we have so far left on one side will put us on the right scent. Not all the coins of foreign type were imported: a certain number of them had been struck in Catholic lands, copying models that had come from elsewhere. In other words, if there was no more minting of native-type gold coins over three centuries, there was a minting of counterfeit coin, not always the work of false coiners of humble rank, but sometimes commissioned by princes.

Equally eloquent testimony, both in writing and in recovered treasure, comes from England also. In his will, King Eadred ordered 2,000 *mancusi* to be struck in the year 955.[57] Moreover there is in existence a gold piece exactly reproducing the features of an Abassid *dinar*, with the legend in Arabic language and characters, and the date as from the hegira, 157 (774 of our era); but it also carries in Latin letters the words *Offa Rex*. It was found in or near Rome, and is probably a survivor from the tribute-money paid to Saint Peter.[58] In the same way there are in Catalonia fairly numerous documents which mention *mancus* minted by order of the Count; and on certain of these that have come down to us we can read, alongside the proper Arabic inscriptions, the prince's name in Latin letters.[59] Elsewhere, we have in the nature of the case nothing but hints to go upon. One of the principal Mediterranean mints during the Middle Ages was at Mauguis, in Languedoc. We are only acquainted with the *deniers* which it turned out, but these were made in large numbers. We do however know that about the year 1080, gold was being coined there.[60] Can there be any doubt that these coins were imitations? This would also seem to be the most reasonable explanation of a text that has caused historians a great deal of embarrassment, the lease from the Genoa mint in 1149 which affirms that gold as well as silver was struck, although texts and coins alike agree in placing the first appearance of gold pieces officially issued by the great Ligurian port more than a hundred years later – in 1252.[61] Moreover the *mancus* that happened to bear the name of the Christian sovereign, who was responsible for their issue, could after all only be called half-counterfeit. The out-and-out forgeries always run the risk of being confused by us with the originals, unless their clumsiness sometimes gives them away. Thus there is more than one suspect *dinar* in our collections. And, no doubt, when the *besants* also spread through Europe, people were at pains to copy them, but without ever – so it seems – having the honesty to distinguish them, even by a discreet mention of their origin, from the genuine *hyperperon*. How are we to know where the Genoese false coiners looked to for their models – Byzantium or Islam? Perhaps it was sometimes the one and sometimes the other.

In the Arabic coinage, gold was not the only metal to act as a lure to imitators. There were silver *dirhems* in circulation alongside dinars throughout the East. They too were copied in large numbers: on the shores of the Mediterranean (where the *dirhem* was generally known under the name of *millare*), in Germany, where it was needed for trade with the Slav East, and even as far as the Atlantic ports. In 1268 a mint for 'false saracen coinage' was still at work in the Île d'Oleron; as it used 'base metal' picked up at La Rochelle, it looks as though it must have concentrated specially on the reproduction of silver coins, without prejudice to the minting of a certain amount of gold as well. But it seems that these would-be *dirhems* were slower to appear than the counterfeit *dinars*, and could in any case not be more than a supplement to the circulation, most of them being meant for use abroad, expecially for Spain and the Magrab. The merchants there took up what was produced in this way as payment, thus sparing themselves the risks attaching to the process of exchange. It is significant that Jayme I of Majorca, confirming in 1268 that *millares* should continue to be coined, thought good to order that they should be regulated 'according to the law fixed by the merchants who desire to buy them'. The native *deniers* continued to a large extent to finance domestic transactions – a very different situation from gold, where the whole of the minting was spurious.[62]

The Arabic money thus produced, whether gold or silver, invariably carried certain quotations from the Koran or devices proclaiming the faith of Islam. It was no small scandal to Christian princes – sometimes even bishops – incurring the responsibility for these blasphemies! Protests were in fact raised, at least in the 13th century.[63] Alphonso VIII at Toledo and his grandson Saint Louis, striking coin at Acre during the crusade, got out of the difficulty by substituting Christian maxims for the Mohammedan religious legends – though still printing them in the Arabic characters and language.[64] For a long time it had been purely and simply a case of copying. The fact that such imitation was considered shocking only shows how necessary it must have seemed to be. Why was there such insistence of this point?

In order to understand this, we must have an accurate grasp of the exact part played by the two precious metals in the process of circulation. Small and medium-sized payments – such as dues, wages and current purchases – were far the most common. Those that did not simply involve an exchange of goods were carried out exclusively in silver. The high value of gold did not make it suitable for such petty transactions. So much so that in 1215 we have the spectacle of John Lackland, who possessed gold, being forced to use it in order to procure a loan of *deniers* which he needed to satisfy his mercenaries.[65] There did exist some regulations however which, though ordinarily concerned with larger sums, were nevertheless designed specifically to put relatively distant markets in touch with one another. They may sometimes have arisen because people outside the circle of Latin Christendom had an interest in them; or they may have originated within the Western world, in the relationships that were arising between the various political and economic areas – for the social fragmentation characteristic of this period was responsible for an infinite diversity of such groupings. Here too, because of the dearth of gold, it was sometimes necessary to fall back upon silver; but this was only a second-best, for gold in this case was always the favourite.

Unfortunately we know almost nothing until the 13th century about mercantile accounting. But some facts may be taken as symptomatic. Even the last mintings of gold in Carolingian Gaul were solely intended, it seems, for use in foreign exchange. This is supported by the location of the mints themselves – one at Uzès for the Arabic countries, and one at Dorstadt – at that time the great port in the delta of the Rhine – for trade with the north. Notable quantities of gold, either coined at this latter centre or in other ways, were for a long while held by the Frisians, who were at that time the great traders on the northern seas and northern rivers.[66] At Cologne in the 12th century a duty levied according to the usual custom at the enfeoffment of certain estates was paid exceptionally in gold. Payment was by weight, but the very designation of the unit of weight selected – a *mancus* – clearly takes us back to the already fairly distant days when this coin circulated freely in Europe. Situated as it was on the banks of the Rhine, right in the centre of the trading quarter, and comprising warehouses and wharves, the property which paid these dues was certainly all in the hands of the upper class merchants.[67] It seemed perfectly natural to require gold from people of this class by way of dues on landed property because they habitually used it in their transactions. We have little information about commercial payments, but we are much better informed about the loans, the proceeds of sale, and various kinds of income which accrued to the benefit of members of the seignorial class. It is clear that these great personages were eager for gold, for the fact is that their interests were not restricted to the purely local horizon. In the same way the Papacy, a truly European institution, was always at pains to collect in gold the various taxes that were due to it.

Besides, a variety of reasons, all equally cogent, ensured that the more precious of the two metals functioned as a supra-regional instrument. We might even call it international, so long as we do not assign any too precise meaning to the word 'nation'. Gold enjoyed a kind of supremacy conferred on it by an old tradition whose origins went back into an obscure period when money had possessed an almost religious power. Moreover the *deniers*, which were too light, and silver, with its relatively low intrinsic value, would have been extremely inconvenient to handle over long distances. There were also causes of an economic nature, arising from the very environment, which prevented silver from playing any extensive part. The fact that there were so many centres of production, that they were so widely dispersed, and that the general state of society was highly unfavourable to the establishment of any one market, had the effect of condemning silver to perpetual variations in value. The instruments of exchange favoured by large-scale trade during the Middle Ages were always commodities that were rare, available from a limited source only, and in universal demand. Hence pepper acted for a long period as a genuine kind of money, and was used both as a measure of price and for loans; and gold in particular fulfilled the same functions.

This much-sought-after gold might circulate in the form of bars, or powder, or coin. If it took the latter form, it needed some kind of hall-mark that would serve as a reassurance to merchants of various races scattered far and wide. The crowd of petty princelings who exercised the right of coinage in the West, even if they were kings, were always lacking in power and desperately poor; they were in no position at all to give such a guarantee. The only coin that inspired confidence was the imperial *hyperperon*, which were admirably stable. 'Commerce', wrote Cosmas Indicopleustès, writing in the 6th century, 'is carried on everywhere by means of the νόμισμα, which is in use from one end of the world to the other.'[68] Alternatively, recourse was had to the *dinars* of the rich Arabian monarchies. If the Catholic princes wished to share the benefits of this coinage, they could only fall back upon imitation. No doubt, the copies did not always deceive; sometimes they were not even intended to do so; but they took their place in the monetary series to which the trading world was accustomed. All money rests upon confidence, and so to a large extent upon custom. Moreover the history of the silver *denier*, and of the larger coin, is enough to show the necessity for these imitations, and to reveal the motive that lay behind them. When a mediaeval mint was intent upon securing a large currency for its products, the regular custom was to copy a piece that was already in wide circulation, or at any rate familiar in the region with which it was desired to trade. When the minting of a national gold coinage ceased in the West, it was not, properly speaking, the effect of an unfavourable balance of trade; for however marked the lack of gold had been, it had never amounted to a complete and irrevocable disappearance of the metal from the West. It is to be explained by a complex web of causes, some economic and some more particularly social. The slowing down of internal trade had confined gold – too valuable for current payments – to the role of an exceptional and supra-regional instrument; and the poverty, fragmentation and bad administration existing among the minting States meant that their coinages failed to command universal confidence, an indispensable requirement for any money that was to have such a wide circulation. All this reflected conditions in the world economy which, after so many centuries when the scales have been tipped in the opposite direction, it is difficult today to imagine: the economies of the Latin and Germanic countries were dominated by their richer neighbours – Byzantium and the Islamic countries of the Mediterranean. To find a parallel, we would have to imagine in our own time a European monetary crisis which reached such a pitch that all payment by bills of exchange came to an end, and the only means of payment between one place and another was by dollars, whether genuine or counterfeit.

A few words on the causes of the resumption of gold minting in the 13th century, and then on its consequences, will finally throw light on the function of gold in the circulation of the Middle Ages. But on this last point we must confine ourselves to a very rapid sketch. A more thorough study would have to reckon with the new procedures in accounting and settlement of debts resulting from improved commercial techniques, such as banco money and bills of exchange. Such a study would need to be elaborated at considerable length.

* * *

Undoubtedly it was the new commercial conditions, having tilted the balance in favour of the West, that allowed a return to minting. This was preceded, as we have seen, by important arrivals of gold.

At Genoa, fiscal policy was consciously designed to draw off this inflow. The tariff of port dues, drawn up in 1142, generally envisaged payment in merchandise; but by way of exception it required each ship coming from Spain or from beyond Sardinia to pay one *marabotin*; the rents paid by lessees for farms in the eastern colonies had regularly to be paid in *besants*.[69] It is significant that Genoa and Florence, both of them great exporters, should have returned to the minting of gold well before Venice. Not that Venice was any less wealthy; but she bought more from the East than she sold to it; and it was more often than not in gold that she paid for these products, recovering the price at inland trading-centres usually only in silver. When she made up her mind to follow her competitors' example, her mints had to provide themselves with metal largely obtained from South Germany, which was then one of the great markets for gold.[70]

Such were the conditions that made this revolution possible; but it was circumstances of quite a different order that made it necessary. Coins to finance transactions began to multiply at a steadily increasing rate. The *denier*, whose silver-content had from the start been low, became more and more depreciated, and proved a decidedly inadequate instrument for purposes of trade. First of all attempts were made to find the remedy in terms of silver. From this point onwards it became necessary to strike heavier pieces (as well as the traditional *deniers*), whose value was generally fixed at 12 *deniers*, that is to say one *sou*. There were Venetian *matapans* in 1203, Veronese *sous* about the same time, Florentine *sous* shortly before 1237, large Saint-Louis *tournois* in 1266, Milanese *sous* and *Aquilini grossi* from the Tyrol about the middle of the century, Montpellier *sous* in 1273, *groschen* from Prague in 1296 – to name only the oldest and most characteristic examples. This important modification in the monetary position of silver, therefore, occurred earlier than the resumption of a gold coinage, which cannot be separated from it; for these first measures, having to some extent met the need in transactions involving large sums, were doubtless soon found to be inadequate. But they naturally suggested the idea of producing an increased quantity of coins in a more precious metal, so that, weight for weight, the value could be increased.

For some time the imported money, growing larger and larger in volume, seemed to be sufficient for the task. The decisive moment arrived when it was found to be incapable of performing what was required. The political map of the Mediterranean, like the commercial map, was just then undergoing profound changes. The greater part of Spain had escaped from the Moors. The Musulman States that continued to exist were of no great economic importance; we have already seen how from the 12th century onwards, when gold ceased to be minted at Marcia, Castile was thereby led to take it up. As for the Byzantine Empire, its preponderance in trade had diminished considerably since the days of the great Comneni; and internal troubles and the crusade of 1204 left it permanently disabled. The decadence of the State and the general impoverishment brought the usual monetary abuses with them. The metal-content of the *hyperperon* lost all stability and went rapidly downhill. The story of this decline has been too often and too well told to warrant any elaboration here. I shall confine myself to a single piece of evidence, which, although very characteristic, has seldom been put forward. In 1250, Alphonse de Poitiers, who was then in the Holy Land, had some gold coin sent to him from France. His representative bought them by weight, the price in silver coins varying for each type, no doubt according to the fine metal content. The dearest were the Castilian *anfous*, which were the local successors of the marabotins; then came the *augustales*; and finally, at the bottom of the scale, the *besants*.[71] This lack of a customary medium of exchange was a most vexing embarrassment to the trade of the East. The great Italian centres overcame it by themselves forging the necessary instruments, under their own hall-mark, of course; for why should they have taken the trouble to counterfeit coins that were from now onwards devoid of all prestige? The day came in the 14th century when one saw *hyperperons* accepted simply on the basis of their value in ducats: this, though it appears to be only a minor detail in the merchant's accounting arrangements, is in reality an eloquent symptom of the way the economic equilibrium throughout the world had been upset.

It is moreover no cause for astonishment that the States or principalities beyond the Alps should have promptly imitated the Italian example, or at any rate attempted to do so. It was in the nature of such a reform that it should spread. In the first place the minting of gold seemed to serve the interests and prestige of the coming powers; also it served commercial needs which to a large extent inspired the English decisions of 1343;[72] and it was helped by the additional fact that merchants, being obliged to settle their transactions abroad in gold, were suffering very heavy losses in the process of exchange, whose repercussions were to the detriment of the consumer. This last consideration, it is true, can only be explained by the fact that gold coins, unlike silver, no matter where they came from, almost always enjoyed a quasi-universal currency. In other words, gold kept its role as an instrument of international exchange – a fact that will become clearer as we proceed.

* * *

But the return to the minting of gold came up against a good many obstacles, not all of which had been foreseen. Proof of this is to be seen in the stoppages to which the first experiments were subject, in France and especially in England. Further proof is to be seen in the reaction of Germany against the new regime, conspicuous at any rate from the 14th century onwards. At this time several towns and principalities agreed to deny gold any value as legal tender.[73] What was the origin of these difficulties?[74]

It need hardly be said that the success of these measures depended in each case on circumstances of an economic order. If the balance of trade was in disequilibrium, gold deserted the country. But it is difficult to believe that England, with her large exports of wool, could have been forced by such considerations to give up her first attempt at a new gold coinage. Yet even where the rates of exchange with other countries were more or less favourable, may it not have been that the domestic exchange facilities were inadequate and the coins too small in value? The new coins were only intended for making large payments, and failed to be as serviceable as might have been expected; there was even a risk that they would fail to circulate. This was no doubt the chief reason for the English failure. Indeed, there is a significant parallel in this same country; a similar fate overtook the high-value silver coinage when it was first issued. The first *groats* were struck not long after the florins of Henry III, under his successor, Edward I; but they failed to establish themselves, and the attempt was not repeated till 1351, when it was successful, seven years after the definitive return to the minting of gold.

Whatever may have been the state of regional economies, the stocks of metal throughout Europe proved insufficient for this increased demand. Hence the marked rise in the exchange rate for gold.[75] True, this movement came to a halt in 1342 or thereabouts. But for reasons that are still a mystery, silver at that period underwent a marked increase in value on the oriental markets, thus allowing the West to purchase gold at a much more favourable rate than before.[76] It is none the less true that the relationship between the two metals remained much more favourable to gold than it had been before the resumption of gold minting. During the last two centuries of the Middle Ages it continued to be an agonising problem how to provide the mints with sufficient precious metal. Unfortunately the history of the trade in precious metals is for the present, like so many other chapters in monetary history, a complete blank; and this is due to the lack of any system for guiding research workers rather than to any scarcity of documents. In the 14th century, an important market was held at Bruges, to which large quantities of goods were carried by sea; and in 1341 Lübeck acquired from this source the wherewithal for its new minting.[77] Moreover, considerable quantities of gold, coming from Hungary and no doubt from Asia too, entered by way of southern Germany, and particularly through Ratisbon, which supplied not only Venice but also, on occasions – along with Augsburg and Nuremberg – the busy mint of Tournai.[78] And the resources of the East were not the only ones to be pressed into service. Long before America came upon the scene, the Sudan and Guinea were the Eldorado of adventurers in the trading world. From the beginning of the 14th century, the Genoese, in league with the Touareg caravaners 'with their veiled faces', frequented the Sahara oases and bought the precious gold-dust that had come from the south. They were first seen at Tafilalet, the principal palace of which, Sidjilmassa, minted money with the purest gold in the world; then in 1447 at Touat,* where they made contact with the Abyssian merchants. A little later the Portuguese succeeded in reaching the coastal markets by sea. In 1479, an inhabitant of Tournai followed them there, exchanging his cheap wares at Sierra Leone for slaves, which he would have exchanged again for gold at Elmina, if the Portuguese, who were jealous of their monopoly, had not taken possession of his person and his goods, greatly to his loss. A trade as hazardous as this favoured speculation: but it was no mere chance that induced the Centurioni of Genoa, who had specialised in this line, to do their utmost to set up a thoroughgoing monometallism for gold in their native city.[79]

These uncertainties surrounding the supply of gold only underlined the defects inherent in the system itself. 'Because gold was not adjusted to silver, the realm of France was robbed by rogues and rascals,' says a memoir from the time of Philip the Fair.[80] Authorities have recognised the internal contradic-

* Touat is a group of Saharan oases in Aïn-Sefra territory, W. Central Algeria [Ed.].

tions from which all bimetallic systems have suffered. They are condemned to imposing, at least for fairly extended periods, a fixed relationship between the monetary values of the two metals, when the commercial rates do not necessarily move in the same direction; and even when the direction of movement is the same, they do not necessarily move according to a uniform rhythm. The difficulties of this 'adjustment' made themselves felt from the beginning – witness, for instance, the fumbling efforts of the English Government in the period when minting was resumed in 1344. In the Middle Ages they were especially serious, because economic conditions and in particular the wide dispersal of markets militated against stable rates of exchange. The sovereigns' interests – seeing that they paid most of their officials, and particularly their troops, in silver – tended to make them set too high a value upon it in relation to gold, as the King of Sicily freely admitted in 1301.[81] Finally, it is clear that the two means of payment which it was desired to bring into mutual harmony really belonged to two different stages of the economy.

Gold, to be sure, whether in money or in ingots, remained what it had always been since the beginning of the Middle Ages – an instrument familiar especially to large-scale commerce, and made to circulate between one market and another. But do not let us be led into saying 'just like today'. There is too great a gulf between the economy of this period and our own; both the extent of the market, and the human relationships involved in it, were completely different then as compared with now and there are too many differences in the respective techniques of exchange for such comparisons to be anything but repugnant to a true historical sense, unless they are accompanied by the necessary correctives. Let us rather say that in spite of these contrasts, and in spite of the intrusion of periods when gold served largely as a means of internal exchange, the tradition governing this use of the metal, whether in coin or other form, has continued down to our own days. When the minting of gold was resumed in the Middle Ages, the question arose whether the new gold coins would constitute the same legal tender as silver. The problem, it is true, was often ignored; but when it came to a final decision on the point, the solution was generally unfavourable to gold, for it was resolved that gold need not be accepted unless by mutual consent, or unless the contract expressly stipulated its acceptance. Bimetallism – to use a phrase dear to the hearts of economists today – was beginning to 'sag', but with silver, and not as in the 19th century gold, as the chief support.[82] The English regulations of 1344 were more precise. They laid it down as a matter of principle that gold could not be insisted upon. With one exception, however: between one merchant and another it was absolutely legal tender, and could not be refused.[83] Could there be any clearer recognition of its character as money associated with a particular class?

As for its international role, there are many significant facts available to throw light upon it, and we can select where we like. Villari has described the budget of expenditure for the years 1336 to 1338 at Florence. All the salaries and wages of public officials, even including those of the Podestà and the captain of the people, were paid in silver; the only exception to this rule was the honorarium of the castle guardians – condottieri, no doubt, and therefore foreigners – and that of the ambassadors. In 1294, when the monks of the Bavarian monastery of Aldersbach wished to pay a contribution towards their abbot's story in Paris, they bought gold ingots in exchange for silver, and sent them to him.[84] Moreover, gold currencies were to some extent free from national restrictions, inasmuch as they enjoyed in practice their own special rate of exchange, fixed by the general conditions of the European economy. This commercial or 'voluntary' rate was distinct from the legal rate, and – because of the excessively high official value set upon silver coinage – was usually superior to it; it produced fruitless protests from the princes in one edict after another. It served as a standard for merchants' payments, particularly those of fixed date, even when the payment had perforce to be made in silver, a fact which is attested by the books of the brothers Bonis of Montauban. Naturally, it was especially the most solidly based coins, such as the florin, or the Rhenish *gulden* in Germany, that fulfilled this role of regulator for the exchange rates between one country and another.[85]

But an additional difficulty entered into the situation: there could be no watertight divisions between the various economic systems. Gold currencies were very far from escaping the ups and downs which were the plague of the mediaeval monetary system; but, owing to the protection afforded by their international character, they did not ordinarily feel the full force of these vicissitudes as strongly as the silver currencies; moreover, wherever the legal rate became too artificial, the commercial rate acted as a brake. The result was that in times of crisis the custom of stipulating payment in gold, or at any rate of submitting it, whatever the nature of the transaction, to the gold standard, began to spread from merchant circles to the whole of the propertied classes. We have seen precisely the same thing happening today in times of inflation, yet with this difference: the flight from money was not a flight from paper-money, but from metallic (silver), though it was in truth often adulterated and nearly always overvalued. The States, who were intent on protecting the medium of internal exchange, asserted their right to forbid such practices;[86] but they were hardly ever successful in doing so. Here, too, we are witnessing a drama that recurred again and again down the ages.

*   *   *

Such, it seems, in outline were the vicissitudes in the use of gold or purposes of exchange in the Middle Ages, as far at any rate as it is possible for the time being to trace them. I only hope the uncertainties in this sketch, and even the mistakes from which it is probably not exempt, will help to call attention to the gaps in our programmes of research. The economic – or let us rather call it the human – history of mediaeval money has not yet been written. It would probably need to be preceded by studies of an archaeological and numismatic nature, and there is no doubt at all that it needs to go hand in hand with work of this kind, patiently carried out. But the time is overdue for a frontal attack on the problem. Anyone attempting now to sketch in some aspects of the story must needs proceed by way of examples; but it is important that we should be able to replace this random collection of facts by methodical studies supported by figures, especially studies of payments. And this piece of economic history cannot be written without becoming a social history as well; we must remember that society consists of various groups, whose opposing ways of life are expressed in their monetary habits. What would be the use of a statistical study of cheques today without giving precise information as as to what kind of operations are carried out by these means, and what classes make use of it? The same applies to the history of gold, silver, currency, ingots and payments in kind during the Middle Ages.

NOTES

1. *Annales d'histoire économique et sociale*, no. 19, Vol. I, January 31st 1933, p. 1, 34. For the problems of gold in the contemporary world, cf. *Annales*, Vol. III, 1931, p. 361 and Vol. IV, 1932, p. 359.
2. For the bibliography of the subject, the reader should refer to the bibliographical survey to be found as an appendix to the present article. The only references given in the notes relate to the documents themselves, or to scholarly works which, with rare exceptions, do not appear in the Survey. I have moreover taken the liberty of dispensing with references to facts which are common knowledge.
3. J. Kulischer, *Russische Wirtschaftgeschichte*, 1925, p. 19.
4. H. Dannenberg, *Die deutschen Münze der sächsischen und fränkischen Kaiserzeit*, Vol. I, nos. 797 and 1385, distinguishes two gold coinages belonging to two Henrys (probably Henry II and Henry IV). If the pieces are authentic, the unanimous opinion of the experts is that they could only be ornamental medals.
5. Bitterauf, *Die Traditionen des Hochstifts Freising*, Vol. I, nos. 177 (799, Oct. 38) and 620 (836, Nov. 23).
6. Cf. Cl. Sánchez-Albornoz, *La primitiva organización monetaria de León y Castilla*, in *Annario de historia del derecho español*, 1928, p. 335. It is as well to add that in 1193 the king of León, Alphonso IX, granted the archbishops of Compostella the right to mint gold (*ibid.*, p. 337); from there, gold minting spread to regions that had never really come under Islamic influence. But the situation of a mint in this out-of-the-way corner can only be explained by the great religious prestige enjoyed by the church of Saint James, and the economic result of the measure remained the same – namely to substitute for the *dinars*, which had circulated in the markets of León, at a time when the greater part of the country was under the authority of the Musulman princes, the coins struck by Christian princes.
7. See for example A. Molinier, *Correspondance administrative d'Alphonse de Poitiers*, Vol. I, nos. 643, 644, 702, 863, 870, 881.
8. Huillard-Bréholles, *Historia diplomatica Frederici secundi*, Vol. II, p. 688 (1226, Nov. 8th).

THE PROBLEM OF GOLD IN THE MIDDLE AGES 219

9. A. Schaube, *Ein italienischer Coursbericht von der Messe von Troyes aus dem 13 Jahrhundert*, in *Zeitschrift für Social-und Wirtschaftsgeschichte*, Vol. V, 1897, p. 299.
10. *Pratica della Mercatura*, in Pagnini, *Della decima*, Vol. III, 1766, p. 260. This observation would tend to prove that at least the part of the work that concerns England was put together before 1344. This would be an important point to remember for the scholar who will one day – we hope – give us a much-needed critical study of this famous text.
11. For the countries incorporated later on under the Austrian crown, see Luschin von Ebengreuth, in *Numismatische Zeitschrift*, Vol. XLII, 1909, p. 169. The *Annale Reinhardsbrunnenses*, which we only possess in the form of a late and frequently remodelled compilation, make the Emperor Otto IV responsible for the plan of imposing a tax on each plough, fixed at first at one gold piece then at two. It also credits him with the intention, whenever a married couple had produced three daughters, of taking the third of them for the brothels, from which the king himself would make his selection. This would appear sufficient evidence for estimating the quality of the document's testimony in general (edit. Wegele, in *Thüringische Geschichtsquellen*, Vol. I, pp. 128 and 134).
12. For the reasons referred to above, I have left on one side all the facts concerning Spain. There, too, it is noteworthy that Aragon does not seem to have taken to the minting of gold before 1346: cf. A. Heiss, *Descripción general de las monetas hispano-cristianas*.
13. G. C. Crump and A. Hugues, *The English currency under Edward I*, in *The Economic Journal*, 1895, p. 58 (with a mention of the Limoges money); J. Petit, *Essai de restitution des plus anciens mémoriaux de la Chambre des Comptes*, 1899 (Université de Paris, Bibliothèque de la Faculté des Lettres, Vol. VII), supporting document no. XXIII, p. 166 before Oct. 18th 1312.
14. Henry de Huntingdon, *Historia Anglorum*, edit. Th. Arnold (*Rolls Series*), p. 5. The work in its first form was put together in 1129.
15. G. von Karajan, in *Das österreichische Geschichtsforscher*, hgg. v. J. Chmel, Vol. I, 1838, pp. 497 and 499; cf. pp. 292 and 293. In the same way, in 1261, for the deniers of melgueil: A. Germain, *Mémoire sur les anciennes monnaies seigneuriales de Melgueil et de Montpellier*, in *Mém. Soc. Archéologique Montpellier*, Vol. III, 1850–1854, p. 195.
16. L. de Launay, *L'Or dans le monde*, 1907, p. 89. For the history of gold production, cf. H. Hauser, *L'or*, 1901, and an article, unfortunately rather a hasty piece of work without any references, by M. Zimmermann, *Les foyers de production de l'or dans l'antiquité et au Moyen Age*, in *Bullet, de la Soc. de Géographie de Lyon*, Vol. XX, 1905.
17. For Silesia, cf. C. Faulhaber, *Die ehemalige schlesische Goldproduktion*, 1896, p. 2. It appears that seams rather than placers were worked in Calabria (the 'Bruttium' of the classical world): see Cassiodorus, *Variae*, IX, 3, and in the 11th century Benzo d'Albe, III, 1, in *S.S.*, Vol. XI, p. 622. (Further on, however, on p. 678, this same Benzo

contrasts the gold of Arabia with the *silver* of Calabria.) But southern Italy did not belong to the part of Europe which gave up the official minting of gold in the 9th century. Moreover the Illyrian mines, abandoned at the time of the invasions, seem scarcely to have come into action again before the 13th century: cf. C. J. Jireček, *Die Handelstrassen und Bergwerke von Serbien und Bosnien*, Prague, 1879, pp. 41ff. Were there – in the 13th century at any rate – mines worked in the Massif Central? The mention, in an account prepared for Alphonse de Poitiers (see below, note 71), prompts me to ask this question, but I have not been able to arrive at an answer.

18. Barbier, *La cueillette de l'or à Pamiers* in *Bulletin périodique de la Soc. Ariégeoise des Sciences*, Vol. IX, 1903–1904; H. Heimpel, *Das Gewerbe der Stadt Regensburg*, 1926, p. 159 (*Beihefte zur Vierteljahrschrift für Soz., – und Wirtschaftsgeschichte*, Vol. IX); A. Solmi, *l'amministrazione finanzaria del regno italico nell' alto medio evo*, 1932. (*Biblioteca della Società Pavese di Storia Patria*, 2) pp. 129ff.

19. Ermoldus Nigellus, in *Poetae aevi Karolini*, Vol. II, p. 83, line 125; Otfried, *Evangelienbuch*, I, line 72; *S.S.*, Vol. XV, p. 995; XXIII, p. 436, c.q.; Theophilus, *Schedula*, edit. Ilg (*Quellenschrift für Kunstgeschichte*, Vol. VII), III, 49. A gold-washing site between Bâle and Strasbourg was described as late as 1438 by the Spaniard Pierre Tafur: cf. *Festschrift A. Castellieri*, 1927, p. 33.

20. *Ep. X*, 29.

21. *Cod. Theod.*, XIII, 2, 1; VIII, 4, 27.

22. *Nov. Maioriana*, VII, 14; *Greg. Ep.*, *VI*, 10; Lex Burg., XXI, 7; *Aviti Ep.*, in *A.A.*, Vol. VI, 2, p. 96, 1. 33.

23. Cf. Luschin von Ebengreuth, in *Neus Archiv.*, 1908, p. 449.

24. Havard, *Histoire de l'Orfèvrerie française*, 1896, p. 59. The memory of this impoverishment finds legendary expression in a curious account in the *Anglo-Saxon Chronicle*, in the year 418: 'The Romans gathered together all the gold treasure that was to be found in Britain; part of it they buried beneath the ground, so that no man should ever find it again, and the rest they took with them to Gaul.'

25. *Revue numismatique*, 1845, p. 14.

26. *C.J.*, IV, 63, 2.

27. Adam Bremensis, IV, 6; *Encomium Emmae*, II, 4, in *S.S.*, Vol. XIX, p. 515. Cf. the works of d'O. R. Janse, *Le Travail de l'or en Suède*, 1922, and *Note sur les solidi*, in *Revue numismatique*, 1922. It is known that at the beginning of the 6th century a portion of the *Herulian* people left the Upper Danube and returned to Scandinavia. A Norwegian prince resided at Theodoric the Great's Court.

28. Besides the works on the *hyperperon* (for which see the bibliographical survey), consul Ch. Diehl, *Une crise monétaire au VIe siècle*, in *Revue des études grecques*, Vol. XXXII, 1919.

29. M. Prou and A. Vidier, *Recueil des chartes de Saint-Benoît-sur-Loire*, no. XXV.

30. E. H. Warmington, *The Commerce between the Roman Empire and India*,

THE PROBLEM OF GOLD IN THE MIDDLE AGES 221

1928, pp. 272ff.; J. H. Clapham, *An economic history of modern Britain*, 1926, p. 488. Even in the 12th and 13th centuries, when the balance of trade had become much more favourable, the ports on the Tyrrhenian Sea were compelled to export large quantities of coin and precious metal. *A fortiori* these exports must have been proportionately the same, during the preceding centuries.
31. Ch. de la Roncière, *La découverte de l'Afrique au Moyen Age*, Vol. I, p. 163.
32. *S.S.*, Vol. XVII, p. 29. For the economic use of the treasures, see the very acute observations of M. Van Werveke, in the article referred to below, note 34.
33. In England, during the 12th century there was an additional payment of 10%, called the *aurum reginae*, due to the queen from persons who purchased any licence or favour from the king (T. F. Tout, *Chapters in the administrative history of mediaeval England*, Vol. V, 1930, p. 264). The term is a strange one; but it does not warrant the conclusion that all payments in this respect were really made in gold.
34. An excellent example of this kind of research has been provided, for France and Lotharingia, by M. H. Werveke's *Monnaie, lingots on marchandises?* in *Annales*, Vol. IV, 1932, pp. 452ff. If I can get the necessary support I hope to set on foot similar enquiries in various regions of France.
35. Mabillon, *Aux. ord. S. Bened.*, 1080, no. LXXI; L. Lex, *Eudes, comte de Blois*, 1892, appendix no. X; the word *sepias* (cf. Du Cange, *Glossarium*) does not appear to me to mean anything else but fish, probably dried.
36. *Revue des études juives*, Vol. LXVIII, 1914, pp. 64 and 73.
37. L. Blanchard, *Le besant d'or sarrazinois pendant les croisades* in *Mémoires de l' Acad. des Sciences . . . de Marseille*, Vol. XXIV, 1879-1880.
38. It is of course possible that old Roman *sous* continued in circulation for some time, at least in some places; cf. for the finds of treasure, U. Monneret de Villars, *Rivista italiana di numismatica*, Vol. XXXII, p. 29, and for the texts (and the expression *solidos romanos*), the article by M. Sánchez-Albornoz referred to above, note 6; M. Sánchez-Albornoz seems moreover to be of the opinion that it was the silver coinage that survived.
39. *Bulletin des musées royaux . . . à Bruxelles*, 1909, p. 74; *Numismatic Chronicle*, 1914, pp. 79 and 84; G. Colson (in *Revue numismatique*, 1850, pp. 240 and 243) has called attention to a find of about a hundred *dinars* 'in the ancient chapel of the Del Camp monastery'. I have not been able to identify this place.
40. *Versus contra indices*, in *poetae aevi karol.*, Vol. I, p. 498, lines 173ff.; *Gesta abbatum Trudonensium*, 1, 3, in *S.S.* X, p. 231, and edit. C. de Borman, Vol. I, p. 9. The two editions give: *mancosos 5 pensantes denarios 6*, and this reading, as M. F. L. Ganshof and M. l'abbé De Clerc have kindly informed me, is in agreement with that of MSS. no. 18181 and 7647-7651 in the Bibl. Royale at Brussels, and no. 6 in the Grand Séminaire at Malines. But it is in itself an impossible reading. Perhaps

222 THE PROBLEM OF GOLD IN THE MIDDLE AGES

we should emend 'den. VI' to 'den XI', which would give as the total weight of the *mancus* a reasonable figure (between 19 and 20 g., that is a little less than 4 g. per *mancus*).

41. Bitterauf, *Die Traditionen des Hochstifts Freising*. The last mention of a gold *sou* in the 9th century is there said to be in the year 846 (Vol. I, no. 679); and the money might still be paid either in gold – one *sou* – or in silver – 30 *deniers* (the usual equivalent in Bavaria). The first mention of bezants occurs between 1024 and 1031 (Vol. II, no. 1609). From this moment onwards, gold coins, whether simply as *aurei*, or under the specific name of *bezants*, figure frequently in the clauses relating to the right of redemption which was recognised to belong to the heirs of the donor, in cases where the gift had been put to something other than its proper purpose.

42. Petri Damiani, *Ep. V*, 3.

43. *Cantatorium sive Chronicon S. Huberti*, C. 65; edit. Hanquet, p. 68. On p. 121 this sum is given as the equivalent of 700 silver marks, which – supposing it refers to Cologne marks, and valuing it in round figures at 230 g. – would give 1,610 kg. of silver. Unfortunately, we do not know the date of the *hyperperon*, which makes it very difficult to establish the relationship between the two metals. For this operation and others at the same period and in the same circles using gold, this time in the form of ingots, cf. Van Werveke in *Annales*, Vol. II, 1932, pp. 459ff.

44. L. Delisle, in *Bibliothèque de l'École des Chartes*, 1848–1849 (2nd series, Vol. I) p. 207.

45. R. L. Poole, *The Exchequer in the twelfth century*, 1912, pp. 84–85; M. Prou and A. Vidier, *Recueil des Chartes de Saint-Benoît-sur-Loire*, Vol. I, no. CL; M. Quantin, *Cartulaire général d l'Yonne*, Vol. II, no. CCLXXIX. The abbot of Saint-Benoît appears to have preferred to be paid 500 *bezants* rather than 200 silver marks.

46. Marc Bloch, *Les rois thaumaturges*, 1924 (*Publications de la Faculté des Lettres de Strasbourg, XIX*), p. 240, note 2 (with bibliography). For the reign of Philip Augustus, add Le Blanc, *Traité des monnoies*, p. 170. The account from the *Hôtel*, from which Le Blanc here gives some extracts, seems to have been omitted by Borrelli de Serres in his *Étude sur la comptabilité publique au XIIIe Siècle*, which forms the first part of his *Recherches sur divers services publics*, 1895.

47. Le Blanc, op. cit., p. 170; *Livre des Métiers*, I, XVIII, 13; Calendar of Patent Rolls, Henry III, 1247–1258, p. 314 (1254, July 21st). The treasure included, besides, some gold not in the form of coins and various other gold coins, whose origin (if I understand the analysis of the document correctly) was not specified, no doubt because there were only a few of them.

48. Examples abound in the text and the notes of P. Fabre's edition of the *Liber Censuum*. It will be noticed on p. 110 that the quit-rent due from Saint-Marie-Majeure de Verceil was fixed indifferently at a *bezant* or a *marabotin*. The numerous Anglo-Saxon *deniers* found in Rome

THE PROBLEM OF GOLD IN THE MIDDLE AGES 223

appear to prove that although stipulated in *mancus*, the dues owing to Saint-Peter were in fact often paid in silver; cf. O. Jensen, *Denarius Sancti Petri*, in *Transactions of the Historical Society*, 1901, p. 191. It is significant that the form of one of the *deniers* of Edward the Elder (901–924) was probably copied by Pope John XII (955–969); cf. C. Oman, *The Coinage of England*, p. 55.

49. *Liber testamentorum S. Martini de Campis*, edit. Depoin, 1905, no. XXXVII.
50. V.-L. Bourrilly, in *Les Bouches-du-Rhône, Encyclopédie*, 1st part, Vol. II, 1924, p. 316; the count undertook besides to make an annual payment of 15,000 gold marks.
51. H. A. Erhard, *Regesta historiae Westfaliae*, Vol. II, p. 135, no. CCLXXXV.
52. M. Quantin, *Cartulaire général de l'Yonne*, Vol. II, no. CLXXVII. But the crusade also gave rise to movements in the opposite direction, for those going on crusade sought to take gold with them; it is impossible for us to say in which direction the balance inclined. In 1189, the Comte de Frensdorf, preparing to accompany his master the Emperor to the Holy Land, made over his rights of advowson to the church of Bamberg; the amount of the loan had been fixed at 400 silver marks. The count received at his own request 40 gold marks instead. Cf. A. Köberlin, *Fränkische Münzverhältnisse*, 1899, p. 3.
53. *Codex Hirsaugiensis*, in *Bibliothek des literarischen Vereins*, Vol. 1, 2, p. 51. The small amount of information obtainable on the reciprocal rates of the two precious metals before minting was resumed proved more especially how variable they were, as E. Born has been quick to grasp in *Das Zeitalter des Denars*, p. 115. In a general way what information we can gather does not suggest a very strong appreciation of gold. In 1044, Henry III borrowed from the church of Worms 20 gold livres and 200 silver marks; at the same time the bishop got the Chapter to give him 57 silver marks to be spent 'in the service of the king'. It is clear that the church of Worms had much more silver than gold at its disposal. If one admits that the mark was worth in round figures two-thirds of a *livre*, the canons on this occasion must have disbursed 171 silver *livres* against 20 gold livres. But a demand for gold did not find the church at a loss to provide it (*Dipl.* H. III, no. 125; *Neues Archiv*, 1899, p. 725).
54. The interesting work by M. Levi Provençal, *L'Europe musulmane au Xe siècle*, 1932, does not give any exact information on the sources of imported produce, except as regards slaves.
55. G. de Tournadre, *Histoire de comte de Forcalquier*, 1930, p. 39.
56. The obligation rested in principle on all the Lombard rivers; but from the time of Otto III, the privileges given to various churches introduced certain exceptions; cf. Solmi, *L'amministrazione*, p. 138, note 1.
57. *Liber monasterii de Hyda*, edit. E. Edwards (*Rolls Series*), p. 154.
58. There is a whole literature on the subject of this coin. U. Monneret has made a list of it in his *Rivista italiana di numismatica*, Vol. XXXII, p. 95, note 5.

224 THE PROBLEM OF GOLD IN THE MIDDLE AGES

59. H. Lavoix, *Catalogue des monnaies arabes*, Vol. II, p. 25; cf. pp. 25ff. for evidence of counterfeit *dinars* still being produced at Majorca in 1273.
60. *Histoire du Languedoc*, Vol. V, no. 346 ('de ipsa moneta de ipso auro').
61. *Liber Jurium*, Vol. I, no. CL. At first sight one might be tempted to compare this document with the text relating to Marseilles, referred to above, note 8. But these two pieces of evidence are in fact amenable to quite different explanations. Both of them certainly refer to the striking of a coinage which does not correspond with any known minting; but at Marseilles we are dealing with a privilége which could scarcely apply to anything except an official minting, which was decided upon but not actually carried out; whereas at Genoa the lease bears witness to a minting that was actually carried out, though we cannot trace any of its products.
62. For the *millares*, see the memoirs of A. Germain (still the fundamental work on the subject), *De la monnaie mahométane attribuée à un évêque de Maguelonne*, in *Mémoires de la Soc. Archéologique de Montpellier*, Vol. III, 1850–1854 (cf. for the Majorcan minting of 1268, p. 694), and L. Blanchard, *Le millares; étude sur une monnaie du XIII siècle imitée de l'arabe par les chrétiens pour les besoins de leur commerce en pays maure*, Marseilles, 1876. For the German *dirhems*, H. Dannenberg, *Die deutschen Münzen der Sächsischen. . . . Kaiserzeit*, Vol. I, no. 1185, and Vol. II, no. 1738. For Oléron, A. Molinier, *Correspondance administrative d'Alphonse de Poitiers*, Vol. I, no. 695. The County coiner of Montreuil-Bonnin, anxious about his supplies, had complained about the purchases of counterfeit coins made at La Rochelle by the island's mint, the island being then in English hands. Alphonse directed the seneschal of Saintonge to find out whether these purchases were in fact illicit; if so, he was to see that the embargo was maintained. Quite clearly there was no question of contesting the legality of the mintings in themselves.
63. A Bull of Innocent IV in reply to a request from Cardinal Eudes de Châteauroux, legate to the Holy Land, Feb. 8th, 1253; Raynaldi, *Ann.*, 1253, §52; cf. Potthast, no. 14868; a Bull of Clement IV to the Bishop of Maguelonne, 1266, Sept. 16th (*Gallia christ.*, Vol. VI, instr., p. 374, no. XIV); cf. A. Germain, *De la Monnaie musulmane attribuée à un évêque de Maguelonne*, in *Mémoires de la Société Archéologique de Montpellier*, Vol. III, p. 685, note 1, and E. Cartier, in *Revue numismatique*, 1855, p. 198; Letter from Saint Louis to Alphonse of Poitiers, 1267, July 19th, in *Layettes du Trésor des Chartes*, Vol. V, no. 812, and a directive from Alphonse, in A. Molinier, *Correspondance administrative d'Alphonse de Poitiers*, Vol. I, no. 556. In the two latter cases, it was a question of *millares*, that is to say, silver; but the Bull of Innocent IV mentions some gold coins (*bisanciis*) as well as silver (*drachmis*).
64. Lavoix, *Catalogue*, Vol. II, *Préface*, p. 31; G. Schlumberger, *Numismatique de l'Orient latin*, 1878, pp. 140ff.
65. *Rotuli litter. patentium*, Vol. I, pp. 135 and 141. Cf. earlier the shrewd

THE PROBLEM OF GOLD IN THE MIDDLE AGES 225

remark of Tacitus on 'Germania' (Bk. V): 'Their preference is for silver rather than for gold, not because their tastes lie in that direction, but because silver coins are quantitatively more useful to people who chiefly trade in common objects of only moderate value.'

66. A considerable part of the gold in circulation was naturally in the hands of the money-changers, who were often at the same time coiners. The most ancient edition of the laws of the city of Strasbourg – about 1150 – direct (C.77) that any new coiner must pay the bishop half an ounce of gold, and the master of the mint 5 'gold *deniers*' (*marabotins* or *besants*? – we do not know).

67. R. Hoeniger, *Kölner Schreinsurkunden*, Vol. II, 1 (*Publikationen der Gesellsch. für Rheinische Geschichtskunde*, I), p. 273. Neighbouring properties (pp. 274, 276, 277) paid a pound of pepper. The use of the *mancus* as a unit of weight for gold may perhaps be explained by English influence, for Cologne had fairly old and close trade relationships with England.

68. *Topographia christiana*, II, 148; cf. Procope, *De bello gothico*.

69. The growing importance of gold as a medium of exchange well before the resumption of gold minting is clearly brought out by the successive measures taken by the Dukes of Austria. In 1192, they forbade the Ratisbon merchants to buy silver in metal form in Austrian territory; it was clearly reserved for the ducal mint. But they were allowed to buy gold (*Regensburger Urkundenbuch*, Vol. I, no. 44, in *Monumenta boica*, Vol. LIII); in 1221, the veto was placed upon gold as well as silver: neither of them could be acquired except by the Duke himself (*Stadtrecht* de Vienne, c. 23, in Keutgen, *Urkunder zur städtischen Verfassungsgeschichte*, p. 209).

70. *Regensburger Urkundenbuch*, Vol. I, no. 445 (1324); Luschin von Ebengreuth, *Goldgeschäfte Meinhards II, Grafen von Tirol, und seiner Söhne*, in *Veröffentlichungen des Museums Ferdinandeum*, 1928, p. 449. One should note the part played by the Counts of Tyrol, who carried on a flourishing trade in gold, buying it in Germany and re-selling it in Italy.

71. E. Cartier, in *Revue numismatique*, 1847, pp. 120ff. The money sent also included a gold mark, of 'Montferrant'; cf. above, note 17. The only author, it seems, who has referred to this text in relation to the *hyperperon* is Casaretto, *La moneta genovese*, pp. 136ff.

72. *Rotuli parlamentiorum*, Vol. II, p. 137, c. 14; the remedy proposed was not only a native gold coinage, but a common gold coinage for England and Flanders.

73. Inama-Sternegg, *Die Goldwährung des deutschen Reiches während des Mittelalters*, in *Zeitschrift für Social-und Wirtschaftsgeschichte*, Vol. III, 1894, p. 55; W. Jesse, *Das wendische Münzverein*, 1928 (*Quellen und Darstellungen zur hansischen Geschichte*, N.F.VI), p. 115.

74. Perhaps we should consider, in the early stages at any rate, the part played by the hostility of merchants which are not sufficiently explained by mere routine. In 1257, when Henry III of England formed the project of initiating a gold coinage, he sounded the opinion of the

226 THE PROBLEM OF GOLD IN THE MIDDLE AGES

chief burgesses of London. They declared the reform to be inopportune. Their reasons, as given to the King, have been set down for us by one of their number, Alderman Fitz Thedmar, in his *Chronica maiorum et vicecomitum Londoniarum*, which he drew up not many years later (*De antiquis legibus liber*, edit. Stapleton, *Camden Society*, 1846, pp. 20–30). These reasons are very strange. Our people, he says, foresaw grave difficulties for the poor, 'many of whom do not possess moveable goods worth as much as one gold piece', and expected a fall in the price of the metal. If we are to believe Fitz Thedmar, this fall would in fact have taken place (the king having overruled the objection). But it is hardly necessary to say that, taking into account local variations, which were always a possibility, the overall effect wherever gold minting had been resumed was exactly the opposite: the demand on the part of the mints raised the rates of exchange. But it is also probable that it helped to stabilise them. May not this have been what the rich burgesses feared, seeing that they were more or less interested in speculations on gold?

75. For the exchange rates for the metals, after minting was resumed, see especially: A Nagi, *Die Goldwährung und die handelsmässige Geldrechnung im Mittelalter*, in *Numismatische Zeitschrift*, Vol. XXVI, 1894, p. 79; E. Luschin von Ebengreuth, *Das Weitverhältnis zwischen den Edelmetallen in Deutschland während des Mittelalters*, in *Congrès International de Numismatique organisé... à Bruxelles*, 1891, p. 471, and *Goldgeschäfte Meinhards II*, p. 444. Cf. also the controversy between various numismatists in *Annuaire Soc. Franç. Numismat.*, 1890 and 1891. Naturally, the rise in the rates for metal reacted on the coinage rates. It is characteristic that shortly before the first English minting came to an end, the value of gold pieces should have moved from 20 to 24 silver deniers. The same movement, slightly obscured by the monetary speculations of the monarchy, but quite clearly discernible nonetheless, is to be observed in France under Saint Louis, Philip III and Philip IV.

76. R. Cessi, *Problemi monetari e bancari veneziani del secolo XIV*, in *Archivio Veneto-Tridentino*, Vol. IX, 1926, p. 241; Villani, XII, 53.

77. *Zeitschrift des Vereins für lübeckische Geschichte*, Vol. I, 1855, p. 52; W. Jesse, *Der wendische Münzverein*, pp. 70 and 161. In 1399–1400, gold was sent from the Low Countries to Hamburg: H. Nirnnheim, *Das Hamburgische Pfund-und Werkzollbuch*, 1930 (*Veröffentlichungen aus dem Staats-archiv der Freien und Hansestadt Hamburg*, Vol. II), p. lvii.

78. Besides the texts referred to above, note 33, *Regensburger Urkundenbuch*, Vol. I, nos. 41, 44, 466 and (for Tournai) 539; F. Bastian, *Oberdeutsche Kaufleute in den älteren Tiroler Raitbüchern*, 1931 (*Schriftenreihe zur bayerischen Landesgeschichte*, 10), pp. 121 and 124, nos. 2, 4 and 5.

79. On this subject as a whole see the very informative book by Ch. de la Roncière, *La découverte de l'Afrique au Moyen Age*, 3 Vols., Cairo, 1925–1927 (*Mém. de la Soc. Royale de Géographie d'Égypte*, Vol. V, VI and XIII). Cf. H. Sieveking, *Genueser Finanzwesen*, Vol. II, 1899, p. 92,

and Eustache de la Fosse, *Voyage*, edit. Fouché-Delbosc, in *Revue hispanique*, 1897.
80. Borrelli de Serres, *Les variations monétaires sous Philippe le Bel*, in *Gazette numismatique*, 1901, p. 377, note 3.
81. L. Blanchard, *Du rapport de l'or à l'argent en Sicile de 1278 à 1302*, in *Mém. Acad. Sciences Marseille*, Vol. XXIX, 1888–1892.
82. Cf. in England, in 1257, *Chronica maiorum*, p. 30, and the various German texts summarised by Inama-Sternegg, *Die Goldwährung*.
83. *Rotuli parlamentiorum*, Vol. II, p. 138, c. 14.
84. *Villani*, XI, 93; Inama-Sternegg, *Die Goldwährung*, p. 14, note 17.
85. Cf. the report by Pepe Bonaprise (about 1323), quoted by N. de Wailly, *Mémoire sur les variations de la livre tournoise*, in *Mémoires de l'Acad. des Inscriptions*, Vol. XXI, p. 213.
86. A directive by the Duke of Brittany, John V (1425, Feb. 12th), in M. Planiol, *La Très-Ancienne Coutume de Bretagne*, 1896, p. 385; cf. *ibid.* a directive of Feb. 1st, 1385 and May 15th 1386, and L. Lièvre, *La Monnaie et le change en Bourgogne sous les ducs Valois*, 1929, pp. 80 and 108.

A Bibliographical Survey

To give an approximately complete list of references for the monetary history of gold in the Middle Ages would almost amount to giving a bibliography of mediaeval money. It would certainly not be a useless task – especially if it were a critical bibliography – and there are no reasons for believing it to be impossible. But I need hardly apologise for not having undertaken it here. The notes above will have provided pointers to some detailed works. Here, I shall not do more than refer to the chief general works which, since they contain bibliographical lists, will help the beginner to find his bearings; and I have added some studies relating particularly to the problem of gold.

*   *   *

Although the historian may consider that the author gives undue space to the interests of the collector, the most reliable manual is undoubtedly the work by A. Luschin von Ebengreuth, *Allgemeine Münzkunde und Geldgeschichte des Mittelalters und der Neueren Zeit*, 2nd edit., 1926 (*Handbuch der mittelalterlichen und neueren Geschichte*, hgg. von G. v. Below und F. Meinecke). Unfortunately, the parallel work by F. Friedensburg, *Münzkunde und Geldgeschichte der Einzelstaaten*, which also came out in 1926 in the same collection, is much less satisfactory. The researches of A. Soetbeer, *Beiträge zur Geschichte des Geld-und Münzwesens*, in *Forschungen zur deutschen Geschichte*, Vol. I, II, IV and VI, 1860, 1861, 1864, 1866, remain fundamental.

For workers already familiar with the interpretation of texts, the skilfully chosen collection of documents brought out by M. W. Jesse in 1924, entitled *Quellenbuch zur Geld-und Münzgeschichte des Mittelalters*, will immediately lead them to the main problems.

For France, consult A. Blanchet and A. Dieudonné, *Manuel de numismatique française*, Vols. I and II, 1912–1916 (as far as the Capetian period is concerned), so far only cover the royal coinage. For England, see the list – sometimes a little hasty – given by Ch. Oman in *The Coinage of England*, 1931; for the Anglo-Saxon epoch cf. H. Munro-Chadwick, *The Monetary System*, in his *Studies on Anglo-Saxon Institutions*, 1905 (for gold coinage, see especially p. 5). For Germany, Erich Born's book, *Das Zeitalter des Denars*, 1924 (*Wirtschafts-und Verwaltungsstudien* . . . hgg. von G. von Schanz, Vol. LXIII) attempts a general survey which, though sometimes questionable, should not be neglected. The reader will need to refer also to the older work of Th. Eheberg, *Uber das ältere deutsche Münzwesen*, 1879 (*Staats-und Socialwissemschaftliche Forschungen*, hgg. von G. Scomoller, II, 5). For Italy in ancient times the reader will find a good deal of important information collected by Ugo Monneret de Villars, *La Moneta in Italia durante l'alto medio evo*, in *Rivista italiana di numismatisca*, Vols. XXXII and XXXIII, 1919–1920. What is more, this excellent memoir covers much more than the Italian scene, and will be found to contain (notably Vol. XXXII, pp. 78ff.) a study on the *mancus*, to which I am greatly indebted. The facts relating to this coin quoted without references are taken from his work. I have likewise made equally generous use for a more recent period of the unfortunately unfinished work of P. F. Casaretto, *La Moneta genovese* (*Atti delia Soc. Ligure di Storia Patria*, Vol. LV, 1928); cf. the review by our collaborator A. E. Sayous, in *Annales*, Vol. II, 1930, p. 266; any information given, without particular references, on the subject of Genoa has been derived from this source. For Florence, and incidentally Italian coining in general, the reader should refer to R. Davidsohn, *Geschichte von Florenz* (see particularly, for the resumption on gold minting, Vol. II, p. 441; for the silver *sou*, Vol. II, p. 213, and the *Forschungen* by the same author, Vol. IV, p. 318; for the first papal gold coinage, Vol. IV, 2, p. 290).

The catalogues of the great collections, often with useful introductions, are indispensable. Several of them have been mentioned above in the notes. The little volume by M. Menadier entitled *Die Schausammlung des Münzkabinetts im Kaiser-Friedrich Museum*, 1919, has the subtitle: *Eine Münzgeschichte europäischen Staaten*, and it lives up to the promise (see particularly p. 215 for the resumption of gold minting in the Empire). Mention must also be made of the valuable introductions that precede Maurice Prou's *Catalogues des monnaies merovingiennes et carolingiennes* in the Bibliothèque Nationale (1892–1896); for Frankish coining, which is a particularly thorny subject, but only of indirect interest to us here, these two works and the general ones that have appeared since provide all the necessary bibliographical information. One should add the memoir by M. Segre, *La circolazione monetaria del regno dei Franchi*, in *Rivista storica italiana*, 1931.

*   *   *

THE PROBLEM OF GOLD IN THE MIDDLE AGES

The works by Inama-Sternegg and Luschin von Ebengreuth on the problem of gold in the Middle Ages have been referred to above (notes 73 and 75) on the subject of the monetary system following the period of resumed minting; it is in fact to this period that they chiefly refer.

The return of a gold coinage and its relationships with the decay of Byzantine money has been studied by G. I. Bratianu in his suggestive work '*L'hyperpère byzantin et la monnaie d'or des républiques italiennes*, in *Mélanges Diehl*, Vol. I, 1930. This memoir also contains a very useful account of the fate of the *hyperperon* itself, with some bibliographical indications; cf. A. Andréadès, *De la monnaie et de la puissance d'achat des métaux précieux dans l'Empire byzantin*, in *Byzantion*, Vol. I, 1924.

For the minting of gold in England, consult the two articles by J. Evans, *On gold coins struck in late Saxon times*, and *The first gold coins of England*, in *Numismatic Chronicle*, 1879 and 1900; for the first mintings in the Low Countries, V. Tourneur, *Le florin du type florentin dans les principautés belges*, in *Revue belge de numismatique*, 1926.

8

NATURAL ECONOMY OR MONEY ECONOMY: A PSEUDO-DILEMMA[1]

Sclerosis, an illness well known in the medical world, is no less dangerous to man in the world of nomenclature. We historians need to classify, but we also have to be constantly on our guard against continuing to accept rigid schemes which have been drawn up in the past. The thoughts that follow have no other aim but to bring out, by considering one clear case, the need for this periodical re-thinking of all our categories. If they are intentionally confined to a relatively limited historical problem, it is not because there is no awareness of their possibly wider application – with various slight modifications – to many other phases of economic development; very rich rewards could be reaped particularly from research into colonial economies and even that of the United States down to quite late in the 19th century, if it was carried out in a similar spirit. But it seemed to me that an analysis concentrated on one field would be both clearer and more penetrating.

The notion of an economy dependent upon payments in kind was put forward for the first time in 1864 by Bruno Hildebrand, and it has flourished exceedingly.[2] Again and again attempts have been made to see it as the cardinal feature in the economic civilisation of the Great Days of the Middle Ages right up to the Renaissance of the 12th and 13th centuries. But a closer look shows that this over-simple classification leads in this particular case to a failure to come to grips with a fundamental problem. For – make no mistake – to reduce a very complicated system of payments to one simple process of barter between producers or one-sided payments in kind by peasants forced to surrender a part of their harvest to their feudal lord, saves the historian the trouble of enquiring whether in this kind of society, so very remote in all respects from ours, the instruments of exchange may not themselves have fulfilled functions very different from those of today or yesterday. This simplification encourages us to ignore a problem which, in fact, requires careful analysis: it is a lazy solution whose apparent simplicity would soon be exploded by a more searching enquiry.

*   *   *

By way of definition, it seems necessary to draw a preliminary distinction. The exchange of one commodity for another by means of something other than gold or silver does not by that fact escape the rubric of a money economy. In other words, we should beware of arguing that there is no money except metallic money. Stated in a general form, this is certainly a commonplace truth to be found by the most cursory examination of any text-book. The important point, once the facts are really examined, is to get at the reasons which obliged the various societies in the High Middle Ages to adopt such practices. Any one explanation would not cover the situation as it really was. Sometimes, it is clear, we are simply dealing with the survival of types of economy that are still very primitive. Thus in Frisia certain pieces of material of a specific length and no doubt weave were used as a measure and medium of exchange.[3] The custom continued long after the knowledge of metal money had spread among the groups who were familiar with it. In itself it probably preceded a metal coinage and was justified by the infrequency with which new money was minted. But payments in peppercorn raise quite different problems.

There can be no doubt that this condiment did really – at least in the 10th and 11th centuries – act as money.[4] But let us beware of imagining a system of direct barter by which the grocer took a few pinches from the contents of his bins in order to buy himself shoes from his neighbour the cobbler. To quote only one example out of a hundred, a certain Norman manorial official, about the year 1180, received a grant from his master of a piece of land, part of an assart. He undertook to pay a pound of peppercorns annually as rent.[5] But this does not mean that the importation or sale of oriental goods was part of his ordinary occupation. Still less are we to imagine him growing pepper-plants in his orchard. On the other hand it is not impossible that the produce from the rent was used to season the sauces and roasts of the seignorial table. But even this is not certain. There is no reason why we should not imagine it reserved once again for making further payments. In Genoa particularly peppercorns were commonly used in loans both by private persons and by the commune.

It is pretty clear what reasons had led to the choice of this particular commodity among all the possible substitutes for precious metals. As a matter of fact, pepper fulfilled all the conditions demanded by classical theory of a material suitable for use as money. It was relatively scarce, and so had a relatively high value over against a relatively low volume and weight.

It was easily kept. It came more or less into the category of 'fungible' articles, there probably being little perceptible difference of quality between the different varieties. Finally, while serving as a more or less abstract medium of exchange, it was also genuine merchandise, with a value-in-use quite independent of its monetary function. One was practically always certain of finding someone ready to accept accumulated stocks, perhaps more readily than in the case of gold or silver. We know that our ancestors were fond of highly flavoured foods, a preference that was after all largely based on the very rudimentary methods of stock-rearing, which made venison the only form of more or less edible meat. And in this preference we can recognise one of the reasons for their monetary habits.

But we must carefully note that the case of societies using this strange money was very different from that of Frisia, with its lengths of cloth. There was nothing economically backward about them: for Genoa itself was one of the most lively centres of mediaeval trade; and Normandy conjures up the picture of a countryside that was at that time pre-eminently flourishing and well developed. Moreover, the use as a monetary medium of an exotic substance shows how far these communities were from practising or seeking to establish any kind of closed economy. On the other hand a long tradition had familiarised them with the idea and the use of metallic money, which they

A PSEUDO-DILEMMA

never ceased to employ along with payment or credit in peppercorns. Why then were they not content to do their accounting in pounds, shillings, and pence, and settle their balances in metallic coin?

At first sight, one is tempted to put this down to the scarcity of precious metals; and this explanation should not in fact be altogether rejected, provided that we recognise the varying significance of this fact, according to the period under consideration. For the period before the great turning point marked approximately by the end of the 11th century, there can be no doubt that the precious metals were in short supply. Not only was the native production of gold negligible, and that of silver very modest; but the balance of trade, which was then definitely unfavourable, had the further effect of draining away many gold coins and ingots to the East; and the sluggish working of the exchanges, by slowing down the circulation, reinforced the effects of deficient supplies. Yet on the other hand it is clear that these latter considerations cannot apply to the Genoese economy, or even to Normandy, during the 12th and 13th centuries.[6] But there, too, it appears that a certain dearth of money frequently made itself felt, for the increase in the stock of metal, however considerable it might be, had not kept pace with the inordinately increased demands of trade and credit. Mediaeval capitalism was constantly handicapped because it did not manage to invent the banknote. In one sense, the use of peppercorns as money was one of the results of this shortage – a form, if you like, of necessary inflation.

There was another reason, however, which encouraged this practice, and its importance should not be neglected. This was the imperfect nature of the mintings. Here, the responsibility lay with the fragmentation of political authority, the origins of which fall outside our present subject. Not only were the mints very numerous and the pieces in circulation very various as regards their place of origin, but even the issues of each mint were subject to almost constant jumps in value. Hence the tendency to resort to a commodity whose value was more or less stable. This flight from metallic money never became complete; but it was repeated sporadically, and is a thoroughly characteristic phenomenon in the mediaeval economy, sometimes assuming the most highly developed forms. It amounted in the last analysis to a flight from the State. For if payments in pepper carry the stamp, in several respects, of the most classical type of monetary payment, they lack one feature which would be needed to make the similarity complete. Although it was precious, durable and fungible, this monetary commodity lacked the stamp of the public authorities. There is thus some doubt whether such usages were fully in keeping with the idea of a money economy; but it would seem still more doubtful to range them under the heading of a natural economy.

*   *   *

Metallic money, inherited by the Middle Ages from the Mediterranean civilisations, never ceased to be a familiar feature, however; but there were different modes of use which should be more precisely described. To this end we shall find it convenient to adopt the definitions that current doctrine, based upon the experience of the first capitalist age, affords for the part played by money. As is well known, three distinct functions are recognised: the conservation of value (which makes money, as Simiand puts it, a marvellous instrument for economic 'anticipation'); an instrument for payment; and a measure of value. In the light of these three notions, taken one at a time, let us see what we can learn from documentary evidence about the practices followed in Western and Central Europe from the Carolingian period to about the year 1200.

Clearly, the precious metals never ceased during this period to constitute the most favoured instrument for the conservation of value. But not, most frequently, in the form of specie, nor even, it seems, in ingots. In the church treasuries for certain, and probably also in those of great men and royalty, the greater part of the metal reserves was in the shape of gold ornaments – vases, liturgical ornaments, table-ware, and all kinds of jewellery. If need arose to make a payment beyond the scope of one's regular income, these objects would be pledged to a money-lender, in the hope – which was often disappointed – of being able to redeem them later on. Or they would be taken to the foundry. This operation did not then appear exceptional, as it did later on in the France of Louis XIV, for example, or during the Revolution. Even then the instability of money was not without its effect. What was the good of keeping in one's strong-box a medium of exchange of variable value which easily went out of fashion? But a custom like this also bears witness to the low value set upon the element of human labour in the economy of this period. If anyone could so easily resign himself to losing the value of the work embodied in the material, it is evident that this could not have represented a very high proportion of the loss. Finally, there can be no doubt that those who hoarded treasures were yielding also, and perhaps principally, to the desire to extract from their fortune at the present moment a more direct pleasure than a pure and simple 'anticipation' of the future. The abstract gloating over their golden crowns by a Harpagon or a Père Goriot would probably have been incomprehensible to men who were primarily moved by what was material and immediate in its appeal.

On the other hand it is no longer necessary today to show that many payments of all sorts were carried out in a coined currency. Let me just pick out one small fact among the many brought to light by recent research. In the first half of the 9th century, along with large gifts of food, the abbey of Corbie used also to distribute to the poor vagrants who knocked at its gate a certain amount of alms in the form of *deniers*;[7] which is sure proof it must have been known far and wide that a small silver coin could, at this date, provide a wandering traveller along the roads of Gaul with the modest wherewithal to satisfy his hunger.

True, one may well wonder whether, even among the best-attested of these payments in metal coin, all of them deserve to be classified as coming under a monetary economy in the strictest sense of the term. We notice, to be sure, that the coins, before being accepted, were frequently put on the scales or submitted to other tests calculated to check their precious metal content. The reason for these practices is obvious. There were only too many grounds for suspecting the quality of minting or fearing that the chisels of the astute 'clippers' had been at work, paring down little by little the edges of the *deniers*, the *mangons* and the *besants* that passed through their hands. The most careful administrations, like the Norman or Angevin exchequers in England, even when they consented to give their coins a specific denomination, used to deduct a certain percentage from their nominal value by way of compensation for the almost inevitable losses incurred.[8] Now the essential characteristic of a 'true' money as understood by the 19th-century economists is that it should carry its value in itself; and a coin that has to be weighed is not so very unlike an ingot.

But here is another reservation that will no doubt seem more serious still: far fewer payments in fact took the form of specie, whether weighed or not, than one would be inclined to infer from a casual and incautious reading of the documents. A particularly instructive example is found in the payment of the personal due, ordinarily known in France as '*chevage*'. Originally the sign of a protective relationship between lord and man, it became – at any rate in France – one of the symptoms of servitude in the new sense of the term; and under a variety of names it certainly constituted one of the most widespread of the seignorial dues in the Europe of the first feudal age. It is to be found commonly fixed at an annual rate of a few *deniers* per head. A literal interpretation of these requirements would make it appear that innumerable persons of both sexes and generally belonging to the humblest classes were in a position to make a payment each year of a number of small silver pieces. But the true situation was something quite different. Certain charters, or other documents which happen to be less guarded in language, explain clearly how the *deniers* required for the *chevage* might be replaced by goods – the nature and quantity of which was sometimes specified and sometimes passed over in silence. Sometimes they could even be replaced by a few days' work. Among the great majority of texts which do not indicate the possibility of such substitution, most do not, it seems, assert that such a procedure was ruled out; they simply deemed it superfluous to allude to a universally known custom, and one that was often imposed by inescapable necessity. Everyone knew that to pay in *deniers* meant in *deniers* or their equivalent – their 'price', as a legal document at Passau called it;[9] besides, it was obvious that to insist on always receiving what the peasant could not always give would have meant in the end that the lord risked getting nothing. Why then was money mentioned at all in such a case? Because it fulfilled the third of the functions enumerated above: it served as a measure of value.

As all readers of cartularies are aware, there was nothing exceptional about this method of procedure. It is attested in a whole variety of transactions in innumerable documents of the same period, and even as early as Merovingian times.[10] The sum to be paid was fixed in *sous* and *deniers*, and later in *livres* as well. But settlement was provided for in goods, which, as certain documents specify, should be duly 'priced' – in *appreçiadura*, as the *Cantor del mio Cid* succinctly put it.[11] This reliance upon a standard distinct from the material in which payment was made is precisely what marks the difference between such a practice and the procedure referred to above with non-metallic money. Lengths of Frisian material were at one and the same time the measure and the means of payment. The case of pepper represented in certain respects a transitional system; for the spice was also sometimes 'priced' in terms of money. Not always, however, as our Norman contract showed; and not in the usual course of events, at any rate according to the oldest examples in our possession.

The facts just recalled are common knowledge: that is why it has seemed unnecessary to untie a vast bundle of easily accessible examples. On the other hand the conclusions to which they lead undoubtedly need to be set down in the clearest terms.

One of them concerns the interpretation of the texts. Obviously, when a legal document stipulates that a price or a due shall be paid in money, one cannot legitimately conclude that the settlement was actually made in the form of specie – unless there are more precise indications to this effect. We possess two successive references concerning the gift of a serf to the monks of Saint-Père de Chartres made on November 2nd 1107 by a certain Josselin de Lèves. The first informs us that as the price of his consent, the donor's brother received twenty *sous*; the second, that instead of this sum in money he had been promised a palfry of equivalent value.[12] If we only had the first document, should we not be inclined to place this transaction to the credit of a money economy? In other words, in all statistics dealing with the means of payment in mediaeval times – and we require more and more closely marshalled facts and figures – we first need a careful list of the payments that were both measured and carried out in money; and another of the payments measured in money, but carried out in goods. Even then, we shall require a supplementary column for the doubtful cases.

In these monetary practices one can scarcely fail to recognise, moreover, the expression of one of the most significant features of so-called 'feudal' societies, observable in almost all aspects of their life – I mean their loyalty to a certain civilising tradition. Although it was, to be sure, often obscured, it nevertheless remained sufficiently deeply embedded in men's consciences to be capable of revival as soon as the atmosphere had become more favourable. Just as the political institutions of feudalism contributed to the profound enfeeblement of the State, while nevertheless preserving the memory and bearing the traces of a past in which the State had been strong, so likewise did the economy, in the days of slow-moving trade, cling unceasingly to a monetary system the principles of which had been inherited from preceding civilisations. It thus remained possible to relate variable payments to a general framework of reference.

It appears certain, moreover, that the frequent disparity between the standard and the instrument of payment was destined to leave a long and deep impress upon the economic mind of the age. To be sure, the regime of money as a system of accounting under which Europe was to live for several centuries when its economic system was already well developed, only assumed its true form from the beginning of the great monetary revolution of the 13th century; it was only then that the resumption of gold minting, the appearance of large silver coins, and the whittling down of the *denier*, which was now definitively reduced to a subsidiary role, finally succeeded in separating the intrinsic value of money from money of account. There is no doubt, moreover, that the causes which produced

A PSEUDO-DILEMMA

and maintained this dualism were extremely complicated. It would however be difficult not to believe that the way was paved by the habits of a more distant age in which money was used quite as much for 'reckoning' as for paying.

Finally, we come up once more against the problem of classification. What name should one give to a system under which money never ceased to be a standard of values, but only acted very imperfectly as a means of payment? Should one call this a natural economy or a money economy? Does not the posing of this question rather reveal how artificial and consequently dangerous is our dilemma?

*   *   *

One final question confronts us: were these objects used for payment directly produced by the man liable for the debt or by his dependants? In other words, ought we to reckon the presence of such a method of payment as – if not one of the symptoms of a 'natural economy' – at least among those belonging to a 'closed economy'? There can be no doubt that such was most frequently the case when the payer belonged to the humblest classes. Yet it even appears that peasants here and there owed dues in wine without possessing any vines.[13] Some of the best-known transactions between persons of higher rank confront us with a church paying a certain price and a member of the knightly class receiving it. Most of these do not seem to fall within the strict framework of an exclusively domestic production. We can make a guess in a good many cases; for to suppose otherwise would mean that there were quantities of war-horses in the monastic stables and secular – not to say feminine – articles of apparel in the wardrobes which were supposed to be confined to rough homespun. Sometimes the writers of documents have been at pains to guard against any ambiguity. Between 1090 and 1102, when the monks of Saint-Vincent du Mans received the consent of Hamelin the Forester to a gift of land at Ferrières, made them by one of Hamelin's uncles by marriage, they were obliged to compensate his wife for her interest, since she was the niece of the donor in the direct line. It was agreed that she should have a present of 'an assortment of furs'. But the monks obviously did not possess such an article. They sent one of their number to buy for six *livres* of Rouen, in the market at Falaise, the desired finery; and as the lady had no doubt only moderate confidence in the taste of this worthy saint, Hamelin sent one of his own servants with him, specially commissioned to 'choose the furs'.[14] Thus in an exchange transaction a payment in kind was immediately preceded and conditioned by a purchase in money.

Why, in such a case, did not the church pay directly in good ringing coin? Probably this strange roundabout method can only be explained by taking into account the preferences of the receiving party. M. Dopsch showed not long ago how the settlement of a due in coin was sometimes only a second-best. The lord would resign himself to accepting this method of payment, for example, in the case of a bad harvest. In normal circumstances, he thought it more advisable to insist on payment in kind. All this, taken in company with other evidence, goes to show that in aristocratic circles the 'closed economy' was, if not always a reality, at least an ideal.[15] In certain situations clearly defined by custom, the proprieties imposed their own laws even more firmly. In this connection there is nothing more striking than the lesson to be drawn from the deeds of sale or gift drawn up for the benefit of churches. Quite early on, in the first type of transaction, the seller frequently received the price in money; at any rate if we can take the texts at their face value. On the other hand, when it was a question of a gift, whether real or so-called, or of a genuine sale, the agreement of the near relatives was obtained by means of payments in kind, more often than not valued in terms of money. We even find stipulations like those in a notice from Saint-Martin-des-Champs, about the year 1100: an exchanger, having realised a balance in silver, makes over six *deniers* of it to his daughter but expressly 'in order to buy herself some shoes'.[16] The sum paid over for these family *'laudationes'* was always comparatively small. No doubt it would have seemed unbecoming to offer a person of distinguished rank a few insignificant small coins. An object, even a modest one, could be more easily presented and accepted, in the same way that nowadays a person who would not accept a tip does not refuse a small present. The lesson of these last examples is clear enough: they remind us in their own way of the great truth that it is not enough for a study of payments to distinguish, as it naturally must, between times and places; it must take at least equal pains to discriminate in a manner demanded by the facts between the different reasons for payment and the different classes of payers or recipients. Not only because the range of possibilities is different in different social circles – as everyone knows, money transactions spread much more quickly and completely among the rich and in the towns – but also because of a whole highly variable system of traditions and conventions. Moreover, the historian only needs to look around him to be reminded of this precept. It is still common enough at the present day for a landowner of modest means in our countryside to pay his architect by cheque, his butcher by postal order, and his grocer in cash. And if it should chance that one of his neighbours wishes to repay him for some service rendered, politeness strictly requires that this should take the form of a chicken or a present of butter. What is true now was also true in the past, *mutatis mutandis*. In other words, all research into payments must, if it wishes to achieve its goal, become a social study; and so indeed must all research-work in economic history.

NOTES

1. *Annales d'Histoire sociale*, Vol. V, 1933, pp. 7–16.
2. In an article in the *Jahrbücher der Nationalökonomie*, Vol. II: *Naturwissenschaft und Kreditwirtschaft*. The literature on the subject is immense and there would be no point in attempting to list it here. I will only refer the reader to the work of Alphons Dopsch, *Naturalwirtschaft und Geldwirtschaft in der Weltgeschichte*, Vienna, 1930, and to the excellent critical review of it by M. Van Werveke in the *Annales d'historie économique et sociale*, Vol. III, 1931, p. 428. Cf. also my remarks on a memoir by M. Heckscher, *ibid.*, p. 435, and my article on *Le problème de l'or au Moyen Age*, Vol. V, 1933, and above, p. 186.
3. Cf. M. Jaeckel, *Die friesische Wede*, in *Zeitschrift für Numismatik*, XI,

242   NATURAL ECONOMY OR MONEY ECONOMY

1884. The use of cloth as money was equally widespread among the Slavs; cf. Helmold, *Chronica Slavorum*, I, 38, edit. Schmeidler, p. 77; G. Jacob, *Arabische Berichte von Gesandten au germanische Fürstenhöfe*, Berlin, 1927, p. 13. In 1124, when Bishop Otto of Bamberg went to evangelise the Pomeranians, he sold his corn in order to buy lengths of cloth to serve him as money ransoming the captive Christians: Herbordi *Dialogus*, in *S.S.*, Vol. XX, p. 717.

4. There are numerous textual references, abundantly quoted, but the literature is unfortunately very widely dispersed. I will not do more than refer to P. F. Casaretto, *La moneta genovese*, in *Atti della Società Ligure di Storia Patria*, LV, 1928 (particularly pp. 3ff.), and to the references collected by A. E. Sayous, in *Revue Historique*, CLXX, 1932, p. 9, note 2; also to A. Schulte, *Geschichte des mittelalterlichen Handels*, Vol. I, p. 73 and note 1, and to J. Kulischer, *Allgemeine Wirtschaftsgeschichte*, I, p. 317. There are some fairly late examples in H. du Halgouet, *La Vicomté de Rohan*, 1921, Vol. I, p. 151. It would be easy to go on multiplying references.

5. P. Le Cacheux, *Chartes du prieuré de Longueville*, no. LXIX (*Publications de la Soc. de l'hist. de la Normandie*, 1934). There is another example from the same region and approximately of the same date (the reign of Henry II, Plantagenet), referring likewise to the grant of an assart. S. Deck, *Étude sur la forêt d'Eu*, 1929, p. 47.

6. C.-H. Haskins, *Studies in Norman Institutions*, 1918, p. 45, notes that in the 11th and 12th centuries money-rents played a large part in the grants made by dukes, whereas the contemporary kings of France preferred to grant revenues in kind.

7. *Statute d'Adalhard*, edit. I. Levillain, in *Le Moyen Age*, 1900, p. 355.

8. R. L. Poole, *The Exchequer in the 12th century*, 1912, pp. 3off.

9. *Die Traditionen des Hochstifts Passau*, edit. Heuwieser (*Quellen und Erörterungen zur bayerischen Geschichte*, N.F., Vol. VII), no. 108.

10. Cf. Bishop Bertrand's will (March 27th, 616), in G. Busson and A. Ledou, *Actus Ponticum Cenomannis in urbe degentium*, p. 137: 'in aurum aut in caballos solidos V'.

11. Ed. Menendez Pidal, Vol. III, line 3236 b and ff. The whole passage is of the greatest interest for the history of payments.

12. B. Guérard, *Cartulaire de l'abbage de Saint-Père de Chartres*, Vol. II, p. 274, no. XVII. Milo subsequently contested the gift, less, it would seem, because he had received a horse instead of money than because of the delay that had occurred in handing over the present. He ended by withdrawing his objection.

13. Cf. Ch.-E. Perrin, *Recherches sur la seigneurie rurale en Lorraine*, 1935, pp. 303–304.

14. R. Charles and S. Menjot d'Elbenne, *Cartulaire de Saint-Vincent du Mans*, no. 802.

15. *Naturwirtschaft und Geldwirtschaft*, p. 138. Prudent administrators estimated that in order to guard against fluctuations in price, it was as well to levy two sets of dues on each piece of land, one in money and

one in kind, without sacrificing one or the other; see the remarkably intelligent explanations in the *Gesta abbatum Trudonensium* (X, 6; edit. de Borman, Vol. I, pp. 176-177) on the subject of the tenure of office by Rodolphe, (abbot from 1108-1138). But in 1184 these same fluctuations in value of commodities made Saint-Denis substitute money revenue for revenue in kind: Archives Nationales, LL, 1157, p. 57. For the impropriety involved in a king having to buy victuals, cf. Lambert de Hersfeld, *Annales*, edit. Holder-Egger, pp. 100 and 173.

16. R. de Lasteyrie, *Cartulaire général de Paris*, no. 127, and J. Depoin, *Recueil de Chartes et documents de Saint-Martin-des-Champs*, I, no. 102. A similar mention in *Cartulaire de Notre-Dame de Josaphat*, edit. Métais, no. 62.

INDEX

Aachen, 2, 122 n
Ableiges, Jacques d', 121 n
absolutism, 31
Abyssinia, 180
accounting, 207, 210, 212, 238
Acquebouille, 110 n
Acre, 202, 206
Adam of Bremen, 195, 220 n
Adam du Petit-Pont, 165 n
Adelaide (Queen, widow of Lothar of Provence), 04
Adelaide de Forcalquier, 204
administrative classes, *see* classes
Adriatic, 204
Aebischer, P., 168 n
Africa, 180, 193
Agnes (daughter of the knight Etienne Jouvin), 93
Agobard of Lyons, 54
agrarian customs, *see* customs
agricultural revolution, 127 *ff*, 176
agriculture, 49 *ff*, 62 *f*, 119 n 126 *ff*, 140; in ancient world, 145; French, 128; Roman 128
Ahrens, J., 114 n
Aix-la-Chapelle, 13, 18 *f*
Alans, 174
Alard (Abbé), 151
Alaric I (Visigoth king), 193
Alart, E.-G., 112 n, 113 n
Albert de Behaim, 29
Aldersbach, monks of, 216
Aleaume, 93, 101, 115 n
Alexander III (Pope), 37
allods, 90 *f*, 100 *f*, 113 n, 200
Alphonse of Castile, 12
Alphonse de Poitiers, 211, 220 n
Alphonso VIII, 189, 206
Alphonso IX (king of León), 218 n

Alps, 192
Alsace, 150, 155
Altaï, 192
Ammianus Marcellinus, 161 n
anachronism, 70, 80 n, 88
Andréadès, A., 229 n
Andreas, Willy, viii
anfous, 189, 212
Anglade, J., 113 n
Anglo-Saxons, 187 *f*
animal-power, 136, 141, 147, 176, 182; *see also* horse-power
Annals of Quedlimbourg, 6
Annolied, 2
Antichrist, 26 *ff*, 40
Antipatros of Thessalonica, 160 n
Antiphilus of Byzantium, 160 n
Apocalypse, 28
Aquilini grossi, 211
Arabs, 148, 175, 187 *f*, 196, 199
Arago, 134
Aragon, 219 n
d'Arbois de Jubainville, 120 n
Archipoeta, 18, 23
Ariège, 192
Arles, 4, 13
Arnold, Brother (German Dominican) 28
Arnold of Brescia, 21, 23
Arnold, Thomas, 163 n, 219 n
Arnold, W., 160 n
Arnulf the bastard, 3
Arras, 123 n
art/artists, 23, 172, 184 n
artisans, 132 *f*, 171, 176, 201; of St Albans, 157; specialisation of, 140
Asia, 196, 214
Assembly of Forchheim, 10
Assyria, 110 n

L.A.W.I.M.E.—R   245

246 INDEX

L'Attelage et le cheval de selle à travers les âges (Lefebvre des Noëttes), 176
Auberon (Archbishop), 64
Auger, Matthew, 95 *f*, 120
Augsburg, 214
augustales, 23, 189, 201, 212
Augustus, 18, 20, 31
aureus solidus, 186 *f*, 200
aurum reginae, 221 *n*
Ausonius, 160 *n*, 161 *n*, 162 *n*
Austria, Duke of, 190
Authentiques, 22
Auxerre, 200
Averroist philosophy, 28
Avignon Papacy, 37, 190

bakers, 140, 146
Baldwin VI (Count), 91
Balkans, 188
Ball, John, 158
Ballard, A., 166 *n*
Baltic, 138, 195
Bamberg, 105, 122 *n*
banalités, 150, 152 *ff*
banco money, 210
banknote, 233
barbarians, 150, 180, 187, 193 *f*
Barbarossa, *see* Frederick Barbarossa
barley, 129
barter, 230 *f*
Bartole, 10
Bartsch, K., 115 *n*
Basileis, 187
bas-reliefs, 172
Bastgen, H., 111 *n*
Bastian, F., 226 *n*
Baudrillart, A., 167 *n*
Bavaria, 151, 192, 200
Bavaria, Duke of, 191
Beaugisière, 194
Beaulieu, 97, 101
Beer, Henri, 76 *n*
Beirut, 202
Belisarius, 144
bellows, 142

Below, Georg von, 41, 81 *n*
beneficium, 86, 111 *n*
Bennett, R., and Elton, J., 161 *n*, 166 *n*, 167 *n*
Benoît, F., 109 *n*, 119 *n*
Benzo d'Albe, 219 *n*
Berenger of Ivréa, 4
besant, 198 *ff*, 205, 210, 212
bills of exchange, 209 *f*
bimetallism, 215 *f*
Birch, W. de Gray, 161 *n*
bishops, nomination of, 36 *f*
Black Sea, 127, 175
Blanchard, L., 221 *n*, 224 *n*, 227 *n*
Blanchet, A. and Dieudonné, A. 228 *n*
Bloch, Marc, vii, *ff*; bibliography, vii; his historical method, viii *ff*; and religion, x *f*
WORKS: *Les Caractères originaux de l'histoire rurale française*, vii, x; *Feudal society*, vii, xi; *The Historian's craft*, vii; 'Mediaeval inventions', ix; *Mélanges historiques*, vii *f*, 185 *n*; 'Natural economy or money economy', ix; *Rois et serfs*, 120 *n*; *Les rois thaumaturges*, 113 *n*, 222 *n*; 'Technical change as a problem of collective psychology, viii; *Les transformations du servage*, 114 *n*
Blümner, H., 168 *n*
Bohemia, 138, 188, 190
Bologna, 22
Bonaprise, Pepe, 227 *n*
bond service, 89
Bonis brothers, 216
Bonnefoy, J. A. and Perrin, A., 109 *n*, 113 *n*
Bonneval, 97
Borman, C. de, 221 *n*
Born, E., 223 *n*, 228 *n*
Borrelli de Serres, 227 *n*
Bourrilly, V.-L., 223 *n*
Bourilly, V.-L. and Busquet, R. 119 *n*
Bouthors, A., 113 *n*
Brabant, 190, 197, 199

INDEX 247

Bratiana, Georges, 175
Bratianu, G. I., 229 n
Brindisi, 189
Bristol, 166 n
Brittany, 155, 159
Broussillon, B. de, 111 n, 116 n
Bruges, 214
Brun, A., 78 n
Brun, R., 112 n
Bruno (Saxon cleric), 10
Brutails, J. A., 163 n
buckwheat, 156
Burgundy, 4 f, 13 f
burial customs, 194
Bury, 159
Busson, G. and Ledou, A., 242 n
Byzantium, 32, 187 ff, 195 f, 200, 203, 205, 209, 211

Cabira, 137, 139
Cahen, Leon, 163 n
Calabria, 219 n
Caligula, 136, 144
Cam, Helen, 77 n
Canada, 153
Cantor del mio Cid, 237
Capet, Hugh, 65
Capetian dynasty, 9, 14, 19 f, 33 f, 63, 83, 154, 175
capitalism, 91, 233 f
Capitol, Rome, 144 f
Capitulare de villis, 150
Capitularies, 52 f
Capua, 23
caravan routes, 200
Cardiff, 156
Carolingian Empire, 1 f, 18 ff, 36, 52 ff, 63, 66, 77 n, 149, 154, 178, 187
carriages, 131
Cartier, E., 224 n, 225 n
Casaretto, P. F., 225 n, 228 n, 242 n
Cassiodorus, 152, 162 n, 164 n, 219 n
caste, 61, 64 ff
Castile, 211
Catalonia, 199, 205
Cathari, 27

Caucasus, 192
Cauvet, E., 77 n
Cavaignac, G., 165 n
Cedrenas, 161 n
Celtic languages, 139
Cessi, R., 226 n
Cevennes, 192
Champagne, 190
Champeaux, M., 109 n, 118 n, 120 n
Champeval, J. B., 112 n
Chanson d'Aspremont, 121 n
Chanson de Roland, 18, 198
Charles of Anjou, 190
Charles of Lorraine, 64
Charles the Bald, 2, 67
Charles the Fat, 3
Charles, S. and Menjot d'Elbenne, S., 242 n
Charlemagne, 18 ff, 31, 39, 54, 92, 188, 194; charter of, 18
Chartier, Alain, 78 n
Chartres, Bishop of, 89
Chartres, Count of, 97
Chaucer, Geoffrey, 141
chevage, *see* poll tax
China, 161 n, 175
Chinard, Gilbert, 76 n
Christ, *see* Jesus Christ
Christianity, xi
Chrysostom, Dion, 196
circulation of money, *see* coinage
Clapham, J. H., 221 n
classes: administrative, 82 ff; middle, 127, 141, 156; noble, 92 ff, 98 ff, 106, 127; social, 60 ff, 102 ff, 107, 135, 241
Claude of Turin, 54
cloth, as medium of exchange, 231 f, 237
Cnut the Great, 195
cogwheels, 143, 148
coinage, 23; Arabic, 203, 205 f; circulation of, 191, 206 f, 210, 213, 233; copper, 187; counterfeit, 191, 204 f, 209, 212; depreciation of, 57, 78 n, 103, 187, 193,

INDEX

210 *f*; foreign, 198 *ff*, 204; gold, 18 *ff*, 191, 193 *f*, 197, 200, 208 *ff*, 215 *f*, 233; Merovingian, 191; silver, 187 *ff*, 191, 195, 208 *ff*, 213, 238
Colin (son of the steward of Choisy), 93 *f*
Cologne, 207
Cologne, Archbishiop of, 190
colonial expansion, 49
colonus, 63
Colson, G., 221 *n*
Columba, St., 164 *n*
common, rights of, 129
Common Law, *see* Law
communal obligations, 49 *ff*
comparative method, 44 *ff*, 105
compass, *see* magnetic compass
Compostella, 218 *n*
Conrad I, 89
Conrad II (Emperor), 5
Conrad III (king), 15, 18, 20 *f*, 42 *n*
Conrad IV, 10
Conrad Hohenstaufen, 6 *f*
Conrad (priest), 17
consecration ceremony, 13, 15, 18, 24 *f*, 39, 52
Constantine (Emperor), 20, 23, 36, 146, 186, 194
copper coinage, *see* coinage
Coquille, Guy, 102
Corbie, 89; abbey of, 151, 235
Correspondence des contrôleurs généraux avec les intendants, 131
Cosmas Indicopleustès, 209
cotton, 197
Coulanges, Fustel de, 81 *n*
Council of Pavia, 32
counterfeit coinage, *see* coinage
Couronnement de Louis, 103
courts of justice, 59
craftsmen, 172
Cram, W. E., *see* Winlock, E. H. and Cram, W. E.
criminals, and labour in the mills, 146

Crump, G. C. and Hughes, A., 219 *n*
crusades, 202, 206, 211, 223 *n*
'culverts', 123 *n*
currency, *see* coinage
customs, 47; agrarian, 69, 127; burial, 194

Dagobert, 122 *n*
Damien, Peter, 200
Daniel, prophecies of, 20
Dannenberg, H., 218 *n*, 224 *n*
Davidsohn, R., 228 *n*
Davillé, Louis, 76 *n*
de la Roncière, Ch., 221 *n*, 226 *n*
de la Tour, Imbart, 77 *n*
De l'histoire au martyre Marc Bloch 1886–1944 (Febvre), xiii *n*
De Ortu et Tempore Antichristi, 26
Déchelette, J., 160 *n*, 162 *n*
Deck, S., 242 *n*
Delisle, L., 111*n*, 163 *n*, 164.*n*, 222 *n*
Demont, A., 166 *n*
denier, 188 *f*, 199 *f*, 206 *ff*, 210 *f*, 235 *ff*, 238, 240
Denis, Abbé, 80 *n*
Denis, St., 89
Denmark, 138
Depoin, J., 243 *n*
Des Marez, 118 *n*
Deutschland vor der Reformation (W. Andreas), viii
Diana (goddess), 46
Diehl, Ch., 220 *n*
dienstmann, 105
Diet of Dole, 33, 37
Diet of Roncaglia, 22
Dijon, 151, 155
dinar, 189, 199, 202, 205 *ff*; Abassid, 204 *f*
Diocletian (Emperor), 22
dirhem, 205 *ff*
Diutischin lant (*Deutschland*), 2
documentation, 47 *ff*, 171 *ff*
doges of Venice, 9
Dole, Diet of, 33, 37
dollars, 210
Domesday Book, 150, 198

INDEX 249

Donation (Constantine), 23, 36
Dopsch, A., 114 *n*, 161 *n*, 240, 241 *n*
Dorinder, A., 165 *n*
Dorstadt, 207
Douais, C., 112 *n*
drapers, 157
Drival, van, 109 *n*
drop-hammer, 181
du Halgouet, H., 242 *n*
ducats, 190, 212
dues and rents, 57, 78 *n*, 86, 90, 92, 94, 96, 101, 150, 152 *ff*, 156 *f*, 160, 178 *f*, 198, 206, 236; exemption from, 85
Dumas, Aug., 112 *n*
Dunstable, 171

Eadred (King), 204
Eastbourne, 199
Ebengreuth, A. Luschin von, 219 *n*, 220 *n*, 225 *n*, 226 *n*, 227 *n*, 229 *n*
Ebert, Max, 167 *n*
economics: and agriculture, 125, 129; and inventions, 131 *f*
Ecorcheurs, 155
education: and invention, 135; and rural societies, 126
Edward I (King of England), 213
Edwards, E., 223 *n*
Egypt/Egyptians, 124, 136, 139, 161 *n*
Eheberg, Th., 228 *n*
election: of the Emperor, 5 *ff*, 14 *ff*, 21, 39; in the Mediaeval Church, 10; of the Pope, 37 *ff*
electorate, 11 *ff*
Elmina, 214
Elton, J., *see* Bennett, R., and Elton, J.
emancipation, 95 *f*, 104
Emperor: power over Rome and the Papacy, 35 *ff*; sacred character of, 24 *ff*, 31, 38; temporal power of, 30 *ff*
Empire, under the Hohenstaufen, 1 *ff*; concept of, 16 *ff*; national character of, 40 *f*; its territorial formation, 2 *ff*; and universal monarchy, 30 *ff*
'enclosure awards', 50
enclosure movement, 49 *ff*
end of the world, 26 *f*
engineers, 133
England, 6, 14, 34, 37, 191, 197; agricultural revolution in, 129; enclosure movement in, 49 *f*; feudal system in, 57 *ff*, 87; land-systems in, 69 *f*; monetary systems in, 187 *f*, 190, 198 *ff*, 204, 212 *f*, 215 *f*, 236; Parliament in, 56; and the slave trade, 203; social classes in, 104, 107; water-mill in, 150, 156
Énlast, C., 163 *n*
environment: and invention, 132
Epistle to the Hebrews, 38
Érembaud (Flemish Lord), 103
Erhard, H. A., 223 *n*
Erlendsson, Hank, 184 *n*
Ermoldus Nigellus, 220 *n*
Ertaud, 103
Ervig (King), 53, 77 *n*
Essenes, 54
Estates General or Provincial, 55
Ethelred II, 188
ethnography, 69, 77 *n*
Eude de Blois, Court of, 85
Eustache de la Fosse, 227
Evans, J., 229 *n*
exchange media, 198, 208, 212, 230 *ff*
exchange rate, 187, 190, 193, 200 *f*, 203, 212 *f*, 215 *f*
experiment, 171

Fabre, P., 222 *n*
fallow, 127, 129
Far East, 196
farm rents, 210
Faucher, Daniel, 126 *ff*, 135 *n*
Faulhaber, C., 219 *n*
Febvre, Lucien, vii, xi *f*, xiii *n*, 170
Feldhaus, F. M., 161 *n*, 166 *n*
Ferrières, 239

250 INDEX

feudal system, 53 *ff*; and monetary practices, 238
Ficker, Julius, 41
Ficker, J. and Puntschart, P., 122 *n*
fiefs, 86 *ff*, 94 *f*, 101, 105, 110 *n*
Finch, William Coles, 167 *n*
Flanders, 83, 92, 99, 105, 190, 197
Flanders, Count of, 88
Flodoard, 165 *n*
Florence, 189 *f*, 210, 216
florin, 190, 213, 216
Foerster, W., 119 *n*
Font-Reaulx, J. de, 118 *n*
forced labour, *see* servile labour
Forchheim, Assembly of, 10
foreign exchange, 207
France/French, xi, 2, 6, 14, 32 *ff*, 37, 41, 212, 235 *f*; administrative classes in, 83 *ff*; Carolingian legend in, 19 *f*; 'Eastern', 2 *ff*, 13; enclosures in, 50 *f*; feudal system in, 55 *ff*, 61; land-systems in, 69 *f*; monetary systems in, 190, 212, 214; peasant holdings in, x; social classes in, 104, 106; towns in, 71; water-mills in, 155; 'Western', 2 *ff*
'franchises', 63
Francis, St., 27, 30
Franciscans, 27, 30
Franks, 53 *f*, 187 *f*
Frazer, Sir James, 46 *f*, 76 *n*
Frederick Barbarossa (Emperor Frederick I), 7 *f*, 13 *f*, 17 *ff*, 21 *ff*, 31 *ff*, 36, 40, 42 *n*
Frederick II (Emperor), 7, 9, 11, 14, 17, 22 *f*, 28 *ff*, 31, 34, 37 *f*, 40 *f*, 149, 189
Frederick Hohenstaufen, 6
freedmen, 99 *f*
freedom, notion of, 179
freeholds, *see* allods
freemen, 60, 65, 79 *n*, 99 *f*, 106
French language, 68, 78 *n*
French monarchy, 9
French Revolution, 235
French Rural History (J. Sondheimer), vii

Friedensburg, F., 227 *n*
Frisia, 150 *f*, 207, 231 *f*, 237
frontiers, 70 *f*
Fuller, E. A., 166 *n*
fulling-mills, *see* mills

Galbert de Bruges, 103, 112 *n*
Gall, St., 89
Ganshof, M. F. L., 83, 86 *f*, 90, 92, 97, 99 *f*, 103, 105 *ff*, 116 *n*, 118 *n*, 120 *n*, 122 *n*, 123 *n*, 221 *n*
Gansi, 93
Gaul, 53 *f*, 63, 68, 127, 129, 203; monetary systems in, 188, 193, 199, 207; water-mill in, 136 *f*, 143, 150, 159
Gautier, E., 144, 183 *n*
Gautier, L., 121 *n*
Geneva, 151, 193
Genoa/Genoese, 189, 191, 197, 201 *f*, 214, 232 *f*; mint, 205, 210
Germain, A., 219 *n*, 224 *n*
Germain d'Auxerre, 152
German monarchy, 5 *ff*, 40
German princes, as allies of the Pope, 11
German scholars, viii
Germany/Germans, viii, x, 14 *f*, 41, 63, 210; Carolingian tradition in, 19 *f*; classes in, 65 *f*; in Gaul, 127; land-systems in, 69 *f*; *ministeriales* in, 105 *f*; monetary systems in, 186, 188, 199, 202, 205, 213 *f*, 216; slavery in, 179, 203; *Stände* in, 56; water-mills in, 137, 149, 155
Gesta Friderici, 8
Girard d'Athée, 120 *n*
Girard de Roussillon, 102
Gisèle (Empress), 18
Godefroy of Viterbo, 25
gold: coinage, *see* coinage; as instrument of international exchange, 212, 216 *f*; mining of, 192; minting of, *see* minting; ornaments, 194 *f*, 197; shortage of, 191 *ff*, 233

INDEX

gold-dust, 204, 214
gold standard, 217
golden age, 29
Golden Bough, The (Frazer), 46
goldsmiths, 194, 197
Gonesse, 63
Gordian (Emperor), 22
Görz, Comte de, 190
Gothic arch, 172
Goths, 175
Grand, Roger, 183 *n*, 184 *n*
Gratian, 32, 194
Great Charter of the Teutonic Order, 35
Greco-Roman civilisation, 143 *ff*
Greece, 137
Greek *Anthology*, 134, 143, 145 *f*
Greek Emperors, 1, 195
Greeks, King of the, 32 *f*
Gregorian reforms, 10 *f*, 24
Gregory the Great (Pope), 193
Gregory VII (Pope), 10, 15, 36
Gregory IX (Pope), 28
Gregory of Tours, 80 *n*, 162 *n*, 164 *n*
Grimm, J., 42 *n*, 164 *n*
groat, 213
groschen, 211
Guérard, B., 109 *n*, 111 *n*, 114 *n*, 115 *n*, 116 *n*, 118 *n*, 121 *n*, 164 *n*, 185 *n*, 242 *n*
guilds, 133, 140
Guillaume le Breton, 120 *n*
Guinea, 214
gulden, 216
gunpowder, 169
Gutsherrschaft, 57
Guy of Osnabrück, 24 *f*

Hainault, 91, 190
Hainault, Countess of, 200
Hamelin the Forester, 239 *f*
handmills, *see* mills
harness, 172 *f*, 175 *f*, 184 *n*; and the abolition of slavery, 177 *ff*, 185 *n*
Harz mountains, 191
Haskins, C. H., 242 *n*
Hauser, H., 219 *n*

heating, methods of, 131, 145
Hebrews, Epistle to the, 38
Heckscher, M., 241 *n*
Heerschild, 65, 107
Heimpel, H., 220 *n*
Heiss, A., 219 *n*
hennin, 175
Henry II (Emperor), 5, 8, 38
Henry II (King of England), 34, 61, 200
Henry III (Emperor), 38
Henry III (King of England), 38, 213, 225 *n*
Henry IV (Emperor), 15, 24, 38, 97
Henry V (Emperor), 6
Henry VI (Emperor), 7, 9, 11, 25, 32, 34
Henry de Huntingdon, 219 *n*
Henry the Liberal (Count of Champagne), 103
Henry the Proud (Duke of Bavaria), 6
Hentzner, Paul, 162 *n*
hereditary rank, 106
hereditary service, 84 *ff*, 93 *ff*, 102, 105
heredity, 5 *ff*, 65 *f*
heresies, 27
Hering, Hans, 140
Hérivaux, abbey of, 98
Hermaville, 166 *n*
hierarchy, 97, 101, 108
Hildebrand, Bruno, 230
Hindustan, 192
Hirsau, monks of, 202
Historia de duabus civitatibus, 17
historical method, 44 *ff*
historical research, 72 *ff*
history: and psychology, 124 *ff*
Hoeniger, R., 225 *n*
Hohenstaufen period, 1 *ff*
Holy Empire, 25
homage, 34, 65, 88 *f*, 92, 100, 107, 112 *n*, 119 *n*
Hoop, J., 167 *n*
horse-power, 136, 144 *f*, 147 *ff*

252　INDEX

horse-shoe, 172, 177, 181
house-warming, see heating
Hüfen, 66 *f*
Hugo V (abbot of Saint-Germain-des-Prés), 94
Huguccio of Pisa, 32
Huizinga, J., 43 *n*
human labour, value of, 235
humanism, 20 *f*
Hungary, 190, 214
Huns, 175
hydraulic saw, 142, 181
hyperperon, 187, 199, 202, 205, 209, 211 *f*

Iceland, 138, 184 *n*
Île-de-France, 98
Île d'Oleron, 206
illuminated manuscripts, see manuscripts
immigrants, 127, 138
India, 196, 161 *n*
individualism, 49
Indo-European languages, 67 *f*
industrial revolution, 49
inflation, 217, 233
inheritance, 64, 84, 98
Innocent III (Pope), 7 *f*, 10, 15, 39
Innocent IV (Pope), 10, 28, 35
Inquisition, 27
insignia, 34
inventions, xi, 125 *ff*, 136 *ff*; borrowings and, 175 *f*; and economics, 132; in France, 131
inventiveness, periods of, 131, 145
inventors, 132 *f*
'Investiture dispute', 36 *f*
Inwärts-Eigen, 114 *n*
Ireland, 138, 151, 159, 192
Irish legend, 145
irrigation, 139 *f*
Isaiah, 29
Islam, 175, 188 *f*, 203, 205 *f*, 209
Istria, 199
Italy/Italians, 3 *f*, 13 *f*, 21, 23, 27 *f*, 36, 63; millstone in, 136 *f*; monetary systems in, 188 *ff*, 193, 199,
201, 212; *Parliamenti* in, 56; slavery in, 179, 203; social classes in, 105

Jacob, G., 242 *n*
Jaeckel, M., 241 *n*
Jakob de Köningshofen, 162 *n*
Janiculum, 144
Janse, d'O. R., 220 *n*
Japan, 175
Jarry, E., see Thillier, J. and Jarry, E.
Jayme I of Majorca, 206
Jean de Blanzac (bishop), 163 *n*
Jensen, O., 223 *n*
Jerome, St., 9
Jerusalem, 26 *f*
Jesse, W., 225 *n*, 226 *n*, 227 *n*
Jesus Christ, 54; imitation of, 30
Jewish religion, x *f*
Jews, 199
Jireček, C. J., 220 *n*
Joachim of Flore, 27
Joachites, 29
Jocelin de Brakelonde, 163 *n*
John de Charpentier, 171
John Lackland, 120 *n*, 207
John of Salisbury, 33, 40
Josselin de Lèves, 237
Jouvin, Etienne, 93
Jumièges, 154
Justinian (Emperor), 20, 31; codes of, 21 *f*

Kaiserchronik, 18, 20
Karajan, G. von, 219 *n*
Keller, F., 163 *n*
Kent, 150
Kiev, 200
kingship, 13, 24 *ff*, 38, 77 *n*
Kingsthorpe, manor of, 158
knighthood, 65, 96 *ff*, 101 *ff*, 106, 121 *n*
Knonau, Meyer von, 117 *n*
Köberlin, A., 223 *n*
Koehne, C., 164 *n*, 165 *n*, 167 *n*
Koran, 206

Kulischer, J., 218 n, 242 n
Kur, 12
La Rochelle, 206
labour supply, 132
Lacrocq, Louis, 183 n
Lafitan, Father, 46
Lambert d'Ardres, 113 n
Lambert de Hersfeld, 243 n
Lambron de Ligny, 120 n
land: appropriation of, 94; leasing of, 96; tenure, 51, 59 ff
land-systems, 69 f
Landsberger, B., 168 n
landscape, effect of enclosures on, 50
Landulphe, 97
Langlois, Ch. V., 76 n
Languedoc, 71
Last Judgment, 26
Lasteyrie, R. de, 243 n
Latin language, 68
Latouche, R., 165 n
Launay, L. de, 192, 219 n
Laurent, H., 108 n
Laurière, E., 111 n
Lavoix, H., 224 n
law: Bavarian, 151; Carolingian, 52 ff; Common, 104; English, 107; and feudalism, 59 ff, 79 n; German, 107; Italian, 21 f; and ministeriales, 105 ff; Roman, 21 f, 32 ff; of royal election, 8, 12; and tradition, 18
Le Cacheux, P., 242 n
Lefebvre des Noëttes, R. J. E. C., 169, 172, 175 ff, 181 f, 182 n, 184 n
Lehr, Henry, 80 n
Leroux, A., 116 n
Levant, 175, 188, 196
Levillain, L., 109 n, 164 n, 242 n
liber, meaning of, 100 f
Liège, 190
liegemen, 107
Lièvre, L., 227 n
Ligurinus, 15, 17, 31, 40

Lindet, L., 162 n, 167 n
linguistics, x, 45, 47 f, 58, 67 f, 73, 138 f
Lippmann, O. von 183 n
literature: French, 19; German, 19
Little Flowers of St. Francis, 30
livre, 237, 240
Livre de Guillaume de Ryckel, Le, 117 n
Livre des deux cités, 20
Loches, 152
Lodge, E., 113 n, 114 n
Lomagne, Viscount of, 95
Lombards, 4, 13, 36, 187
London, 156, 159, 166 n
lords: of the manor, 57, 85, 93 ff; territorial, 14
Lorraine, 3 f, 13 f, 83, 95, 99, 105
Lorraine Charters, 100
Lot, F. and Fawtier, R., 163 n
Lothar I (Emperor), 2 f
Lothar II, 3
Lothar (Duke of Saxony), 6, 11
Lothar of Provençe, 4
Lothar, State of, 2
Lotharingia, 90, 199
Louis of Bavaria (Emperor), 190
Louis the Pious, 2, 20, 54, 188, 192
Louis, St., 20, 104, 190, 206
Louis VI, 200
Louis VII, 200
Louis XIV, 131, 235
Lübeck, 190, 214
Lucca, 190
Lucretius, 139, 161 n
Ludus de Antichristo, 26 f, 32 ff, 40
Luxembourg, 190
Luzarches, Eude, stewards of, 98, 118 n, 121 n

machinery, 132, 145; opposition to, 146 ff
magnetic compass, 175
magnetic needle, 183 n
Magrab, 188, 199, 206
Mailly, Garnier de, 103
Maintenon, Mme de, 131
Mainz, Archbishop of, 12

Mainz Cathedral, 198
maires, see stewards
Maitland, F. W., 79 *n*, 107, 122 *n*, 123
Majorian (Emperor), 193
Making of the Middle Ages (Southern), xi, xiii *n*
malting, 158
Malvin, M., 168 *n*
mancus, 198 *ff*, 203 *ff*, 207
manorial rights, see *banalités*
manors, 57, 59, 60, 62; in France, 83 *ff*
manpower, shortage of, 160, 182
manse, 80 *n*
Mantoux, P., 166 *n*
manufactories, 142
manumissions, 101, 104
manuscripts, illuminated, 172, 175, 177
marabotins, 189, 199, 201 *f*, 210
Marcia, 189, 211
Marion, J., 161 *n*
Marius d'Avenches, 162 *n*, 164 *n*
Marlenheim, 150
Marquardt, J., 168 *n*
marriage: dues, 60; prohibited, 93, 115 *n*
Marseilles, 189, 201
Marx, Karl, xi
Masset, G., 109 *n*
Massiet du Biest, 113 *n*
matapans, 211
Matile, G. A., 121 *n*
Mauguis: mint at, 205
Maurizio, A., 165 *n*, 167 *n*
Mayer, Ernst, 108 *n*, 110 *n*
Maysan, 199
Méautis, G., 184 *n*
Mecklenburg, 57 *f*
Mediterranean region, 46 *f*, 51, 127, 180, 189, 198, 205, 209, 211, 234; water-wheels in, 136 *ff*, 174
Megingaud (Archbishop of Trèves), 111 *n*
Meillet, A., 58, 68, 76 *n*, 167 *n*
Meitzen, P. A., 69, 77 *n*

Melle, 191
Menadier, M., 228 *n*
mercenaries, 195, 207
merchants, 206 *ff*, 212, 214, 216 *f*, 225 *n*; Norman, 149
Meringer, R., 167 *n*
Merovingians, 52 *ff*, 129, 144, 191, 237
messianism, 24 *ff*
Messina, 189
Métais, Ch., 80 *n*, 112 *n*, 113 *n*, 243 *n*
metals, precious, 233 *f*
métayage, 57
Metrodorus, 161 *n*
Metz, Bishop of, 200
middle classes, see classes
Milan, 190
military service, 96
mill-wheels, see water wheels
millares, 201, 205 *f*
millers, 140 *f*, 156 *f*
mills: fulling-, 142, 157, 161 *n*, 181; hand, 147 *ff*, 154 *ff*; horse-, 148 *ff*, 153, 156, 171; privately owned, 150, 154 *ff*; steam, 147; tanning, 141, 181; water-, 134, 136 *ff*, 148 *ff*, 161 *n*, 174, 181 *f*; wind-, 147 *ff*, 153, 160, 163 *n*, 175, 181
millstone, 134, 136, 139 *f*, 144 *f*, 147 *f*, 157
miniatures, 172
ministeriales, 83, 90, 92, 96, 99 *ff*, 109 *n*; legal status of, 105 *ff*
Minns, E. H., 183 *n*
minting of coins, 187 *ff*, 195; florins, 190; French, 191; gold, 191, 202, 204 *ff*; imperfect nature of, 233, 235; return from silver to gold, 189, 210, 238; silver, 191, 202, 204, 206
Miret y Sans, 199
'Mirror of Swabia', 104
Mithradates, 137
Molinier, A., 218 *n*, 224 *n*
Mommsen, Th. and Marquardt, J., 168 *n*

INDEX

monasteries: and gold, 192; and the water-mill, 151 *f*
Mone, F. I., 165 *n*
monetary systems, 186 *ff*; *see also* coinage
money: definition of, 231; metallic, 232 *ff*
money-lenders, 197, 199, 234
Monneret de Villars, U, 221 *n*, 223 *n*, 228 *n*
monopolies, 131, 153, 156, 158 *f*
Montégut, H. de, 118 *n*
Montiérender, Adso de (Burgundian monk), 26
Montpezat, canon of, 155
Moors, 211
Morel, E., 113 *n*
mortar, *see* pestle and mortar
Mortet, V. and Deschamps, P., 163 *n*, 165 *n*
mortmain, 120 *n*
Moselle river, 137, 159
motive-power, 131
Mühlhausen, 138, 160 *n*
Müller, Emil, 114 *n*
Munro, W. B., 165 *n*
Munro-Chadwick, H., 228 *n*
Musset, R., 184 *n*
mythomania, 125

Nagi, A., 226 *n*
Némi, Lake, 46 *f*
Newcastle, 156
Niederle, L., 161 *n*
Nîmes, 149
Nirnnheim, H., 226 *n*
noble class, *see* classes
nobles: French, 65, 108; German, 108; Roman, 36
nomads, 128
Normandy, 200, 232 *f*
Normans, 156, 189
Norway/Norwegians, 142, 159, 184 *n*
Nuremberg, 214

oath of loyalty, 24 *f*, 89
Odenwald forest, 138

L'œuvre historique de Marc Bloch (Perrin), xiii *n*
Offa (king of Mercia), 199
Olbik, Axel, 161 *n*
olive-presses, 141
Olsen, Magnus, 184 *n*
Oman, C., 166 *n*, 223 *n*, 228 *n*
open field system, 70
ornaments, 194 *f*, 197, 234 *f*
Orsonville, 148
Otto I (Emperor) 4 *ff*
Otto III (Emperor), 5 *f*, 19
Otto IV (Emperor), 7 *f*, 27, 219 *n*
Otto of Bamberg (Bishop), 242 *n*
Otto of Freising (Bishop), 8, 14, 17, 20, 31, 40, 42 *n*

Palestine, 136
Palladius, 145
Papacy, 8, 10 *f*, 15, 21, 23, 27, 33, 35 *ff*, 201, 208
papal election, 37 *f*
Paris, 149, 201
Parîs, Matthew, 29
Parma, 149
Pascal III (Pope), 19
Passau, 237
patriotism: German, 40 *f*
Pavia, 13; Council of, 32; mint at, 204
payment: methods of, 85 *ff*, 95, 198 *f*, 201 *f*, 206 *ff*, 210, 215 *ff*, 230 *ff*
peasant routine, 126 *ff*
peasants: payments by, 236 *f*, 239; and the water-mill, 150 *ff*
Pegolotti, 190
Pepin, 52
peppercorns, as medium of exchange, 208, 231 *ff*, 237
Perrin, Ch. E., xiii, 185 *n*, 242 *n*
Persia/Persians, 180, 187
Perugia, 189
pestle and mortar, 136, 145, 147, 160
Petit, J., 219 *n*
Petot, Pierre, 112 *n*, 113 *n*, 118 *n*, 119 *n*, 122 *n*

Pherecrates, 161 n
Philip of Swabia, 7 f, 15 f
Philip the Fair, 190, 214
Philip Augustus, 19 f, 32, 34, 149, 154, 188, 200
Pierre Raimon de Toulouse, 113 n
piracy, 195
Pirenne, Henri, x, 76 n, 82, 111 n, 196, 122 n
Pisa, 191
Placenta, 202
Plautus, 136
Pliny, 137, 143, 145, 160 n, 196
plough, 172, 176 f, 219 n
Po river, 192
poets, 93, 102, 192
Pöhlmann, C., 122 n
Poitiers, battle of, 149
Poitiers, Comte de, 83
Poland: land-systems in, 69; monetary systems in, 188, 190
poll tax, 89, 103, 113 n, 236
Pollock, F. and Maitland, T. W., 79 n, 122 n
Polyptyques, 150
Pomerania, 57 f, 155
Pontus, 137
Poole, R. L., 222 n, 242 n
port dues, 210
portaturae, 185 n
portraiture, 172
Portuguese, 214
Poullain du Parc, 165 n
Pourpardin, R., 115 n
poverty, evangelical, 38
Power, E. and Postan, M. M., 184 n
Prague, 211
prebends, 86 f, 95, 99, 110 n
prehistory, 47, 69, 77 n, 173
Prentout, H., 78 n
prices, 132
primogeniture, 6, 8
Procope, 225
Procopius, 162 n
property rights, 62, 91, 94 f
Prou, M., 228 n

Prou, M. and Vidier, A., 114 n, 118 n, 220 n, 222 n
Provençal, Levi, 223 n
Provence, 4; disappearance of communal obligations in, 50 f; language of, 78 n; slavery in, 179
Provence, Marquis of, 204
Prussia, 155, 159
psychology: and history, 124 ff
Puntschart, P., 114 n, 122 n
Pyrenees, 192

Quantin, M., 222 n, 223 n
Quedlimbourg, Annals of, 6

race: and hereditary right, 107
Radegonde, 152
Rahewin (chronicler), 36, 42 n, 43 n
railways, 133 f
Rainald of Dassel (Archbishop), 18, 33, 37 f
ransom, 194
rate of exchange, *see* exchange rate
Ratisbon, 214
reeve, 62 f
religion: and gold, 194; and slavery, xi, 181; and tradition, 18
'Renaissance of the 12th century', 20 f, 32
Rennes, *Parlement* of, 156
Reno, 199
rents, *see* dues
Repgow, Eike von, 12
research, historical, 72 ff
rewards, *see* payment
'Rheingold', 192
Rhône region, 3 f
Richard Cœur de Lion, 34
Richard, Earl of Cornwall, 12
Richard II (Abbot of St. Albans), 158
Richter, O., 162 n
ritual murder, 46 f
roads, 182 n
Robert, G., 112 n

INDEX

Roberts, house of the, 4
Roman Catholic Church, 10 *f*, 35, 38 *f*, 52 *ff*, 102, 181
Roman Empire, 18, 20 *ff*, 46, 174, 180, 186
Roman law, *see* Law
Romans, King of the, 13 *ff*, 25, 36, 39, 42 *n*
Rome, 1 *f*, 4, 10, 15 *f*, 23, 47, 140, 180, 187; Abassid coin from, 205; Emperor's power over, 35 *f*; population, 145 *f*; rebellion in, 21; watermills in, 144, 151
Roncaglia, Diet of, 22
rotary motion, 136
rotation of crops, 126 *ff*, 174
Rouen, 155
Roumania, 142
Round, J. H., 112 *n*
routine, social attitudes to, 126
royalty: sacred character of, 24 *ff*, 31; titles of, 13 *ff*
Rozoy, 99
rudder, 183 *n*
Rudolf of Hapsburg, 7
Rudolf of Rheinfelden, 10
Rudolph III, 5
Rufinus (Canonist), 24
Ruge, W., 167 *n*
Rumorr, C. F. V., 112 *n*
rural life, 152 *ff*
Russia: land-systems in, 69; monetary systems in, 188; trade, 196, 200
rye, 128 *ff*

Sachsenspiegel, 12, 106
Sahara, 214
Saint-Adalbert of Aachen, 105
Saint-Alban, Abbot of, 149
St Albans, insurrections at, 157 *f*
Saint-Anatholy, lords of, 87
Saint-Ayoul of Provins, 190
Saint-Benoît, Fleury, 92
Saint-Benoît-sur-Loire, 94 *f*, 97, 102, 200
Saint-Bertin, 152

Saint-Corneille de Compiègne, 89
Saint-Denis, Concevreux, 152
Saint-Denis-en-France, 95
Saint-Etienne de Dijon, 103
Saint-Gall, Alemannia, 97
Saint-Germain-des-Prés, 185 *n*
Saint-Germain-Laval, charter of liberties of, 84
Saint-Hubert, 200
Saint-Jean-d'Angély, 83 *f*
Saint-Laurent, abbot of, 198
Saint-Martin-des-Champs, Priory of, 201, 240
Saint-Martin de Tours, 85, 99
Saint-Maximin de Trèves, 111 *n*
Saint-Mesmin de Mecy à Némois 97
Saint-Père de Chartres, 84, 91 *f*, 94, 99, 116 *n*, 237
Saint-Sernin, abbey of, 87
Saint-Trond, 95, 200
Saint-Vincent du Mans, 239
Saint-Vrast d'Arras, 94
Sainte-Geneviève of Paris, Abbot of, 93 *f*
Salic dynasty, 18
Salic law, 143
Samson (abbot of Bury St Edmunds, 163 *n*
Sanchez-Albornoz, Cl., 77 *n*, 183 *n*, 218 *n*, 221 *n*
Sander, P. and Spangerberg, H., 119 *n*
Saracens, 191, 203
Sardinia, 191, 210
Sarmatians, 174
Sassanidae, 187
Savina, J. and Bernard, D., 165 *n*
Saxon kings, 36, 38
Sayous, A. E., 228 *n*, 242 *n*
Scandinavia, 32, 127, 138, 188, 194 *ff*
sceatta, 188
Schaube, A., 219 *n*
Schleswig, 138
Schlumberger, G., 224 *n*
Schneider, F., 122 *n*

INDEX

Schrader, O., 167 *n*
Schramm, Percy E., 183 *n*
Schröder, R., 122 *n*
Schulte, A., 242 *n*
Schwab, 199
scientific knowledge, and invention, 132 *f*
Scotland, 159
seals, 172
Sée, Henri, 50, 76 *n*
Sée, H. and Lesort, A., 165 *n*
Seeliger, G., 112 *n*
Segre, M., 228 *n*
seigneuries, see manors
serf-knights, 65, 102, 104, 106, 120 *n*
serfs, 59, 61 *ff*, 84, 88 *f*, 91, 99 *ff*, 104, 106 *f*, 179, 221 *n*
sergents, 83 *f*, 89 *ff*, 101 *f*, 104, 106 *f*, 114 *n*, 140
servi, see serfs
servile labour, 62 *f*, 84, 86, 180, 185 *n*
servile status, 99 *ff*, 102 *f*, 106
Shetland islands, 142, 159
shoulder-collar, 177, 181
Sicily, 188 *f*
Sicily, King of, 31, 215
Sidjilmassa palace, 214
Sieveking, H., 226 *n*
siege-engines, 145
Sierra Leone, 214
Silesia, 192
silk, 196
silver: mining, 191 *f*; shortage of, 233
silver coinage, see coinage
Simiand, F., 132, 234
sincerity, concept of, 124 *f*
Sion, Jules, 176, 185 *n*
slave-trade, 179, 203, 214
slaves/slavery, xi, 79 *n*, 96, 134, 137, 140, 150, 184 *n*, 185 *n*, 196; abolition of, 177 *ff*; origin of word 'slave', 179; Roman, 59, 63, 136, 145 *ff*; and the Roman Catholic Church, 186

Slav(s), 32, 34, 138, 155, 159, 203, 205; languages, 139
social classes, see classes
social history, 68 *ff*
Soetbeer, A., 227 *n*
Solmi, A., 220 *n*
Sondheimer, Janet, vii
sou, 186 *ff*, 193, 199 *f*, 211, 237; *de grains*, 189
Souplainville, 94
Southern, R. W., xi, xiii *n*
Spain, 53 *f*, 179 *f*, 210 *f*; *Cortes* in, 56; monetary systems in, 188, 199, 203, 206
spinning-wheel, 132, 172, 175, 181
Stadtmüller, H., 160 *n*
steam engine, 141, 159
steam flour-milling, see mills
Stengers, J., xiii *n*
Steppes, 128
stewards, 92 *ff*, 101, 104 *f*, 110 *n*, 114 *n*, 115 *n*, 118 *n*
stirrup, 130, 174
Strabo, 139, 160 *n*, 161 *n*
Sudan, 214
Suetonius, 144, 160 *n*
survivals, 47, 76 *n*
Swabian dynasty, 18
Sybel, Heinrich von, 41
Symmachus, 193
Syria, 142, 199, 204

Tacitus, 225 *n*
Tafilalet, 214
Tafur, Pierre, 220 *n*
tallage, 85
Talmont, *seigneur* of, 101
tanning-mills, see mills
taris, 189
Tauberbishofsheim, 138
taxes, 85, 208
technical progress, xi, 124 *ff*, 169 *ff*; difficulties of research, 170 *ff*
technical regression, 142
technical terms, see terminology
technology, history of, 141
Templiers en Eure-et-Loir, Les, 70

tenements, 66 f, 86, 101
terminology, 74 ff, 90, 109 n, 147 f, 171
testamentary wills, 79 n, 199
Teutonic Order, Great Charter of the, 35
text-books, 75
Theodulfe of Orleans, 54
Theodulphus, 199
Theophilus (monk), 192
theow, 61
Thibaut (abbot of Saint-Germain-des-Prés), 94
Thillier, J. and Jarry, E., 113 n, 121 n
Thomas, St, 89
throat-collar, 177
Thuringians, 137
Tiber, 144
tiers de sou, 193 f
Tigy, 118 n
Timbuctoo, 197
tin, 203
titles, 98; royal, 113 ff
Toledo, 189, 206
Totila, 144
Touareg caravaners, 214
Touat, 214
Toulouse, 110 n, 192
Toulouse, Count of, 89
Tournadre, G. de, 223 n
Tournai, 214
Tourneur, V., 229 n
tournois, 211
Tout, T. F., 221 n
towns, 71
trade, 179 ff, 195 ff, 200, 202 ff, 211 ff, 232 f
tradition(s), 17 ff, 159; Carolingian, 18 ff; of rural societies, 126 ff
Traité singulier des moulins (Hering), 140
Trajan's aqueduct, 144
transhumance, 51
Transjurania, 4 f
translation, difficulties of, 73 f, 104 f

transport, 141
treasures, *see* ornaments
treaty of Verdun, *see* Verdun
Treichel, A., 165 n
Treviri, 174
tribute, 194, 199, 205
trip-hammer, 142
Tye, Th., 122 n
Tyler, Wat, 158

unction, *see* consecration ceremony
universities: French, 80 n
Urals, 192
Urgel, Comte d', 204
Usher, A. P., 162 n, 166 n
Uzès, 207

Valence, 193, 204
Valens, 194
Valentinian (Emperor), 20, 194
Valéry, Paul, 184 n
value: conservation of, 234 f; measure of, 237
vanes, 141, 143
Varangians, 188
vassals, 87 ff, 94, 97 f, 100 ff, 107, 119 n
Vaudois, 27
Vendryes, J., 161 n, 162 n, 168 n
Venice, 190, 204, 210, 214
Verdun, treaty of, 2 f
Verlinden, Ch., 184 n
Verriest, L., 118 n
Vespasian, 144
Victor IV (Pope), 37
Vienne, kingdom of, 4
Vierendeel, A., 167 n, 182 n
Vignay, G., 110 n
Vikings, 184 n
Villari, P., 216
villeinage, 58 ff, 101 f, 120 n
Vincent de Viviers, St, 89
Vinogradoff, P., 59, 110 n, 122 n
Visigoths, 53 f, 127, 187
Vitruvius, 137 ff, 142 f, 160 n
Vitry, Jacques de, 120 n
Viville, 154

INDEX

Vladimir of Kiev, 196
Vogelweide, Walther von der, 15 *f*, 17, 23, 34
Voltaire, 124

wages, 95, 195, 206
Wagria, 138
Wahabite emir of the Nedj, 52
Wailly, N. de, 227 *n*
Wales, 166 *n*
Walsingham, Th., 166 *n*
Warmington, E. H., 220 *n*
water-lifting machinery, 139
water-power, 138, 148, 159 *f*, 182
water-wheel, 136 *ff*, 148, 159, 172; adaptations of, 139, 141 *f*; in boats, 144; horizontal, 142; vertical, 143
watermills, *see* mills
Watford, 166 *n*
weight, measure of, 201

Weimann, K., 118 *n*, 122 *n*
Werner (Bishop of Strasbourg), 6
Werveke, M. H. van, 221 *n*, 222 *n*, 241 *n*
Westphalia, 155
wheat, 129
William I (abbot of Saint-Père de Chartres), 84
Willigis (Archbishop), 198
wills, *see* testamentary wills
Wilson, E. M. Carus, 184 *n*
windmill, *see* mills
Winlock, E. H. and Cram, W. E., 161 *n*
Winter, G., 114 *n*
Wittich, W., 117 *n*
wool, 213

Zealand, 195
Zeglin, D., 107, 108 *n*, 122 *n*
Zimmermann, M., 219 *n*